Missing Pieces II

An Alternative Guide to Canadian Post-Secondary Education

edited by
Denise Doherty-Delorme
and Erika Shaker

About the authors

Denise Doherty-Delorme is a Research Associate of the Canadian Centre for Policy Alternatives.

Erika Shaker is a Research Fellow at the Canadian Centre for Policy Alternatives and Director of the CCPA Education Project.

Acknowledgements

This work would have been impossible without the valuable contributions of so many individuals and organizations: however, some do deserve special mention. Among them are Ed Finn, Kerri-Anne Finn for their expertise and patience, as well as the staff of the Canadian Centre for Policy Alternatives: Paul Leduc Browne, Bruce Campbell, Ansky Espinoza, Agathe Gautier and Diane Touchette.

We would like to thank a number of supporting organizations who contributed their time, energy, advice and support: the Canadian Federation of Students (CFS), the Canadian Association of University Teachers (CAUT), the Canadian Union of Postal Workers (CUPW-STTP), and the Canadian Union of Public Employees (CUPE/SCFP) local 1979. Thanks also to Gord McWilliams of Studio 2 Graphic Design.

Finally, we would like to thank all the students, researchers, activists, teachers, faculty and support staff who contributed to this report in addition to the valuable work they do every day. We are privileged to work with such a dedicated group of individuals and organizations who continue to strive for a public education system that serves the needs of all Canadians, and look forward to working with them in the future. We also invite you, the reader, to participate in this discussion.

The Editors.

Cover design: Gord McWilliams

Printed in Canada.

Contributors

Normand Baillargeon is a Professor, Université du Québec à Montréal

James Beaton is a doctoral student in sociology at York University.

David Bernans is a researcher for the Concordia Student Union.

William Carroll is a professor of sociology at the University of Victoria

James Clancy is National President of the National Union of Provincial and General Employees.

Robert Chernomas is a professor of economics at the University of Manitoba and president of the Manitoba Organization of Faculty Associations.

Michael Conolon is the National Chairperson of the Canadian Federation of Students.

Dr Livio Di Matteo is an Associate Professor of Economics at Lakehead University and Vice-President External Relations, Humanities and Social Sciences Federation of Canada.

Sarah Dopp is the Coordinator for Operation 2000, a project of the Polaris Institute.

Joel Duff is the President of the Graduate Student Union at the University of Ottawa.

Karl Flecker is a policy analyst in the equity field at Queen's University.

Bernie Froese-Germain is an education writer and researcher based in Ottawa.

Loretta Gerlach, Prairie Organizer, Council of Canadians

Jeremy Gillies is a Communications and Information Technology Specialist with the Canadian Union of Postal Workers' National Office in Ottawa. His background includes research into the commercialization of public education and the commodification of public space. He is currently working on a web site project for CUPW and is a member of CUPE local 1979.

Joel Harden is currently completing his PhD at York University and is the former Chairperson of the Ontario office of the Canadian Federation of Students.

Pauling Hwang is a youth orgnizer and activist.

Dale Kirby was Chairperson of the Newfoundland and Labrador Federation of Students from 1997 from 1999. Mr. Kirby completed a Bachelor of Science (1998) and a Master of Education (2000) at Memorial University of Newfoundland and is currently pursuing a Ph.D. in Higher Education at the Ontario Institute for Studies in Education at the University of Toronto.

David W. Livingstone is Chair, Department of Sociology and Equity Studies in Education, Ontario Institute for Studies in Education, University of Toronto.

Diane Meaghan is a professor of General Education at Seneca College.

Ron Melchers is a Professor of Criminology at the University of Ottawa.

Martin Petit is a Researcher for the Institut de recherche et d'informations socio-économiques (IRIS)

Claire Polster teaches in the Department of Sociology at the University of Regina.

Linda Quirke is a Ph.D. student in the Sociology of Education at McMaster University. She completed the data outlined here for her M.A. in Sociology at the University of Guelph.

Vicky Smallman is a Professional Officer (Organizing) at the Canadian Association of University Teachers.

Jim Stanford is an economist with the Canadian Auto Workers and a CCPA research associate.

Becky Striegler works for the Yukon Department of Education.

Jennifer Sumner teaches the Rural Extension Studies course at the University of Guelph, Ont.

Francois Tanguay-Renaud is a student at the McGill University School of Law.

Michael Temelini is the Government Relations Officer at the Canadian Federation of Students

Nicholas Thompson is an editor of **The Washington Monthly**.

Neil Tudiver taught at the University of Manitoba for 23 years. He is currently Chief Negotiations Officer at the Canadian Association of University Teachers.

Table of contents

Introduction 1

Provincial Rankings 9
    Newfoundland: Cold comfort 15
    New Brunswick 18
    Nova Scotia: From bad to worse 20
    PSE on PEI 23
    Quebec 26
    Ontario 30
    Manitoba 34
    Post-secondary education in Saskatchewan 38
    Higher education in Alberta, 2000 41
    Post-secondary education in British Columbia 44
    Some facts about post-secondary education in the Yukon 47

Equity 51
    Casual labour in Canada's universities: A growing trend 53
    The impact of the restructuring of higher education on rural communities 57
    Access in jeopardy? Social class, finances and university attendance 63
    The face of the faculty is still mainly white 71
    Free Money!... (For those who already have it) 75

Accessibility 79
    Canada Student Loan Program: 1995-2000 81
    Registered Education Savings Plans: A national grant program for the wealthy 85
    Underemployment and life-long learning: Canadian views 88
    The tax cut context 99

Quality 107
    University finance in Canada: 1972-the present 109
    Research, innovation and prosperity 118
    The state of university education and the liberal arts 127
    Online learning: Compromising quality 136
    Unexus University at-a-glance 140
    The classroom vs. the boardroom 141
    Harnessing university research to business needs 147
    Growing the market: Of urinals and university centres—targeting the campus crowd 155

Public accountability 163
Con U Inc.: A shopping mall, and so much more... 165
No exclusivity for Coca-Cola at McGill Or, the silent growth of campus corporatization 173
The advantages and disadvantages of corporate/university links:
What's wrong with this question? 180
Globalization and the restructuring
of Canadian community colleges: Critical perspectives 186
Private universities, public menace 197
Neoliberalism, corporate hegemony and the university 200
Whither education for citizenship in a globalized, free market world? 209

International context 221
Private higher education at McGill and beyond: A fact sheet 223
Public Education: Citizen's rights for sale—cheap! 234
The fire this time? Understanding the movement against trade liberalization 238
UNAM — Students on Strike 248
Playing with numbers: How U.S. News and World Report
mismeasures higher education and what we can do about it 250

Appendix 261

Introduction
By Denise Doherty-Delorme and Erika Shaker

In November 1999, the Canadian Centre for Policy Alternatives released **Missing Pieces, An Alternative Guide to Canadian Post-secondary Education**. **Missing Pieces** was designed as the inaugural report in a series which would attempt to redefine the way in which conventional ranking systems determined the state of higher education across Canada. Instead of reinforcing competition between individual institutions, the CCPA report ranked the provinces on their commitment to higher education based on some of the most recent Statistics Canada data and information from students, activists, educators and researchers.

In this manner, the inaugural volume of **Missing Pieces** attempted to expose the roots, as well as the results, of the restructuring agenda now sweeping post-secondary education in Canada, in addition to the impacts of these changes on students, faculty and support staff, and on the quality of the education provided by the institutions.

Missing Pieces was not intended to be an exhaustive study: there are many issues that were beyond the scope of this initial report—issues that also require thorough examination. Consequently, an additional goal of **Missing Pieces** was to expose the research that had yet to be done on higher education, in order to provide the Canadian public with a more accurate picture of colleges and universities, the impact of federal and provincial restructuring, and the role of private sector involvement.

There has been growing discontent over the inadequacies inherent in conventional ranking reports—concern with the limited subject areas, with the ideological direction, and with the way in which these reports have been used to villify or promote institutions based on a narrow set of criteria and an even narrower philosophical premise. Schools are forced to compete against one another, without taking into consideration the fiscal restraints under which institutions are forced to operate. Concerns have been raised that the competitive model in fact exacerbates diminished access and leads to destructive remodeling of the post-secondary system as a whole.

We were equally dismayed that the popular ranking really only gives voice to senior administrators on the universities, while the voices of students, faculty and support staff were largely marginalized, reduced to a side-bar of "what's hot and what's not on campus"—from the drinking and sexual habits of students to faculty strikes and the alleged abuses of tenure.

As the editors of **Missing Pieces**, we argue that, without examining the forces behind post-secondary restructuring, as well as the gravity of the impact these initiatives have on both our public institutions and the wider society, it is impossible to recognize the nature of the changes taking place. Financially and structurally, post-secondary institutions have undergone a series of profound changes—changes that, arguably, have made these institutions less accessible, less accountable, and of lesser quality: in short, less democratic.

We therefore call for an emphasis and reexamination of the principles of higher education in Canada—equity, accessibility, quality and accountability to the public—and attempt to uncover how these principles have been altered or diminished by an increasing emphasis on "standards," "corporate involvement," "efficiency," and "global competitiveness," for example. In other words, we need to re-examine the role of public education in Canadian society, how it serves to change society as well as reflecting the society in which we live.

We selected the title **Missing Pieces** for two reasons: we felt there was a need to look at what was missing from the public debate surrounding the state of higher education in Canada; and we wanted to help document what is increasingly missing from higher education policy necessary to achieve and maintain a high quality of education—for the institutions, student life, and faculty research and scholarship. Too much of the public analysis of post-secondary education has taken the form of simplistic rankings, devoid of context. Such methods serve only to reinforce the rhetoric of restructuring—rewarding institutions that move away from public accessibility and towards market accountability—without examining the source of this rhetoric, and the undemocratic impact of its influence.

We are committed to ensuring that higher education in Canada remain true to the Canadian Charter of Rights and Freedoms, and the United Nations' Declaration of Human Rights. Education at all levels is a right, not a privilege. But experience, compassion, and a democratic commitment to social development and justice tells us that there are no rights without means. Public education at all levels therefore depends on establishing and enforcing the means to attend those public institutions, or they serve merely to reinforce existing socioeconomic inequities.

With this second edition of **Missing Pieces**, we have maintained an emphasis on the four principles of higher education, but have attempted to provide a broader analysis. This has included: private universities and colleges; the role of international trade deals and student (re)action towards them; international response to the ranking trend; analysis of college restructuring across Canada; and an attempt to look at the restructuring of universities and colleges within the broader context of educating for citizenship.

In this time of globalization and the influence of the World Bank, the World Trade Organization and the International Monetary Fund, Canadian education must also be reviewed in an international context. The majority of Canadians believe that the American higher education system is more expensive than a Canadian one, and do not realize that many of our international trading partners charge no tuition fees for higher education. The similarities of many of the restructuring initiatives taking place—across international borders—must also be examined in order to underscore that many of the efforts undertaken to redefine and reform higher education are anything but innovative.

As one of the fundamental cornerstones of a society dedicated to justice and equality, public education is founded on four major themes: equity, accessibility, quality and accountability to the public. We have illustrated, though use of the most recent statistical data available, the level of commitment on the part of the provincial governments to upholding these principles of public education in their provincial institutions.[1] Additionally, we have included a selection of articles providing in-depth analysis on a variety of issues illustrating the four principles of higher education. This year we have included another category: the international context. As many restructuring initiatives are taking place—and being responded to—across national borders, we felt it was important to provide readers with this framework as well.

Equity

Equity is defined as those policies in place to ensure that all individuals and communities are able to attend or work at the school and program of their choice. It also ensures that all students, faculty and support staff are afforded every opportunity to thrive, teach, learn and work fully—and that those opportunities are not just protected, but reinforced and thoroughly integrated into every aspect of higher education.

In the rush to reduce expenditures, universities and colleges have reduced the number of tenured professors and moved to hiring part-time, low-paid instructors, who are unable to teach to their abilities through inadequate or unbalanced infrastructure. This is discussed in some detail by Vicky Smallman (*Casual labour in Canada's universities: A growing trend*).

As higher education is restructured, and as the corporate sector's role is increasingly dominant, particularly in certain subject areas, there are major implications for rural schools and students, as discussed by Jennifer Sumner (*The impact of the restructuring of higher education on rural communities*). The face of campus is also changing, particularly as tuition fees rise out of the range of lower- and now middle-class students; this is examined by Linda Quirke (*Access in Jeopardy? Social class, finances and university attendance*). And for many of those students, as detailed by Karl Flecker (*The face of the faculty is still mainly white*), inadequate mechanisms are in place to ensure that they are in fact able to participate fully in educational opportunities.

Furthermore, the means by which the federal Liberals have attempted to address the situation of skyrocketing tuition fees—the RESP "grants" program, for example—are wholly inadequate because they least serve the needs of those who need help the

Missing Pieces II   3

most, as explained by Jim Stanford (*Free money!... (for those who already have it)*).

Accessibility

We have defined accessibility (including affordability and opportunity) as the financial means in place to ensure that students are able to afford to attend the university or college of their choice—and have the opportunity to use that education upon graduation. To this end, we have examined the financial context within which universities and colleges exist, which allow students to attend the institution that best suits them.

The Canadian Federation of Students has provided two pieces. One, by Michael Conlon, is on the Canadian Student Loan system, and the changes to it which have made it much more difficult for students to afford their education (*Canada Student Loan Program: 1995-2000*). The second piece, by Michael Temelini, (*Registered Education Savings Plans: A national grant program for the wealthy*) is on RESPs, and examines the extent to which this program claims to ensure—and in fact fails to provide—accessibility.

David Livingston (*Underemployment and lifelong learning: Canadian views*) examines the relationship between education and the jobs gap, and Robert Chernomas (*The tax cut context*) provides an overview of the taxation system and puts education—and changes to it—in the context of federal economic restructuring.

Quality

We have defined quality as the provincial and federal governments' commitment to fostering a well-rounded educational experience and environment. This includes: the quality of student life; the adequacy of university or college finances; and the breadth of disciplines and modes of learning offered.

Without adequate financing of post-secondary education, institutions are unable to offer the physical infrastructure necessary to sustain the needs of the student body or faculty through libraries, research, building capacity, or facilities. Ron Melchers (*University finance in Canada: 1972-1998*) and Denise Doherty-Delorme (*Research, innovation and prosperity*) discuss the impact of funding on post-secondary institutions and university research, and provide an overview of the physical state of university and college infrastructure in Canada.

As higher education is restructured to reflect the demands of the global markets, certain disciplines are emphasized—and funded accordingly—while others are not. Livio Di Matteo (*The state of university education and the liberal arts*) discusses the importance of liberal arts, and documents the impacts of restructuring on this discipline.

As demands on higher education grow and increasingly reflect the role of technology and the education industry, on-line learning is touted as the means by which students can explore "anywhere, any-time learning" and infrastructure costs can be reduced. However, there has been little analysis of the impact of this mode of learning on the quality of post-secondary education. This section explores some of these issues in articles by James Clancy (*The classroom vs the boardroom*), Sarah Dopp (*Unexus University at-a-glance*), and Michael Temelini of the Canadian Federation of Students (*Online learning: Compromising quality*).

Neil Tudiver (*Harnessing university research to business needs*), explores the impacts of restructuring and fiscal constraints on the quality of research. And Erika Shaker's article (*Growing the market: Of urinals and university centres: targeting the campus crowd*) examines how campus life and the learning experience is increasingly commercialized, at a time when the fiscal constraints on students and on university and college infrastructure are growing.

Public accountability

When we talk about the accountability of post-secondary education, we are addressing the necessity that public institutions remain accountable to the public. This requires that education be publicly funded, not funded by private sources such as corporations, or the more common user fees (tuition fees) which download the cost of education to individuals.

Private involvement in—and influence over—education funding, including ways in which universities and colleges run themselves and the choices they make, is discussed in a series of articles: Dave Bernans (*Con U Inc.: A shopping mall, and so much more...*) and Francois Tanguay-Renaud (*No exclusivity for Coca-Cola at McGill: The silent growth of campus corporatization*) examine the ways in which private money has changed the way in which public institutions are being run. Claire Polster (*The advantages and disadvantages of corporate/university links: What's wrong with this question?*) discusses the debate over Intellectual Property (IP) and the implications for public vs. private ownership of research.

Often marginalized in the debate over higher education is the state of community colleges. Diane Meaghan (*Globalization and the restructuring of Canadian community colleges: Critical perspectives*) provides a thorough overview of restructuring in this sector, and the implications for students at these institutions. James Clancy (*Private universities, public menace*) examines the role of privatized universities and colleges, to which Mike Harris opened the door in Ontario earlier this year.

But what forces are attempting to shape higher education? And to what effect? These questions are further addressed by James Beaton and William Carrol (*Neoliberalism, corporate hegemony and the university*) and Bernie Froese-Germain (*Whither education for citizenship in a globalized, free market world?*), respectively.

International context

This year we have added an additional section to address the fact that many of the changes experienced by universities and colleges on campuses, by students, faculty and support staff, are in fact happening across national borders. To demonstrate trends impacting education restructuring, we have included a primer on privatization by Pauline Hwang (*Private higher education* at McGill and beyond: A fact sheet), an analysis of trade deals by Sarah Dopp and Karl Flecker (*Public education: Citizen's rights for sale—cheap!*), as well as a description of student resistance to these deals by Joel Harden (*The fire this time?: Understanding the movement against trade liberalization*). Sarah Dopp has also provided us with a case study of the student strike at the National Autonomous University of Mexico (*UNAM—Students on strike*), a strike prompted by many of the same restructuring tactics we are seeing in higher education in Canada.

Finally, resistance against and discontentment with conventional systems of ranking have also crossed national boundaries. For over two decades, **U.S. News and World Report** has completed a ranking survey which has been criticized for promoting a negative competitive environment, and contributing to a damaging restructuring agenda for universities and colleges. This has been documented in an article by Nick Thompson (*Playing with numbers: How U.S. News mismeasures higher education and what we can do about it*).

Provincial Information

As in the inaugural issue, **Missing Pieces II** provides an overview of the state of post-secondary education in each province (we were also able to include some information about the territories this year). And readers will also note that our statistical analysis is even more thorough than in the previous year, and covers a wider range of issues.

In cases where the available information was no more current than the previous year, we attempted to explore other aspects of post-secondary education restructuring in order to provide as well-rounded an analysis as possible. For this reason, we encourage readers to take both issues of **Missing Pieces** into consideration when determining the state of higher education on Canadian campuses, since we have tried to to build on, not duplicate, the research in both these reports.

As we stated in the previous issue of **Missing Pieces**, we encourage readers to continue to contribute to this ongoing research. Many of the comments we have received over the course of the last few months have helped us shape and redefine the parameters of this report, as well as to explore other aspects of post-secondary restructuring across the country and internationally.

We thank the individual and organizational contributors for their dedication and expertise, and are looking forward to a continued broadening of the debate and discussion about the state of higher education in Canada.

Endnotes

[1] Last year we were unable to provide information on post-secondary education in the Territories. We are pleased to announce that the Government of the Yukon has provided us with an overview of the state of higher education in that Territory; however, we were unable to include it in the rankings. We hope that in subsequent editions of this report we will be able to include all three Territories in both the overview and rankings sections. We are greatful to the Government of the Yukon for their co-operation and assistance.

Provincial rankings

Provincial Rankings
By Jeremy Gillies

Public education rests on the four principles of quality, equity, accessibility and accountability, which have been defined in the introduction and throughout this report. Provincial governments have a responsibility to uphold, protect, and reinforce each of these four principles to ensure that the higher education in each province is in fact democratically administered, delivered and received.

However, as federal transfer payments have been slashed, provincial governments have chosen to respond to fiscal restructuring in a variety of ways—most of which have in fact made higher education of a lower quality, less equitable, less accessible and less accountable to the public. In short, higher education across Canada is becoming less democratic.

As the editors of this report, we contend that conventional ranking surveys do not provide an adequate focus on the provincial and federal context of post-secondary restructuring, concentrating instead on the individual institutions as isolated entities. However, without putting individual institutions in the broader financial context (provincial and federal), as well as the international context for education restructuring, the picture of higher education in Canada will be incomplete.

Furthermore, conventional ranking systems tend to reward individual schools for the speed and degree to which they conform to provincial and federal restructuring, thus accelerating changes which may in fact be ultimately destructive or contradictory to the democratic role of higher education in Canada. And the selection of criteria used to determine institutional excellence also may rest on certain beliefs that do not necessarily have anything to do with quality.

For example, MacLean's determines the reputation of an institution in the following manner: "A solid reputation attracts the best students and professors—and gives graduates an enviable calling card. MacLean's measures a school's reputation with its own graduates through alumni donations. " (MacLean's. Nov. 20, 2000. 90) Clearly, in this survey reputation is tied to wealth, which may have nothing whatsoever to do with quality—but as the authority of this sort of ranking system is entrenched, the use of this definition contributes to inequitable fundraising which reinforces existing economic differences between schools as they increasingly rely on private donations.

In fact, much of the criticism surrounding conventional rankings in both Canada and the United States has focused on the negative competitive nature of these systems.

It is for these reasons that we have again chosen to rank not the individual institutions but the provincial governments for their level of commitment to post-secondary education. Without a thorough focus on what provincial governments have undertaken, it is impossible to provide a fair analysis of individual institutions.

As with the previous edition of **Missing Pieces**, we have ranked the provinces from one to ten, with one being the province with the highest level of commitment to post-secondary education, and ten indicating the least level of commitment. However, the province with the top ranking by no means implies that provincial government's record is perfect where higher education is concerned—its superiority is only on a comparative basis.

Each principle has been examined in isolation, across a variety of indicators: this information has been provided in a series of tables to indicate how each province has ranked across the various qualitative data and indicators to illustrate how each province ranks in each of the four principles. Finally, we have ranked each province overall to determine the government with the highest level of commitment to post-secondary education. Unless otherwise indicated, all information used is the most recent available from Statistics Canada.

Overall Rankings

Province	Equity Rank	Quality Rank	Affordability, Access and Opportunity Rank	Accountability Rank	Overall Rank	Last Year's Overall Rank
NF	10	6	7	3	7	9
PEI	9	5	5	5	6	8
NS	3	8	3	9	4	3
NB	7	1	8	8	6	3
PQ	5	3	1	2	2	2
ON	6	10	7	10	10	10
MB	2	5	3	5	3	6
SK	8	9	9	6	9	7
AB	4	8	10	8	8	5
BC	1	2	4	1	1	1

Equity

Equity is defined as those mechanisms in place at a provincial level to ensure that all students, regardless of gender or socioeconomic status, can make optimal use of higher education in whichever location and discipline they choose.

We have included as one indicator of a province's commitment to equity the fees charged to international students as compared to fees charged to Canadian students. Provinces were ranked accordingly to how closely the fees charged for international students resemble fees for domestic students.

Additionally, while certain gains have been made by the increased presence of women on campus, there is still a marked imbalance in the presence of women in the faculty.

Post-secondary education does not exist independent of society—and of the socio-economic context. We have included the incidence of poor households whose head of the family has completed post-secondary education as a measure of a province's commitment to utilizing and adequately compensating people higher education. Furthermore, we have provided provincial unemployment rates as an indication of the economic well-being of a province's workforce, both within and surrounding the post-secondary environment.

Equity Rankings

Province	% of International Students (College 1995-1996)	% of International Students (University 1996-1997)	% of Women Faculty 1998	% Poor Households with PSE (1997)*	Unemployment rate (1999)	Equity Rank	Last Year's Equity Rank
NF	10	9	10	9	10	10	10
PEI	9	10	3	7	9	9	9
NS	7	3	1	4	7	3	2
NB	6	8	2	6	8	7	6
PQ	8	1	9	1	6	5	4
ON	2	7	8	8	1	6	4
MB	4	4	6	2	2	2	8
SK	5	7	5	10	4	8	7
AB	3	5	7	5	3	4	3
BC	1	2	4	3	5	1	1

* Source: CCSD *Poverty Fact Book 2000*

Quality

Quality is determined by the provincial commitment to a well-rounded, adequately funded system of post-secondary education. This is illustrated by several indicators: the amount per capita spent on post-secondary education (PSE), as well as the provincial expenditure of PSE, in addition to the per capita university operating grants. These, in part, indicate the degree to which provincial governments fund higher education, as well as the physical infrastructure of educational institutions. In large part funding determines an institution's ability to accommodate students, faculty and support staff, to provide students with an education, and to allow universities and colleges to fulfil their mandate to carry out research, teaching, and community service.

The role of the faculty is also significant—it is for this reason that we have included information on the percentage change in the number of faculty on campus, as well as the student/faculty ratio from province to province. The latter is an important indicator of education quality, as one of the surest measures of success is determined by face-to-face student/faculty contact.

Quality Rankings

Province	% University Faculty Change 92/93 - 98/99	% College Faculty Change 92/93 - 96/97	Change in Prov. Expenditure on PSE (99/00)	Avg. Student / Faculty Ratio (1996-1999)	Per Capita University Operating Grants (1999-2000)	Quality Rank	Last Year Quality Rank
NF	10	8	7	2	1	6	8
PEI	1	6	10	1	7	5	8
NS	5	9	9	4	4	8	5
NB	3	1	4	5	2	1	3
PQ	7	3	1	8	5	3	1
ON	8	5	8	10	10	10	10
MB	9	4	6	3	3	5	7
SK	6	10	5	7	6	9	4
AB	4	7	2	10	8	8	6
BC	2	2	3	6	9	2	1

Affordability, Access and Opportunity

The accessibility of institutions is determined largely by how the provinces have participated in eliminating—or at least mitigating—financial barriers to university and college. We have therefore provided information about college and university tuition as well as the percentage change in both.

The 18-24 year old participation rate is a useful means of calculating the financial ability of the majority of students to attend institutions of higher learning.

Affordability, Access and Opportunity Rankings

Province	Avg. Undergrad University Tuition (2000-2001)	Avg. College Tuition (1999-2000)*	% Change in University Tuition (90/91-99/00)	% Change in College Tuition (90/91-99/00)*	Avg. % 18-24 Year Olds' Participation Rate	Afford., Access & Opp. Rank	Last Year's Afford., Access & Opportunity Rank
NF	4	4	9	9	4	7	5
PEI	6	8	3	4	8	5	8
NS	10	2	7	2	1	3	3
NB	7	10	2	10	2	8	7
PQ	1	1	5	1	7	1	1
ON	9	5	8	5	3	7	6
MB	3	3	4	6	6	3	4
SK	5	9	6	7	5	9	8
AB	8	6	10	8	9	10	10
BC	2	7	1	3	10	4	2

Source: ACAATO Environment Scan 2000

Accountability

Accountability is the degree to which provincial governments ensure that universities and colleges are in fact accountable to the public, and not to corporations or individuals. This is determined largely by the amount of public funding dedicated to PSE provincial budgets, as compared to funding from private donations or student fees. We have ranked provinces poorly if they rely strongly on private donations or student fees because universities and colleges are public institutions and should be funded from the provincial budget.

We have also attempted to provide some indication of provincial governments' responsiveness to public concern about the increasing inaccessibility of higher education for more and more students. This has been accomplished by awarding provinces with points in the following areas: if the province has frozen tuition; if the province has decreased tuition; if the province increased student grants and is using them correctly; and if the province has an existing grants system.

The Canadian Millennium Scholarship Fund has been calculated by provinces as a grant—however it is a program which has done little to minimize student debt, and has in fact been extremely ineffective in Ontario and Nova Scotia. Quebec is one province which, by no means perfect, has shown consistently high levels of provincial funding for education, and have chosen to not sign the Canadian Millenium Scholarship Fund agreement—we have awarded them for their decision to refuse a flawed system.

Furthermore, BC's funding includes monies for both public and private institutions; as Ontario has also opened the door to private colleges, additional research much be done to better determine the impact of these institutions on accountability.

(Jeremy Gillies is a Communications and Information Technology Specialist with the Canadian Union of Postal Workers' National Office in Ottawa. He is currently working on a web site project for CUPW and is a member of CUPE local 1979—www.cupw-sttp.org)

Accountability Rankings

Province	% of PSE funding from Gov't (1998-1999)	% of PSE funding from Student Fees (1998-1999)	% of PSE funding from Private Sources (1998-1999)	Needs Based Point System	Accountability Rank	Last Year's Accountability Rank
NF	2	6	1	8	3	7
PEI	3	7	2	6	5	4
NS	10	10	3	10	9	9
NB	8	8	5	6	8	3
PQ	1	1	8	6	2	1
ON	9	9	10	10	10	10
MB	4	4	9	1	5	6
SK	5	2	6	6	6	8
AB	7	5	7	8	8	5
BC	6	3	4	1	1	2

Newfoundland: Cold comfort
By Dale Kirby

The March 2000 budget speech in the province of Newfoundland and Labrador contained good news of marginal proportions for post-secondary students in the province. Although no significant new funding was made available for post-secondary education and training, it was announced that the current freeze on tuition costs would remain for the 2000-01 and 2001-02 academic years. This provides little other than cold comfort and does nothing to offset the burden caused by the tuition hikes of more than 250% over less than a decade.

One of the greatest post-secondary education policy deficiencies in Newfoundland and Labrador lies with the Department of Education's Student Loan Remission Program.

The Student Loan Remission Program

This program, a form of student loan forgiveness, was implemented as a component of the new provincial student loan scheme introduced in 1994. At that time, the Government of Newfoundland and Labrador eliminated a provincial needs-based non-repayable post-secondary study grant program and replaced it with the current program.

The grant program had been available to university and college students from 1978 to 1994. While the loan program enabled students to access an increased amount of financial assistance, the elimination of grants resulted in savings of over $10 million to government coffers while students were obligated to assume a significantly higher amount of loan debt. The provincial government has since acknowledged that the effect of eliminating provincial grants for post-secondary study has led to an increase in the average annual amount borrowed by students. For example, compared to the 1993-94 academic year when grants were available, the average student loan in Newfoundland and Labrador has increased by more than 100%. The introduction of the loan program and the Newfoundland Student Loan Remission Program was motivated by fiscal restraint as opposed to a desire to enhance public access to post-secondary education.

Eligibility criteria

Under the program, the province assumes the responsibility for repayment of a portion of students' loans following graduation. The problems with the program are numerous and relate specifically to the basic eligibility criteria which determine whether students qualify for loan remission. The criteria for the program are as follows:

1. The student must complete a program of study of a minimum of 80 weeks in duration. If the program is completed outside the province of Newfoundland and Labrador, one or more of the following conditions must be met: a) the program was not available in the province, b) the student was enrolled in graduate studies, c) the program was substantially different from any program available in the province, d) the student did not meet the minimum entrance requirements for a similar program in the province, but did meet the minimum entrance requirements for the same program at an institution outside the province, e) the student applied to enter a similar program within the province, but was not admitted due to limited enrolment in the program, f) the student received transfer credits toward or advanced standing into the program, which reduced the program length, and/or g) the student's spouse was undertaking studies outside the province for which he/she was eligible for Loan Remission as a result of one or more of the aforementioned criteria being met.
2. The student must graduate within the required number of study periods normally specified for completion of a program, plus a *grace period* of one academic year. This condition is referred to as *timely completion*. If there are extenuating circumstances that cause students to take a longer period of time to complete their programs of study, they must provide supporting documentation to that effect.
3. Students' combined Canada and Newfoundland Student Loan debt for the academic period, referred to in 1, must exceed the minimum debt threshold of: a) $22,016, for programs of study with between 80 and 128 borrowing weeks, or b) $172 per week multiplied by the number of borrowing weeks in program of study, for program lengths that exceed 128 borrowing weeks.

Students who meet all of the above criteria are eligible to have the portion of their student loan in excess of the minimum debt threshold forgiven. However, no remission is granted on the portion of the loan borrowed during the grace period.

A myriad of problems

As stated earlier, the problems associated with the basic eligibility criteria are numerous. First of all, the criteria are largely confusing. An example of this would be the calculation required to ascertain the minimum debt threshold for program lengths that exceed 128 borrowing weeks. Another problem relates to the required minimum debt threshold–the minimum amount a student has to have borrowed in order to qualify for loan remission. This amount appears to be quite arbitrary and there seems to be an implication that any student loan debt below the threshold amount is an acceptable level of debt for a graduate. Why would this be the case? And, on what basis has this judgment been made?

Another problem lies is the timely program completion requirement. There are several potential reasons why a student may not complete a program in the time period required. All of these reasons may not necessarily qualify as *extenuating circumstances*. For example, students' parental responsibilities or their decision to work on a part-time basis may necessitate that their period of study be extended beyond that required for *timely completion*. As with the defined minimum debt threshold, definitions of extenuating circumstances are variable and subjective.

Further, student borrowers who take a longer period of time to graduate may assume larger amounts of student loan debt but are not eligible for loan remission. Is it not inequitable to deny them loan debt forgiveness? There is also that group of students who borrow for post-secondary studies but fail to graduate from a program. Is it not inequitable to deny them loan remission? Also, consider those students who have a student loan debt but completed programs of less than 80 weeks in duration. Is it not inequitable to deny them loan remission?

Another problem is that students who begin one program of study and decide to switch to another program are ineligible for loan remission on the portion of the student loan borrowed to finance the partially completed program.

A final example of the many problems associated with the loan remission policy is that students are not eligible for debt forgiveness on the portion of their student loan debt accumulated during the so-called "grace period."

The apparent arbitrary nature of the policy for granting loan remission under the Newfoundland Student Loan Remission Program—the basic eligibility criteria—raises many questions with respect to fairness and equity. It is justifiable to suggest that the policy is severely flawed and in desperate need of revision.

(Dale Kirby was chairperson of the Newfoundland and Labrador Federation of Students from 1997 from 1999. He completed a Bachelor of Science (1998) and a Master of Education (2000) at Memorial University of Newfoundland and is currently pursuing a Ph.D. in Higher Education at the Ontario Institute for Studies in Education at the University of Toronto.)

New Brunswick

Faculty

The number of people employed as full professor or associate professor in New Brunswick in 2000 compared to 1999 fell by 13% and 21%, respectively. In contrast, those employed as assistant, lecturer, part-time or contract rose on average 14%.

One of the events that stands out over the last year in New Brunswick is the faculty strike at Université de Moncton. The strike started on March 2, and it was the first faculty strike in the history of the university. The 300 striking members of the Association des bibliothécaires, des professeures et professeurs de l'Université de Moncton, who had been without a contract since June 1999, were asking for wage parity with their provincial counterparts. The salary difference is about 20%.

The starting salary of a lecturer in 1998-99 was only $27,500—about $6,500 less than starting salaries at the University of New Brunswick, St. Thomas, and Mount Allison. The average median salary of a New Brunswick faculty member is 10% lower than the average Canadian salary. The annual salary increases—if they can be called that—reached during the last round of bargaining four years ago was 0%, 0%, 0%, and 1.5%. Low wage rates were the major reason for the strike, but workload, research assistance, and governance were equally important.

The Université de Moncton faculty and librarians ratified a new agreement on April 6 after five weeks on the picket line. A salary increase of just under 15% over four years, starting in July 1999, was gained, as well as a commitment to parity with other New Brunswick universities by 2006. The 36-day strike, with almost 100% participation, was one of the half-dozen longest strikes in Canadian university history.

At the start of this round of bargaining, the Moncton administration tabled a three-year salary offer of 0% for each of the three years. In the final days of negotiations, the government even had back-to-work legislation ready to introduce should no settlement be reached.

Equity

In 1985, the percentage of female faculty and librarians at New Brunswick universities was under 20%, and by 1999 it had increased to over 30%. But this is still underutilizing the pool of available candidates. Over 40% of Ph.D. graduates in the humanities, social sciences, education, and health sciences are female. All New Brunswick universities have employment equity policies or equity clauses firmly established in their collective agreements.

Students

Tuition fees have increased by more than 85% over the last decade, and by almost 6% over 1999. Average fees for undergraduate students is over $3,500. University enrolments remain virtually unchanged since 1992 and community college enrolments have increased 60% over the last five years. There were 5,000 more graduates with university degrees than in 1998, yet the unemployment rate for university graduates fell from 5.1% in 1998 to 4.4% in 1999.

Funding

The Government of New Brunswick provided universities with the largest funding grant in nine years. A total of $164 million is being provided for 2000-2001, an increase of $3.3 million over the previous year, and has guaranteed a 2% funding increase in operating grants each year for the next three years. The government's commitment to a three-year funding formula will allow universities to commit to longer- range plan and may help stabilize tuition fees for students.

Last year, university funding was increased by 1%. Prior to that, the university funding decreased by 2% per year between 1996-97 and 1998-99. The average provincial funding of universities represents 0.85% of the province's gross domestic product (GDP), and is 33% higher than the national average. The provincial government also provided additional funding beyond operating grants, including inter-provincial transfers for New Brunswick students who attend university programs outside the province and incentive funding such as the purchase of 10 new seats at Memorial University Medical School for New Brunswick students.

The provincial government has stated that it is actively lobbying the federal government for a fair share of federal research funding from the Canadian Foundation for Innovation and the Canada Research Chairs. The Atlantic region has received less than its fair share of research funding in past dispersements.

The provincial government allocated $2.75 million for capital spending for the universities over the next two years. This is $250,000 more than was originally intended. This amount is in addition to the $7.75 million UNB has received in capital funding from the province since 1998-99. The Université de Moncton will received $1.2 million and Mount Allison University will receive $1 million to spend on repairs to its physical sciences building.

Nova Scotia: From bad to worse
By Jessica Squires

Nova Scotia is home to eight universities and one community college, with 13 campuses across the province. Nova Scotia imports 40% of its student population to its universities.

Since 1991, tuition fees at some Nova Scotia institutions has risen by more than 120%. The result is that 1999 figures show Nova Scotia held onto its dubious distinction of being the most expensive province in which to attend university, and also gained the additional prestige of per-capita funding levels that were the second-lowest in North America. The community college system is funded at a rate of less than one-half of the national average. Every year thousands of students are turned away—not because they aren't qualified, but because there aren't enough seats in the college system.

Class sizes at Nova Scotia's universities are anecdotally larger in almost every discipline. Art History courses at the Nova Scotia College of Art and Design have nearly doubled, with seminars of 20 students or more. At Dalhousie, administrators were considering holding lower level courses in the movie theatres at a downtown mall, and several courses may now be taught in an on-campus concert hall.

Funding promises made by the previous Liberal government included funding increases of $24 million over three years to the universities, and a one-time increase to colleges of 11%. Both of these promises, however, were put on hold and later scrapped by the newly elected Conservative government. Universities must now deal with a significantly smaller projected amount of grant for the coming academic year.

Overall, the funding situation is unchanged at best, and probably worse than it was 12 months ago. Tuition fees have increased to compensate.

Debt relief disappears

The John Hamm government, elected in July of 1999, tabled a 2000 budget which completely eliminated the Nova Scotia Loan Remission Program, a partial repayment plan available to successful students with debts of over $7,500 in a given academic year. The relief was available on an annual basis: students had to apply for it after each study period for which they received loans. John Hamm's education minister, Jane Purves, justified this cut, announced in the 2000 Budget, on the grounds that the Federal Millennium Scholarship Program would replace it.

The Millennium Scholarship Program helps less than 10% of students. Additionally, figures from the Canadian Federation of Students indicate that some students receiving the grants may actually be worse off than if they took a loan instead, dollar-for-dollar.

Under pressure from students in Nova Scotia and elsewhere, the federal government is currently investigating the use of scholarship funds at the provincial level.

Privatization

Dalhousie University co-runs an information technology degree program with a private institution. Additionally, the Lester Pearson Institute, ostensibly mandated to foster development abroad, has links to ventures underway in any number of countries—including Indonesia and Sierra Leone—in which development attempts have brought about hardship and destruction. Even NSCAD, which was regarded as the last bastion against creeping privatization, recently created a corporate position on the faculty.

This fall, Halifax is host to the Commonwealth Education Ministers' Conference. The Symposium, for which tickets are available at a mere $3,000, is run simultaneously with a trade fair entitled "Shopping for Solutions." This privatization bonanza will doubtless be the focus for many a university administrator seeking private "solutions" to the problems created by the government.

What lies ahead

In January 2000, the government's Voluntary Planning Fiscal Management Task Force tabled its final report, entitled "Taking Control of Our Future." This document, compiled from a preliminary report produced by the task force and with what amounts to lip service to concerns raised by members of the public in an extremely inadequate series of hearings, calls for, among other things, a strategy for lifelong learning.

The Task Force was chaired by Allan Shaw, board member of the Atlantic Institute of Market Studies, a right-wing think tank which holds that transfer payments to Nova Scotia have created a culture of dependency and laziness. Shaw is also a director of Scotiabank and chair of the Dalhousie Board of Governors. Other task force members included lawyer and director of Sydney Steel Ed Harris; Sydney Steel Board Chair Teresa McNeil; and John Risley, President of Clearwater Fine Foods.

The task force claimed as fact that the Nova Scotia deficit represented a crisis, that its debt must be eliminated, and that the way to do it was through downsizing government and cutting public services. Its key recommendations were controlling health care and education spending.

The lifelong learning recommendation, seen in this context, can only be interpreted as a bid for opening the Nova Scotia market to private institutions. Nova Scotia

Teachers' Union President Brian Forbes points to international trade liberalization agreements as the vehicle for widespread creeping privatization at all education levels.

Among the Task Force's recommendations for implementing lifelong learning without additional investment was a provision for "tapping the potential of qualified volunteers" where it is difficult to provide faculty resources.

The bleak picture

The Task Force's own document points out that 55% of Nova Scotia's residents earn less than $20,000 per year. Under the Liberals, research showed that "sticker shock" remained an obstacle to access for post-secondary education in Nova Scotia. This is not surprising considering that most students' annual family income must be considerably less than the total debt likely to be incurred.

The Task Force's report also points out that Nova Scotia ranks last in per capita funding for its community college, last in per-student funding for universities, last in terms of funding as a percentage of GDP, and 41% below the national average in its rate of research investment.

The hack-and-slash approach recommended by the Task Force can only be seen as a bid to improve the economic terrain for the private sector and big business. Its goals for lifelong learning cannot therefore be in much conflict with that agenda.

John Hamm's government is so far following the lead of previous Tory provincial governments under Ralph Klein and Mike Harris. This can only mean more tuition fee increases, more debt increases, less access, and increasing control of the post-secondary sector by private sector agendas and interests.

In the Fall of 1999, for the first edition of **Missing Pieces**, I wrote that, while polls consistently indicated education was a priority for Nova Scotians, the government seemed to consistently de-prioritize it. That contradiction between the needs of Nova Scotia's people and the agenda of the government has not only persisted in the last year; it has worsened.

(Jessica Squires is an artists and activist in Halifax.)

PSE on PEI
By Mary Boyd

Post-secondary education on Prince Edward Island continues to operate on roughly the same funding it received a decade ago. The consequences of this are many, particularly increased tuition fees as the decline in public funding is compensated for by higher tuition. The higher cost of tuition took its toll in the form of major declines in student enrolment as students were unable to pay the high tuition costs—especially when they faced the prospects of low-paying jobs at the end of their studies.

Tuition at the Atlantic Veterinary College is extremely high and keeps rising. Foreign students pay $40,190 per year for the first and second year, and $1,244 in student fees. Tuition for the third year is $35,320, and $35,184 for the final year. Student fees remain constant for each year. Tuition for Canadian students is $6,570 per year for years one to three, and $6,434 for the final year. Student fees are $460 per year.

Many Island and Maritime graduates of the institution head for the United States upon graduation because starting salaries for veterinarians are around $30,000 in the Maritimes and US$45,000 in the U.S. Graduates want to get rid of their heavy debts as quickly as they can.

Another problem with high student debts is that students are not able to choose the kind of work they want to do or that they trained for. Veterinary grads going to the U.S. often settle for jobs on cattle farms or other areas not in their special training or interest. The same is true for undergraduate students who look for jobs to pay off their debt rather than embarking on a career that would allow them to love their work. Tuition in the Atlantic region is higher than in other parts of the country, and, while it is lower in P.E.I. than in Nova Scotia, it is still high when compared with the Canadian average.

There are some small gains over last year, probably because it was an election year, but they are insignificant compared to the needs. The provincial government boosted funding to the university by $1 million in the 2000-01 provincial budget in return for a one-year freeze on tuition. The university lists ways in which the money was quickly consumed. Increases in staff salaries, equipment replacement and supply costs will eat up most of the money.

Furthermore, the University faces large infrastructure costs. Maintenance of the physical plant is a big problem and in the days of cutbacks, maintenance was deferred and the need to renovate buildings was squeezed.

Also, during the time of cutbacks there was an increase in sessional lecturers. The problem has been raised for discussion, but it is unlikely, given the limited increased funding and the need for infrastructure repair, that much will be done about the situation in the near future. Although the freeze is in effect, there is no legislation and it could very well be lifted in the coming budget.

Secondly, the 2000-01 budget brought an individual student grant of $600 for all third- and fourth-year students at UPEI and Holland College. Excluded from the grant are first- and second-year students, Bachelor of Education students, and students at the Veterinary College. The grant is part of the Millennium Scholarship Fund.

The University claims it did not follow the privatization trend to the extreme that many other provinces did. For example, security and the physical plant have not been privatized. But students now pay parking fees, lab fees, and music tutorial fees. On the other hand, the university established the AVC Inc., which, although controlled by the university, searches out corporate sponsors for research.

Enrolment of full-time students at UPEI dropped to 2,800 in 1999-00, representing the largest decline in the country. There has been a slight increase of 150 full-time students for the year 2000-01. This could be due to such factors as higher tuition fees in neighbouring Nova Scotia, emphasis on the importance of a university education, and participation of high school students which is up this year from 26% to 29%.

The increase in enrolment, however, does not make up for the heavy decreases experienced between 1992 and this year.
At the same time, part-time student enrolment decreased by more than 50%. Some of this decline can be explained be explained by lack of employment opportunities, and some may be because the majority of part-time students are women and more of them are enrolling as full-time students and therefore do not have to go back later. Another factor is a switch to the many private colleges that have appeared in recent years offering specific shills.

The university offers free tuition to Islanders over the age of 60 as part of a centennial project established to commemorate the province's entry into Confederation in 1873.

Apart from the Island Student Awards, students rely on student loans which offer a maximum of $9,350 per year. The student grant system fell victim to cuts in 1995, and was replaced by a loan remission plan which can reduce a student's debt by as much as $10,000, once they fulfill the requirements for graduation. Given this write-off, a student could still owe more than $25,000 at the end of four years, a definite deterrent to pursuing graduate studies.

Furthermore, students do not find this program to be as effective or helpful as the provincial student grant. P.E.I. has no public transportation system and students have to rely on cars, which increases costs. Parking fees introduced three years ago add further to the cost.

Given that P.E.I. has the second-lowest minimum wage in the country at $5.60 an hour, and given that the tourist industry is one of the largest summer employers, it is clear that students can hardly meet summer living expenses, let alone save for tuition and other costs.

Tuition fees at Holland College and College L'Acadie vary between 3,500 to 9,000, depending on the course. Fees for Holland College are among the highest in the country. From time-to-time, students have to question the relevancy of what they receive and complain that they are not even getting what they paid for, since staff was cut back at that institution, as well.

The big challenge to the college is to train people for new types of work to replace the traditional fishing and farming which is on the decline, or becoming more mechanized. Many of the graduates have to leave the Island for employment, posing a challenge to stir creative forces in the students to be able to design, create and produce things that people need and will buy. Holland College's funding per capita is the lowest in the country, making this demand quite challenging. Unfortunately, its curriculum is all market-driven and in need of an overhaul to meet current demands.

(Mary Boyd is a PEI activist.)

Quebec
By Normand Baillargeon and Martin Petit

Recent struggles

Commercial universities: Progress and setbacks

Bringing the entire university - both its practices, such as research and teaching, and its standards - to the marketplace, is a long and complicated process, which has been achieved to various degrees in the province. The government of Quebec offers the highest degree of public support for its universities and Cégeps, at 68% and the lowest tuition fees in the country. While the province of Quebec when compared to the rest of Canada seems to be providing the right mix of leadership, funding and support, struggles still exist.

But there is no reason to doubt that the elite and the dominant institutions want to achieve such commercialization. However, it is important to note that this marketplace, whose standards and purposes will determine how the university is redefined will be the one to prevail in our societies, where we (fraudulently) designate as the free market a process of socializing the risks and costs. The same applies to universities and will continue to apply unless there is sufficiently strong resistance: university funding comes mostly from public dollars because their operating costs are huge and could not solely be assumed by the marketplace. However, its purposes and benefits must increasingly be brought back to private interests.

Quebec has not escaped the trend summarily described here, which reaches the entire university sector, particularly in North America. There has already been a substantial rethinking of research, to varying degrees depending on the institution, and a reorientation of its practice to meet the needs and desires of private interests. There are now numerous examples to worry about what will happen to the standards and purposes of academic life as the ethos of research retreats in the face of commercialization. There is little doubt that teaching will be the next item subjected to the same process and that Internet will play a fundamental role. University education will then become merely the learning and teaching of disciplines that are increasingly specific, ad hoc and geared to the job market, and deprived of the universalist and empowering aims that are the foundation of university education and teaching.

But the market's entry into universities also takes more direct forms, which some would like us to believe are innocuous. That is precisely what is happening with advertising in education establishments; it is also what is happening with various types of commercial agreements reached between corporations and university establishments.

❖ ❖ ❖

In Quebec, soft drink bottlers are now faced with real and sometimes successful resistance, which gives hope to all those of us who refuse to accept the advent of the commercial university.

Last December 6, Laval University announced that it would not sign an exclusivity contract with Coke or Pepsi. The university administration chose to respect the democratic decision of its student associations. On January 12, the University of Quebec in Montreal (UQAM) also declared that it was renouncing the contract already negotiated with Coca-Cola, a contract that would have made this company the university's sole distributor of soft drinks. McGill University was set to do the same in early April. It is instructive to go over the events as they occurred at UQAM.

On October 19, 1999, after a few months of negotiations, the university administration proposed to the board of directors that they uphold an agreement with Coca-Cola. It was to be a $5.9 million contract over ten years. The proposal's "sponsor" was none other than Jean-Marc Léger, president of Léger & Léger, a polling agency. It should be pointed it out that this company - which we can't help but describe as "manipulating" the public – is precisely the one that had been retained to survey the Laval University students and had depicted them as being in favour of advertising on campus.

The board of directors' proposal gave rise to strong student protest. One after another, a majority of UQAM students, university professors' unions, lecturers and employees opposed the signing of this contract. On November 24, after a peaceful demonstration, police arrested 66 students. During another demonstration within the UQAM campus, the university president admitted to her audience that she obeyed police requests during those arrests; she apparently followed the police recommendation asking the establishment's security services to lock the doors behind the demonstrators. Trapped, some of them were arrested. That was the last straw. Students and professors publicly demanded the resignation of the university president. Shortly before the Christmas break, the board of directors gave in to the pressure and put everything on hold.

On January 12, the board of directors of UQAM adopted the following proposal rejecting the agreement with Coke: "Considering the rift within the community as a result of the board of directors' decision; Considering the serious challenges facing UQAM and the need for solidarity with all segments of the community to rise to these challenges; considering the importance of ending a debate that is affecting the University's smooth operation; It is moved by Paule Leduc, seconded by Jean-Marc Léger, that the board of directors rescind its resolution 99-A-10864 authorizing, with limitations, the signing of a supply contract with Coca-Cola Ltd."

The "democracy" of universities

This event suggests that a university's board of directors is quite likely to adopt decisions that go against the interests and expressed wishes of a majority of its professoral and student body, not to mention those of the public that finance the university. As such, this event compels us to seriously ponder what is left and, ultimately, what will be left of this defining characteristic of a university. Democracy has played such an important role in the development of universities and allowed them to assert themselves as a gathering of professors and students that is self-determining based on their own academic and universalist purposes. From this perspective, the very structure and power of these boards is quite disturbing. For example, the UQAM board of directors consists of only 15 voting members making important decisions, five of whom are from the business sector and three from the senior administration. Therefore, eight people can impose their power and will as they represent more than half the board of directors. Yet UQAM has more than 30,000 students, hundreds of professors, lecturers.

For example, another contract adopted by this same board of directors fuels is cause for concerns. It includes, "clauses that are very restricting for UQAM and abnormally generous for AEterna," the company that signed this contract with the establishment. In these same minutes, excerpts on the research contract reached with AEterna - a private biopharmaceutical company - deserve our attention. For example:

"UQAM offers important services to a private firm under conditions that make any research publication impossible and under which university freedom looses out. It is also noted that UQAM will not reap any commercial gains that may stem from the results of the research conducted at the university.

The Vice-President of Research, Creation and Planning at UQAM responds that the confidentiality and intellectual property clauses in this contract are standard clauses in any research contract with a private company: they are agreed to by the company and the professor conducting the research. The professors and students' broader publishing rights referred to are those granted when research is publicly funded.

(...)

The President recognizes that the issue of intellectual property is relevant and important: the Minister of Research, Science and Technology intends to devote a lot of attention to it in the draft research policy being prepared. Everyone will have to consider the role of the institution, the professors and the students in issues of intellectual property and research contracts."

UQAM's board of directors then gave the Vice-President of Research, Creation and Planning the mandate to sign the contract with AEterna Laboratories. There were eight votes in favour, three against and two abstentions.

How can we not be surprised by the flippancy with which such crucial issues are dealt with? How can we not worry about the fact that public universities assume, for all practical purposes, the mandate to sign agreements that limit their primary mission? (Note the reminder given that the "standard" clauses in this contract are regularly part of agreements signed at UQAM.)

Also, the process of socializing risks and costs mentioned earlier is so remarkably effective in this case, that it provides a perfect example. Consider the following: AEterna received $29.4 million from the federal government under Technology Partnerships Canada. In addition, Canada offers, precisely in AEterna field of operations, the best tax treatment of all industrialized countries insofar as research and development are concerned.

❖ ❖ ❖

This example shows it well; in the province of Quebec, as elsewhere, the forces (at work) to ensure the highjacking of public universities are remarkably powerful, orgazined, and aware of the interests they defend. But the cancelled agreements with the soft drink bottlers also show that the usual proviso applies once again. This proviso is as follows: the future hasn't been written yet, and what it will be will largely depend on us, our actions, our awareness of what is happening and our willingness to fight.

A humanist concept of education, a free and empowered citizenry, critical thought and, finally, public good and democracy all critically depend on it.

(Normand Baillargeon is a Professor at the Université du Québec à Montréal Martin Petit is a Researcher at the Institut de recherche et d'informations socio-économiques [IRIS])

Ontario
By Chris Charlton

Tuition fees

In March, 2000, the Ontario government announced yet another tuition fee increase for 2000-01 of 2% a year for five years. Nearly one-third (30%) of the annual tuition increase must be held back for student financial assistance. The average Arts and Science tuition fee was $3,950 for 2000-01 for universities. Between 1995-2000, average tuition fees will have risen by 60%, or $1, 450.

Fees have already been fully deregulated for international students and for certain professional programs, allowing institutions to charge tuition on a full-cost recovery basis. For example, Queen's University now charges $22,000 for its executive MBA program, and Western's general MBA program is $18,000. Tuition for Waterloo's Master of Taxation program is $24,000. Fees for Dentistry programs have also been deregulated and in 1999-2000 first-year medical students at the University of Toronto were charged an annual tuition fee of $11,000.

An increasing proportion of program costs are now covered through tuition fees. Already, by 1998-99, tuition paid by students represents an estimated 38% of university program costs. The proportion of university program costs represented by tuition exceeds the 35% mentioned in the 1999 Conservative Party's *Blueprint* and the 25% level advocated by the Conservatives in the 1995 election, as well as in statements contained in *New Directions II*.

The Progressive Conservative government has outlined its tuition policy in the following terms: "Tuition fees are an important part of the way we fund a healthy post-secondary education system...To restore the balance in funding for colleges and universities, we brought tuition fees back to the reasonable and affordable 35% [of the cost of providing university and colleges courses]".

Blueprint claims that increased funding for student assistance allows universities and colleges to remain accessible despite higher tuition fees.

Student loan program

Ontario's student aid system was primarily grants-based until 1993, when the government eliminated the grants. Ontario student aid is now almost exclusively loans-based, with the possibility of loan forgiveness if a student borrows more than $7,000 per year. There are some bursaries available for students with disabilities.

The May 1999 Ontario Budget provides for an '*Aiming for the Top*' tuition scholarships for the top 2,500 students in Ontario who require financial assistance. The scholarship will pay up to $3,500 a year of a student's tuition fees for up to four years, provided students maintain their grades.

The number of Ontario Graduate Scholarships (OGS) as outlined in 2000 Ontario budget will increase from 1,300 to 2,000 and the value of the scholarship will increase from $11,859 to $15,000. Whereas the government previously provided all the funding for the OGS, universities will now be expected to provide one-third of the funding for this scholarship, paralleling the funding arrangements for the OGS in Science and Technology. Another $4 million has been allocated to free tuition for medical students agreeing to practice in rural and northern Ontario.

In November 1999, the Ontario government announced almost $30 million in cuts to post-secondary education. The largest portion of these cuts, **$16.3 million**, is to come from tightening eligibility for student loans. Families are expected to contribute greater amounts to their children's educational costs, regardless of whether or not they have the financial means to do so.

These changes have been criticized by university administrators and students as simply motivated by government concerns to cut costs. They also note that these changes increase student debt loads and act as a disincentive to part-time study.

Funding

The May 2000 Budget contained an additional $286 million from the SuperBuild Growth Fund for new university and college buildings and to upgrade existing buildings. Of this amount, $231 million will be provided for 24 projects. Like the first SuperBuild initiative, funding will be allocated on a competitive basis. The government claims that this will create an additional 15,587 spaces for college and universities students.

If the allocation pattern follows the first SuperBuild pattern, then high-tech and applied science programs would receive a greater proportion of the funding. In May, Trent, Brock, Windsor, and the Ontario College of Art and Design, which did not receive any funding from the first initiative, received funding from Superbuild 2. The remaining $55 million will be provided to universities and colleges to modernize buildings.

Total operating grants for next year will be $1.66 billion, an extra $52 million from last year. The increase in funding is a cut in real terms, as it does keep pace with inflation and enrolment growth.

The government's new performance-based funding consists of two envelopes:

1. A $16.5 million Accessibility Fund will be distributed based on enrolment growth in 2000/01 over the previous year.

2. A $16.5 million Performance Indicator Fund will be distributed on the basis of institutional performance in three indi-

cators: the graduation rate of 1991 for new first-year students; the six-month employment rate of 1997 graduates; and the two-year employment rate of 1997 aduates. Institutions will be ranked according to their score, with the top institutions receiving twice as much funding as the middle group, and the bottom third getting no grant.

Universities must obtain private sector and other non-government funding for approved projects. If this private and other funding fails to materialize, SuperBuild support will be withdrawn. Past governments have provided two-thirds of funding for university capital projects and from 75% to 100% of funding for college projects.

Private universities

In April 2000, the government announced that it would permit private for-profit and non-profit universities to offer degree programs in Ontario. The government stated that these universities would not receive public operating or capital funding, but that students would be eligible for publicly-funded student assistance. The Minister of Training, Colleges and Universities has essentially agreed to allow the private for-profit University of Phoenix, Unexus University, and the British IMC University to offer degree programs in Ontario under the ministerial consent process. The private non-profit University of Southern California was also granted permission in November, 1999, to offer a diploma program in Ontario, although this is also not publicly known.

Increasing numbers of out-of-province universities have sought permission from the Ministry of Training, Colleges and Universities to offer university degree programs in Ontario. At present, approximately 10 out-of-province institutions have been granted consent to offer "niche" degree programs.

Faculty

Compounding the corrosive impact of funding cutbacks to operating, capital and student assistance programs, as outlined above, the faculty shortage crisis in Ontario is threatening students' access to a high-quality post-secondary education in this province. Ontario is facing a shortage of university faculty which will become critical in the next few years unless appropriately addressed by the provincial government and university administrations.

Ontario has already lost more than 2,000 full-time equivalent faculty members since 1990-91, representing over 15% of the total complement. This loss is directly attributable to government policies: funding cuts have led universities to offer early retirement packages in order to save costs, while further savings have been realized through layoffs, unfilled vacant positions, days of unpaid leave, and salary cuts or freezes.

Recent plans to increase faculty hiring at some universities do not begin to address the current needs of the university system. Compounding the problem of faculty loss over the past decade is the anticipated rate of retirement by professors over the next 10 years. Currently, a third of faculty members in Ontario are between the ages of 55 and

64, and they will retire just as student enrolment begins to crest.

Current and anticipated faculty shortages have major implications for the quality of education students receive and the research capacity of Ontario universities. Classes are now overcrowded, while professors have many more students to advise and less contact with individual students.

Already student/faculty ratios at Ontario universities have reached unprecedented levels. Between 1988-89 and 1997-98, the ratio of full-time students to full-time faculty member rose by more than 30%. This represents the highest student/faculty ratio in Canada, exceeding the average of the other nine provinces by more than 20%.

One of key factors affecting the quality of the teaching and learning process is the interaction between students and faculty. Faculty create both a teaching and a research environment that nurtures innovation in all disciplines. Canada depends on its higher education sector for almost one-quarter of its national research and development effort, while Ontario is home to 40% of the scholarly and research activity in the country.

Conclusion

As it has done increasingly with operating funding, the Ontario government has used the SuperBuild program to attempt to steer students away from the humanities and social sciences into disciplines such as computer science, engineering, medical research, and communications. The Ontario government's direction has been guided by a narrow conception of universities as vocational training for the labour market and a very shortsighted understanding of the labour market in a knowledge-based economy.

(Chris Charlton is a Policy Analyst with the Ontario Confederation of University Faculty Associations—www.ocufa.on.ca)

Manitoba
By Chris Dooley and Todd Scarth

It is hard to draw an accurate map of post-secondary education in Manitoba right now, as new programs and initiatives are springing up in a variety of places, while others are being reconfigured. The new government's election promise of a tuition fee reduction has been carried out, and there has been an infusion of money into the badly suffering community college system.

One legacy of the 10 years of the Filmon Conservative government, which throughout its mandate remained hostile to publicly funded post-secondary education, is a system propelled by chronic underfunding into a state of perpetual crisis. Manitoba's institutions have suffered the loss of faculty and programs, deep cuts in library acquisitions, and an accumulated "infrastructure deficit"—the costs associated with neglect when the higher education budgets were insufficient to maintain capital infrastructure, declining enrolments, etc.

Tuition Fees

Undergraduate Arts Tuition

In 2000, one of the major platform initiatives of the new NDP government was a 10% tuition fee reduction. Provincial average figures for 2000-01 are estimated to be $2,873 for an undergraduate Arts program. This compares to $3,018 in 1999-2000 and $1,416 in 1990-01 (all figures unadjusted). International graduate students in Manitoba pay no differential fee. The gap between Arts tuition and the tuition fees levied for other programs has widened at an accelerating rate over the last decade. General Science programs are 15% to 18% more expensive that General Arts programs.

Student Aid

For the year 2000, Manitoba has pledged $6 million for what it calls the Manitoba Bursary Program, and an additional $11 million in Millennium Scholarships will be awarded. This is the first time the province

A 30-hour General Arts course load:	
University of Manitoba	$3,040
University of Winnipeg	$3,240
Brandon University	$2,975

has awarded bursaries since 1992. The Manitoba Bursary Program will assist an additional 2,600 students with awards averaging $2,300. Together, the two bursaries are projected to provide assistance to approximately 5,500 students. In 1999-2000, a student attending a regular four-year program at a Manitoba university had a maximum Canada/Manitoba Student Loan entitlement of $9,350 a year, or $37,400 over four years. As of 2000-01, students approved to receive either the Canada Millennium Scholarship or the Manitoba Bursary Program assistance will have their new maximum repayable portion reduced to approximately $6,000 per year or $24,000 over four years, a 36% reduction in maximum debt.

Currently, the maximum Manitoba Study Assistance award is $40 per week of study (in addition to the amount given by the Canada and Manitoba Student Loans). The proportion of the total Manitoba Student Financial Assistance program monies given in the form of non-repayable grants dropped from over $9 million in 1990-91 to under $2 million in 1999-2000. Grants programs, etc., in the provincial budget estimates for 2000-01 are as follows:

Total Loans and Bursaries	$7.6 million
Interest Relief and Debt Reduction	$1.1 million
Manitoba Scholarships and Bursaries Initiative:	$5 million
Manitoba Learning Tax Credit	$14.4 million
Canada Study Grants:	$2.1 million
Canada Millennium Scholarship Fund	$11.0 million
Manitoba Millennium Bursary Fund	$6.0 million
Total:	**$47 million**

Manitoba offers a "Learning Tax Credit" which is a refundable provincial income tax credit in the amount of 7% of gross tuition costs. The province spends about $15 million annually on this program. Tax credit offer effectiveness in increasing accessibility is limited because it arrives long after the student has already had to raise the money to pay tuition; the student cannot be guaranteed that the credit will still exist when they go to apply for it; and, as a non-refundable tax credit, it is useless to low-income people.

An additional $1.03 million was allocated in the 2000-01 budget to the "Post-Secondary Strategic Initiatives Fund" which will provide money for the targeted expansion of university and community colleges. The government also announced a $5.1 million "Colleges Expansion Initiative" that will provide additional spaces and infrastructure for community colleges, especially to develop programs of strategic labour market importance. Much of the 2000-01 grant will be used to re-introduce the Registered Nurse diploma program.

Provincial Funding

Operating grants to the universities

1990-01	$193,391,400
1999-2000	$222,737,600
2000-01	$231,169,000

Operating Grants to Colleges

1999-2000	$61,792,200
2000-01	$64,156,900

At the close of the 1990s, Manitoba had the lowest rate of post-secondary participation in the country, and the lowest rate of public spending as a percentage of GDP of any province. The recent change in provincial government presents reasons for guarded optimism. The new government provided a 4.3% year-over-year increase in post-secondary education spending in its first budget. The government has also pledged to broaden the province's highly successful ACCESS programs, which seek to attract and retain non-traditional (primarily Aboriginal) students to post-secondary institutions. ACCESS programs, although they were extended to several additional institutions in the 1990s, suffered after 1992, when the financial aid component of the program was folded into the provincial student loan program.

While funding was up by 4.3% between 1999 and 2000, about two-thirds of the new money will be taken up in compensating universities for the tuition reduction. After inflation is factored, university funding is effectively frozen, and the government has not yet outlined a plan to reverse the effective 13% cut in total allocations from the province on purchasing power of grants that the universities have weathered since 1992. Without a commitment to increased funding, tuition fees will continue to rise. Tuition fees continue to represent the second largest source (30%) of university revenues after public funds, as compared to under 20% in 1990-91 and under 15% in 1988-89.

The University of Manitoba Libraries recently announced that a further 500 journal subscriptions would not be renewed. This marks the sixth round of cost-cutting journal subscription cancellations since 1991, and the total subscription count declined of 42%.

Crumbling and inadequate infrastructure has also been a chronic problem for all of the province's post-secondary institutions. It is estimated that it will cost at least $200 million to remedy.

Quality

Quality at Manitoba's post-secondary institutions has suffered, not only from the effects of under funding, but from sheer demoralization. According to the CAUT, full-time faculty members at Canadian universities dropped by 7% between 1993-94 and 1996-97. The largest drop, 11%, was seen in Manitoba, with the University of Manitoba posting a decline of 13%. At least part of this precipitous drop can be seen as a reaction to the hostile climate that was created—some would say, engineered—by the government of the day, and early retirement incentive plans have been embraced with enthusiasm.

The legacy of the funding cuts of the 1990s has been a global loss in teaching and research capacity at university institutions, and an acute shortage of spaces in the community college system. In the last decade, university institutions have hemorrhaged tenured faculty as early retirement incentive plans designed to reduce payrolls have been embraced by many faculty members. Few of these retirements have been replaced with permanent tenure track faculty, and the result, already observable in a decline in the graduate student population, has been an overall loss in research and teaching capacity. Research capacity and overall educational opportunity are further threatened by such things as obsolete teaching infrastructure and declining library acquisitions.

Conclusion

The New Democratic government has shown a commitment to accessibility and an affinity for expanded community college education. It has failed, however, to clarify what it imagines its future tuition policy to be, and it has not addressed the most basic concern of the post-secondary institutions themselves: that the base level of funding has dropped below the threshold of sustainability, so simply focusing on the consumption costs for students will not help to avert a crisis in quality of instruction and research.

(Chris Dooley is an independent scholar and CCPA-MB Research Associate. Todd Scarth is the Director of CCPA-MB.)

Post-secondary education in Saskatchewan
By Loretta Gerlach

It was a critical year for post-secondary education in Saskatchewan. The NDP/Liberal Coalition brought down a budget based on "sweeping tax reform" that included a "historical tax cut," and indicated that the average family of four would save $1,000 per year. While the budget also revealed increases in funding to many aspects of post-secondary education, these increases do not keep up with increased expenses, and as a result students are bearing the burden through increased fees.

Provincial Budget and Related Grants

The 2000-01 budget included a 4% increase, equalling $10.3 million, to the universities, federated and affiliated colleges, and the Saskatchewan Institutes of Applied Science and Technology (SIAST). This was in addition of a 2.5% increase in the base grant that was part of the province's plan to implement the funding model of the DesRosiers Report. This breaks down to $7.5 million for the universities and the federated and affiliated colleges, $2.2 million for SIAST, $400,000 for the regional colleges, and $200,000 for Aboriginal institutions. The budget provided $8 million in capital spending to the two universities.

This year's budget also introduced a $350 Graduate Tax Credit. This tax credit will be provided to any graduate of a post-secondary institute who chooses to live and work in Saskatchewan, and it can be claimed within four years of graduation. The government is projecting the spend $3 million a year on the tax credit.

There were other increases included in the budget. The province provided an additional $1 million to the Employability Assistance for People with Disabilities Program; $1.4 million dollars earmarked to support technology-enhanced learning across the province, especially in rural and northern communities; and $1 million dedicated to the creation of a forestry training initiative. Finally, the 2000-01 provincial budget included the Centenary Fund, created to prepare the province for the next century. This will provide an additional $5 million a year for the next four years for post-secondary projects to be announced in the future.

Tuition Fees

Tuition fees increased dramatically in response to the provincial budget allocations. While the province increased funding levels, the institutions claimed that the increases did not meet with increased expenses. The budget provided only an overall increase of 2.5% for the University of Saskatchewan where tuition fees were promptly raised dramatically for 2000-01. Increases ranged from 6% for the average undergraduate program to 14% for specialized programs such as medicine. The University of Saskatchewan increased tuition fees by about 1.9% last year but remained unconcerned about this year's sharp increase since they are still comparable to those in other universities in western Canada. At the University of Regina, tuition fees were increased 7.73%, up significantly from last year. The University of Regina blamed the provincial government's inequitable distribution of the provincial grant (the University of Saskatchewan gets about two-thirds of the grant for universities) for the dramatic rise in fees.

Student Loans

Recent changes to the administration and distribution of the Saskatchewan Student Loan program removed restrictions on students studying outside of the province. In addition, the interest-free period on new and continuing Saskatchewan Student Loans has been changed to mirror the Canada Student Loan Program. Of course, January 2000 marked the start of distribution of approximately 3,200 Millenium Scholarships, as well as 119 Exceptional Merit Awards.

Other Significant Developments

The provincial government passed the Saskatchewan Indian Technologies Act that acknowledged the Saskatchewan Indian Institute of Technologies (SIIT) as a technical institute governed by the Federation of Saskatchewan Indian Nations. The SIIT issues certificates and diplomas, and the passing of this legislation should allow graduates to be better recognized by employers and other post-secondary institutions. The legislation allows SIIT to formally evolve from a community college to a primary technical institute for First Nations people. SIIT has about 1,400 students in seven campuses across the province.

In May, the Province released the *Futures Close to Home Report: Report of the Regional Colleges Committee of Review*. This report was commissioned to address the growing educational needs of people from rural and northern Saskatchewan. The report provides 52 recommendations intended to meet post-secondary education and training needs over the next decade. There is a growing demand for higher education in these areas; in 1998-99, regional colleges in Saskatchewan provided about 35,000 course registrations through eight regional colleges across the province offering independent university and SIAST courses.

Conclusions

Despite the Saskatchewan government's commitment to increased spending on post-secondary education, institutions have indicated that grants are not sufficient to match increased participation and expenses. As a result, funding shortages are being offloaded to students, making the financial burden of post-secondary education more and more unbearable. Commitments to First Nations and students with disabilities are positive starts in addressing the additional stress felt by these students, but there is still a long way to go in making post-secondary education more accessible to equity-seeking students.

The provincial NDP/Liberal coalition government has yet to make good on its promises of financial relief for students. The NDP promised to provide one year of post-secondary education free of cost to students, and the Liberals campaigned on a promise of $1,000 annual scholarships for each university student for up to five years.

Despite the best intentions, tax breaks and token increases are clearly not sufficient in ensuring that students in Saskatchewan have accessible, affordable education. The average $1,000 tax cut that families can expect to receive will not offset the additional burdens being placed on families with students as members.

In addition, with a growing demand for higher education by residents of rural and northern Saskatchewan, the government seems to feel that technologically enhanced programs are the only answer. This begs the question of the quality of education that will be made available in those communities. It's time for the government to abandon neo-liberal approaches to post-secondary funding in favour of meaningful changes that will allow equal access to quality post-secondary education for all the citizens of Saskatchewan.

(Loretta Gerlach is a field worker with the Council of Canadians—www.canadians.org)

Higher education in Alberta, 2000
By Bob Barnetson

Although most people are reluctant to acknowledge it, the cumulative effect of declining government funding has seriously eroded the quality of post-secondary education in Alberta. Inadequate funding has resulted in obsolete equipment and inadequate libraries, while mounting enrolments and deteriorating working conditions are burning out or driving out faculty members. At the same time, the accessibility of higher education—particularly for students from low-income backgrounds —is declining.

Alberta's public post-secondary system serves over 115,000 full-time equivalent students through four universities, 16 public colleges, two technical institutes, and the Banff Centre. Alberta also has five church-affiliated university colleges that grant degrees, a large apprenticeship training program, and over 80 private vocational schools. The pivotal issue affecting these institutions and their students is nearly two decades of declining government funding.

Government funding has dropped by 50.4% over the past 18 years. In 1982, real-dollar per-student transfers to institutions were $12,478. Transfers declined to $7,953 in 1990 and then continued downward to $6,184 per student in 1999. The government has increased its tuition cap several times to provide institutions with additional revenue. Although this has somewhat mitigated the lost government funding, grant- and tuition-based revenue still fell by 34.9% between 1982 and 1999.

Alberta has tuition-fee legislation that caps tuition fees at 30% of net operating costs. Annual tuition fee increases are also limited to approximately $250. Between 1990 and 1999, real-dollar undergraduate tuition fees rose by 142%, with the average student paying slightly more than $3,600 per year in 2000 (excluding fees). College and technical institute tuition remains 30-40% lower. This tuition break, combined with smaller classes sizes, makes colleges' university transfer programs increasingly popular.

During the 1990s, Alberta's student assistance program became increasingly loan-based. Real-dollar debt levels increased by 38% for university graduates and by 12% for college graduates between 1990 and 1998. No data are available for the debt levels of students in professional or graduate programs. In 1998, the average net debt level of university graduates with loans was

$17,300, while college students owed $7,550. The Millennium Scholarships, as well as Alberta's Opportunity Bursaries, have begun to reduce this level, although the government no longer publishes comparable data, perhaps because it was becoming a political liability. Currently, Alberta provides debt remission for university graduates with over $20,000 in loans and for college graduates with over $10,000.

The impact of rising tuition and debt levels is not known as the government resisted examining the issue until 1999. Students and faculty argue that accessibility is predicated upon 1) the availability of seats, and 2) the affordability of tuition and debt levels. In 1999, 75% of learners and 71% of the public were satisfied that adults were able to access the education or training they desire. Despite this, Alberta lags behind the Canadian average in the percentage of 25-34-year-olds who have completed a post-secondary program. As Alberta approaches an election in 2001, the government has agreed to study this potentially damaging issue.

The government has provided additional funding to post-secondary institutions for specific reasons. For example, the Access Fund has created over 12,000 new spaces since 1994, over 90% of which are in fields with clear labour market outcomes (e.g., information technology, science and engineering, business, etc.). The government has also increased research support to market-proximate disciplines, including the establishment of the $500 million Alberta Heritage Foundation for Science and Engineering Research.

Liberal arts programs have been relatively disadvantaged by the increasingly vocational focus of instruction and pressure on institutions to develop and transfer knowledge and technology to the private sector. Other funding envelopes (including one that links performance indicators to funding) reinforce the effect of the Access Fund by favouring market-proximate disciplines.

The government recently announced $200 million for post-secondary infrastructure. Almost 75% of this funding is designated for new construction to meet enrolment demands, particularly in Calgary. This focus on new buildings leaves over $350 million in deferred maintenance largely unaddressed. Additionally, deteriorating working conditions such as rising class sizes and serious shortfalls in library acquisitions are making it difficult to keep top teachers and researchers. This difficulty is exacerbated by the age profile of Alberta's faculty, Alberta's relatively low salaries, and the growing use of poorly paid term appointments.

Perhaps most troubling is the growing privatization of higher education in Alberta. As a result of government policy, institutions are increasingly reliant upon revenue from students and from corporations. This reliance pressures institutions to refocus their efforts on producing private (as opposed to public) goods. For example, the corporate sponsorship of research increases the transfer of (publicly subsidized) knowledge and technology to the private sector.

As students foot more (or all) of the cost of post-secondary programming, the purpose of education narrows to providing the vocational outcomes necessary to make higher education a good investment. This, in turn, justifies rising tuition fees as education becomes a means to increase one's earning potential. Further, as students become customers, pressure exists to pass students regardless of their effort. These outcomes are themselves reinforced by the government's envelope funding system.

These changes have allowed the provincial government to realign the activities of higher education at little political cost. The consequent decline in accessibility and quality, as well as a growing private orientation of institutions, are significant and negative outcomes of government policy.

(Dr. Bob Barnetson is Research and Communications Officer for the Alberta Colleges and Institutes Faculties Association.)

Post-secondary education in British Columbia
By Donna Vogel and Amanda Camley

The government of British Columbia has made improving access to post-secondary education a priority since the New Democratic Party took office in 1992. In part, this was a catch-up measure following years of stagnation in the system. The new emphasis on post-secondary education was also a response to changes in the provincial economy, as jobs in knowledge and high technology industries gradually replace those in traditional resource sectors.

This re-investment in public post-secondary education has clearly paid off. The post-secondary participation rate has gone from second worst at the start of the decade to the current position of fourth best in the country. Enrolment in post-secondary education increased by 10% over the past ten years while the national average fell by 4%.

Public spending on post-secondary education has climbed by 24% over the last 10 years. B.C. opened three new universities in the 1990s: the University of Northern British Columbia; Royal Roads University; and Tech B.C.

The province's system of colleges and institutes has also been substantially expanded. Five colleges and two institutes have expanded to become degree-granting institutions, two First Nations institutes have been created, and tuition-free access to literacy and adult basic education programs has increased.

In 2000, the provincial government announced a funding increase for post-secondary education for the ninth straight year. An additional $96.7 million, up 6% from 1999, has been allocated to: the creation of 5,000 new student spaces (bringing the total of new spaces created over the past decade to more than 20,000); an increase in operating grants to universities and colleges; more money for new equipment and libraries; and new capital initiatives.

Total public spending on advanced education in B.C. now stands at $1.65 billion, or 7% of the total provincial expenditures. Tuition fees in B.C. were frozen in 1992 and again in 1996 by provincial legislation which holds fees at 1995/96 levels. Averaging $2,300 for universities and $1,700 for colleges, tuition fees in B.C. are the second lowest in Canada, next to Quebec.

B.C. also has one of the best systems of loans and needs-based grants in the country. B.C. has used the federal Millennium

Scholarship fund to expand the system of grants for post-secondary education from first and second year to third and fourth year students, as well as implementing interest relief and remission programs for student loans. In 1997/98, the average student debt after loan remission was $15,700. With the changes introduced this year, students who receive the maximum grant of $3,500 a year will see their total debt load for a four-year degree program decrease by $14,000.

This year, the province announced that grants for single parents will be extended to a fifth year and introduced a new loan-forgiveness program for students with permanent disabilities. However, the government appears to be retreating somewhat from its commitment to reducing the financial barriers to post-secondary education. Following the federal government's lead, B.C. will eliminate both the six-month interest-free grace period for student loans and the loans remission program. These policies will add to the difficulties many recent graduates face in repaying their loans.

Despite significant gains made over the past decade, there is much room for further improvement in post-secondary education in the province. Population growth and the rapid expansion of knowledge-based employment are placing a great deal of pressure on the system. B.C.'s post-secondary participation rate for 18-to-24-year-olds remains below the national average. An estimated 40,000 to 60,000 new post-secondary spaces will be needed to meet rising demand levels over the next two decades. B.C. is a long way from having the necessary infrastructure and funding to meet this demand.

The growing gap between the demand for post-secondary education and the publicly-funded programs that are available to students is producing an increasingly privatized and commercialized system. Private spending on all levels of education in British Columbia increased by 60% from 1992 to 1998, from approximately $450 to $743 on average per household (in 1998 dollars). In part, this growth in out-of-pocket spending is reflected in the rapid expansion of private post-secondary institutions in the province. The number of private colleges and institutes in B.C. has nearly doubled since 1992. There are now over 1,100 registered private post-secondary institutions. Of these, only 185 have successfully completed the province's new accreditation process.

The accreditation system was introduced to provide much needed financial and educational safeguards for both students and the government. Starting this year, only those students enrolled in accredited private institutions will have access to provincial student loans and government grants. While certainly a step in the right direction, the accreditation process does not go far enough in addressing some the most serious problems in the private education industry. Private institutions are not subject to the tuition freeze and many charge $10,000 a year or more for courses and programs that may not be recognized by other institutions and for which jobs may be scarce. Admission tends to be based on ability to pay tuition rather than the likelihood of successfully completing the program or finding appropriate employment. Students who obtain loans for study at private colleges have a default rate of 45%, in comparison with rates of 16% at public colleges and 11% at public universities.

Even with non-accredited institutions excluded from access to the provincial student assistance program, high fees and high loan default rates are serious problems for both individual students and taxpayers, as the province takes over responsibility for financing the student loan program from the chartered banks this year. There is a serious need for better regulation of private post-secondary institutions in the province in order to ensure that students receive a high quality education and that public education resources are well invested.

The public college and institute system must also be expanded to meet increasing levels of demand. One notable step in this direction is a new "Training Accord" under which the provincial government has committed to considering public institutions before giving education and training contracts to private providers.

The failure of government funding to keep pace with growing demand for post-secondary education has also put pressure on public post-secondary institutions to find alternative sources of revenue. Universities have become increasingly reliant on private sources of funding over the past decade, including new user fees and "cost-recovery" degree programs that circumvent the tuition freeze, cash or in-kind donations, corporate investment in research, and turning facilities into marketing sites for corporate products and services.

From 1990 to 1998, private support for B.C.'s universities and colleges grew from 35% of total revenue to 44%. In 1998, nearly half of all private funding through bequests, donations and grants came from corporate business enterprises. Almost two-thirds of university revenue from private sources other than tuition fees takes the form of research grants and contracts. An additional 26% is reported as "Special Purpose and Trust" revenues. A mere 7% of this revenue is spent on instruction and non-sponsored research.

The growing dependence of B.C.'s universities on private funds creates inequities among public institutions and places an undue influence on educational and research priorities.

B.C needs to continue its policy of expanding investment in post-secondary education. In the short term, this means more public funding, maintaining the tuition freeze with a view to eliminating tuition fees altogether, reversing the trend towards privatization of the system, improving the regulation of existing private institutions, and introducing province-wide standards to govern corporate involvement in public institutions.

(Donna Vogel is a researcher with the Canadian Centre for Policy Alternatives—B.C. Office. Amanda Camley is the Organizer at the Capilano College Students' Union—Local 5 of the Canadian Federation of Students.)

Some facts about post-secondary education in the Yukon
By Becky Striegler

A discussion on the state of post-secondary education in the Yukon is limited by the fact that we have only one post-secondary institution: Yukon College. The College offers degrees in teaching and social work. Its Arts and Science Division offers the first two years of university transfer courses. As well, the College offers several one- and two-year programs.

Tuition fees at Yukon College have increased since 1991, but are still among the lowest in Canada. In 1991, tuition fees were based on a formula of $25 per credit. In 2000, tuition for all courses is based on a formula of $43 per credit. Today, a full-time student taking five three-credit courses each semester pays $630 per semester for tuition. There are some additional fees, such as $50 per student per semester for computer lab use. There are also activity fees attached to some programs—for culture camps and outdoor education courses, for example.

Tuition fees are lower for those students enrolled in developmental studies, which provide instruction in basic literacy and secondary-school level courses. The tuition per semester is $350.

Yukon College receives its operations and maintenance— as well as capital— funding from the territorial government's Advanced Education Branch. In 1991-92, the territory provided $11,343,107 in capital and O & M funding to the College. In 1994-95, the amount from the territorial government was $10,399,000. Three years later, in 1997-98, it was $10,950,000. In 2000/01, the funding is $11,319,841.

In addition, Advanced Education directly funds two programs—the Bachelor of Social Work and Yukon Native Teacher Education Program. That amounts to about $900,000 per year. Advanced Education also pays for student training programs throughout the year.

No attempts have yet been made to privatize operations at Yukon College. The institution's collective agreement prohibits the college from contracting out any services that will take away jobs from existing employees.

There have, however, been partnerships struck with private businesses. For example, a computer company wanted exposure for its computer equipment. At the same time, the College was looking for a way to provide modern computer equipment for its students. The company and the College signed an agreement in which the company provided 13 computers to be used in the College lab. The company and the College shared revenues on the lab, and the company was able to use the lab to train its staff.

In other instances, the College has worked with private firms to develop training components for construction projects. The training components add value to the contractors' bids when they are vying for work. Recently, the College worked closely with a private company that was upgrading a road to the College grounds. The College provided training for 10 to 12 College students working on the project.

The general policy of Yukon College is that no one private vendor has more opportunities to sell to or benefit from the College market than do other private vendors in the same field.

The Advanced Education Branch also provides financial assistance to college and university students in the form of the Yukon Grant and the Yukon Training Allowance.

The Yukon Grant program was started in 1959. It is a grant program for university students who meet Yukon residency requirements and in some cases complete two years of secondary school in the Yukon. The territory increased funding in the program in both 1978 and 1982, and then again in 2000.

The most recent increase of 20% was brought in to offset the growing costs students are facing in post-secondary education. The increase means a student can now receive up to $1,488 per semester. In addition, Yukon students can receive airfare for one round-trip per calendar year from Whitehorse to Vancouver or Edmonton. It means that, for a full post-secondary year, a student receiving both the Yukon Grant and the airfare coverage can receive up to $4,640 from the territorial government. For the 2000/01 fiscal year, the Yukon government has allocated $1,690,822 in its budget for the Yukon Grant.

The Yukon Training Allowance, too, has existed for several decades and has just been increased by 20%. It supports students attending programs at Yukon College. Because of the recent increase, the maximum amount a student with no dependents can receive has gone from $70 to $84 per week. The amounts are larger for students with dependents. Additional support is provided to students who live in communities outside Whitehorse and have to maintain a second residence in the city to attend college. Those students can receive $66 per week. The territorial government has devoted $1,161,868 in its 2000/01 budget to the Yukon Training Allowance.

In the area of needs-based grants, the Advanced Education Branch signed an agreement in June 1999 to administer the Canadian Millennium Scholarships for Yukon students.

Over the next 10 years, the Yukon is providing 105 students each year with a General Award of $3,000 per student. The award criteria are based on the Canada Student Loan Need Assessment Guidelines. As well, a student has to have successfully completed one year of post-secondary education to be eligible for an award.

The Yukon is also giving out one Exceptional Merit Award of $4,000 per year. The

Canadian Millennium Scholarship Foundation determines the successful recipient of that award.

The Yukon does not have its own student loan program. However, it administers the Canada Student Loan Program in accordance with the program's guidelines.

(Becky Striegler works for the Yukon Department of Education—www.gov.yk.ca)

Equity

Casual labour in Canada's universities: A growing trend

By Vicky Smallman

> "Part-time appointments are the single worst problem higher education faces, and they are linked to every other crisis in the industry. If you start talking about the detenuring of the faculty, you end up talking about part-time employment. If you address threats to academic freedom, you must deal with the part-time scene, where they are worst. Take up the risks in distance learning and you arrive at the certainty of more part-time hires. Discuss the future of affirmative action hiring and you confront the way part-time employment will shape and undermine it. Talk about faculty authority on campus and you must talk about how part-time employment is destroying it. Talk about the place of humanities disciplines cannot occur without confronting their takeover by part-timers.
>
> "University governance? Try addressing it without discussing part-timers' role in its future. The quality of undergraduate education? The future of graduate study? Faculty teaching loads? Funding for higher education? The dignity of teaching? The massive shift to part-time employment is at the centre of everything we do."
> - Cary Nelson & Stephen Watt[1]

The increase in precarious employment has infiltrated most sectors of Canada's economy, and universities are no exception. Cost-cutting administrators, bent on importing corporate management strategies into Canada's public universities, are relying more and more on casual labour to do the bulk of undergraduate teaching.

This growing trend has implications not only for the academics who teach with inadequate pay and working conditions, but for students, their full-time colleagues, and the Canadian public as well.

Contract employment has always been a part of academic life. In the past, temporary appointments were used to fulfill short-term needs, such as replacing a faculty member on sabbatical, or accommodating unexpected increases in enrolment. And every once in a while a department needs to look outside its current staff for expertise in a particular, specialized area. But cash-strapped universities are now using contract appointments to fulfill ongoing teaching requirements.

At the moment, reliable statistics on employment in Canada's universities are unavailable[2]. But American data reveal a disturbing trend. About 43% of American faculty are part-time. Of the 57% who are full-time, about 28% are on limited-term contract. That means only 41% of American faculty are tenured or tenure-track—and the majority of those will be retiring in the next decade. It appears that within 10 to 15 years, unless present trends are reversed, only about 20% of American faculty will be tenured or tenure-track—a proportion so small that academic freedom will be seriously jeopardized.

Anecdotal evidence suggests that the trend is similar in Canada. We know that significant numbers of university faculty are retiring, but they are not being replaced. We know that, overall, full-time faculty numbers have declined by 9.7% between 1992 and 1998[3]. What we do not know is the proportion of undergraduate teaching currently being performed by contract academic staff, and whether that proportion has changed over the last decade.

The decrease in full-time faculty numbers alone should worry Canadians. We need academic staff who have a long-term relationship to one another, to their students, and to their institution, to help maintain a learning environment of the highest quality. What does it say about our universities' commitment to quality education when they refuse to invest in teachers and researchers?

Who are Contract Academic Staff?

Contract Academic Staff go by many names and labels: part-time instructors or "part-timers," sessionals, adjuncts, instructors, limited-term faculty...and there are as many different kinds of contracts as there are names. People are most commonly contracted to teach a specific course, but can be hired to teach several courses over the course of an academic year, or teach full-time for a specified period of time.

The common thread between these different kinds of employment is their precariousness. Unless these academics are protected by a collective agreement with strong language on renewal and seniority, administrators can fire any of them simply by not renewing their contract.

One of the persistent myths about contract academic staff is that they choose to work part-time. Indeed, some do have full-time jobs outside of the university, and provide the university with expertise in a specialized area. And others may have family or other obligations that make casual work an attractive option. But most often contract academic staff would prefer full-time, stable employment if it were available.

Many are younger academics with aspirations to a career in academe. Others have been teaching on contract for years, trying to cobble together a living on a course-by-course or year-by-year basis. Some contract academic staff teach at more than one institution, travelling back and forth between campuses and communities. These itinerant academics have earned the nickname "Road Scholars" or "Freeway Flyers." But, whether they are contractual by necessity or inclination, they are often treated like second-class citizens in the academic community, despite their dedication, their credentials and the quality of their work.

Poor pay and working conditions

Salaries for a per-course contract range from $5,000 to $10,000 for a full-year course, usually without benefits. In order to make a decent living from casual employment, contract academic staff have to take on a much heavier course load than their full-time colleagues (thus making the "part-timer" label a bit of a misnomer). As these contracts are normally for teaching services only, contract academic staff must keep track of new developments in their discipline, research, write, attend conferences and publish on their own time (and their own dime). Even if their goal is a permanent position, it requires superhuman dedication and persistence to meet today's demanding professional requirements with no support.

Working conditions are also less than adequate. Contract academic staff frequently work without consistent access to important resources like office space, library privileges, and e-mail accounts. If they have an office, they normally share it with several others, making it difficult to meet with students. Those who do have library cards or e-mail accounts find their privileges cut off as soon as classes end. They are not paid for the time it takes to prepare their courses or handle appeals. And, while many have been teaching for years, contract academic staff are excluded from departmental and university governance, including the curriculum development process. Their marginal status on campus and in departments renders them invisible to the institution and their full-time colleagues.

Whither academic freedom?

Most importantly, the vulnerability of part-time faculty means they have very little academic freedom. They can be dismissed at the end of their contract for no reason and with no process for appeal.

This may make contract faculty reluctant to teach controversial subjects or adopt unique teaching practices. As their numbers grow and full-time positions decline, students will lose the kind of energetic, innovative teaching that can only occur when academic freedom is protected.

Unless our university administrations can be forced to return to providing permanent, secure jobs as the norm for academic staff, academic freedom will diminish, and with it the quality and integrity of our universities.

The best way of ending the exploitation and overuse of contract academic staff is to improve their wages, job security and working conditions through collective bargaining.

Solidarity works

Contract academic staff in unionized workplaces do fare better than their colleagues without unions. Either by joining with full-time colleagues in faculty associations or by organizing a separate union, they have made major financial and workplace gains through collective bargaining, including:

- improved wages,
- access to benefits,
- increased job security,
- opportunities for promotion,
- office space and teaching resources,
- protection from discrimination and harassment,
- a process to address and resolve grievances,
- access to research and professional development funds, and
- a voice in departmental university governance.

Most of all, organizing has helped contract academic staff achieve recognition of their status as professionals who make an important contribution to the quality of post-secondary education.

In addition to achieving justice for individual academic staff, these gains will help eliminate the incentive to administrations to eliminate tenure lines in favour of temporary appointments. But much more needs to be done. Contract academic staff and their tenured and tenure-track colleagues need to work together to end the exploitation of contract academic workers and address the growing problem of faculty renewal and the increasing casualisation of academic employment.

Our chances of success are greatly improved if all academic staff work together to develop common strategies and solutions.

(Vicky Smallman is a Professional Officer of organizing with the Canadian Association of University Teachers—www.caut.ca)

Endnotes

[1] *Academic Keywords.* London: Routledge, 1999, 210-211.

[2] Statistics Canada has not published a comprehensive survey of part-time faculty since 1993, largely because university administrations refuse to respond to the survey, or submit less-than-complete data. Although preliminary data on part-time faculty was recently released, the report estimated numbers for several major institutions, thereby making it difficult to draw any real conclusions about the amount of teaching being performed by casual academic labour.

[3] *The Daily*, Statistics Canada, August 8, 2000. Unfortunately, the report does not indicate changes in the type of full-time appointments over that period, so we do not know whether full-time contract appointments have increased or decreased.

The impact of the restructuring of higher education on rural communities
By Jennifer Sumner

Rural communities and policy formation

Rural communities are part of our heritage, an integral piece of the mosaic of Canadian life.. Sparsely populated and spatially isolated, rural communities offer ways of life that are qualitatively different from urban ones.

Generally speaking, however, policy formation has traditionally overlooked, omitted or ignored rural areas. A recent report on educational reform and rural communities[1] noted that the dimension of "rural" is seldom considered in the formulation of national or provincial policy; moreover, there is even an implicit bias in policy formulation that actively excludes the consideration of the unique characteristics, qualities and needs of rural community life.

The rise of corporate globalization magnifies this policy deficit, leaving rural communities even more isolated and vulnerable. As corporate values come to dominate government decision-making, policy formation increasingly reflects the corporate agenda of privatization of the public sector.

Corporate globalization

Corporate globalization involves the increasing domination of transnational corporations. These corporations roam the globe looking for sites to maximize profits for stockholders and top-level corporate executives, while minimizing input costs. Supranational institutions such as the World Bank and the International Monetary Fund (IMF) smooth the way for transnational corporations by developing trade agreements—bills of rights for corporations that ease profit extraction by eliminating barriers to trade.

These barriers to trade include not only tariffs, but also the public sector, which historically has been inaccessible to corporate exploitation. The privatization of the public sector gives transnational corporations huge new opportunities to maximize profits, especially in areas like health care and education.

Higher education represents an especially lucrative opportunity for transnational corporations. The World Bank promotes the privatization of higher education, veiled in neo-liberal rhetoric of moving the "higher education cost burden from taxpayers to parents and students"[2]—which translates as full-freight tuition with no grants and no scholarships to hamper pure commodification. Government policy, which increasingly reflects the corporate privatization agenda, supports the push for privatization by reducing funding to higher education. The predictable result is a forced restructuring of higher education that has broad and lasting impacts on many sectors of the population, including rural communities.

The restructuring of higher education and rural communities

The restructuring, or structural adjustment, of higher education through defunding leaves it few choices but to ally with transnational corporations in order to survive. This partnership with business is not a partnership in the true sense of the term—a cooperative venture from which both equally benefit. Higher education is definitely the junior partner in the alliance, dutifully recomposing itself while corporations exploit not only the prestige but especially the public money associated with higher education.

While it may appear that corporations revitalize institutions of higher learning with their capital inputs, in reality that investment is repaid many times over in the form of unlimited access to publicly-funded resources such as research grants, laboratories, and highly educated personnel. For example, at the University of Guelph where I work, it is estimated that the roughly $10 million (1998 figures) that industry invests annually to support proprietary research allows it to leverage a healthy chunk of the much larger (roughly $250 million) taxpayer investment at the university.[3]

This partnership with private interests has predictable results for higher education in terms of its role in society, funding, governance, access, research, curriculum, teaching, learning, technology and outcomes. Some of these results impact directly on rural communities.

Alliances with private interests have changed the research agenda in higher education, especially in those institutions that are involved in agriculture. For example, in the Ontario Agricultural College at the University of Guelph, research was traditionally publicly-funded. In the early 1990s, however, university policy quietly changed and half of all research funding was required to come from private interests. Without the input of private funding, no public funding would be forthcoming. The predictable result is research that supports corporate interests and produces products or knowledge that can be commercialized and sold by corporations for a profit. No research is done for the common good (such as testing the safety of genetically modified organisms) because no private interest would ever fund such research. In fact, as Noam Chomsky[4] pointed out in his convocation speech after accepting an honorary doctorate from the University of Guelph in 1999, "the common good is incidental" when it comes to research in the commercialized university.

Chomsky's point rings especially true for the community of Walkerton, Ontario. In a neo-liberal climate of restructuring, cutbacks, tax credits and infrastructure decimation, the water in this rural community became contaminated with E.coli bacteria. Seven people died and hundreds were made sick. In the wake of this tragedy, a scientist from Queen's University asked, "What agencies today [are doing] science to protect the public interest?"[5]. Certainly not the institutions of higher education, it would seem.

Such a change in the research agenda has also meant the privatization of formerly public knowledge. Research carried out in institutions of higher education no longer adds to the fund of public knowledge, but uses public money to produce knowledge that can be commodified by private interests. One of the first casualties of the new research agenda was agricultural extension services. Originally set up in institutions of higher education such as the Ontario Agricultural College as a means of improving the education of rural people,[6] agricultural extension formed the bridge between research and the community, linking the results of cutting-edge agricultural research to farming practice. Such "free" knowledge was incompatible with the restructuring of higher education demanded by the privatization agenda of corporate globalization because private interests could not compete against this unpriced public good. The demise of agricultural extension has left farmers without a fresh source of knowledge, which leaves them dependent on the propaganda of fertilizer and pesticide corporations—some of the largest transnational corporations in the world.

The changing research agenda has also provided a foothold for genetically modified organisms, with transnational corporations using public money and publicly-funded research laboratories and personnel from institutions of higher education to develop and promote their private products. Farmers are then encouraged to use these products, which many argue have not had sufficient testing, with unknown consequences for their farms and for the larger environment they depend on. In addition, consumer boycotts of genetically modified organisms in places like Europe have left some farmers with no market for these products.

The restructuring of higher education has also resulted in higher education institutions supporting large corporate farms over small and medium-sized farms, now disparagingly dismissed as "lifestyle farms," as if rural ways of life were a fashion you could buy in a mall instead of a deeply-held race memory. Judged only by the percentage of national output instead of their contribution to the web of rural life, small and medium-sized farmers are going bankrupt in a global market where the food industry is making a killing. For example, the CBC reported that farmers in Saskatchewan predict one-third of their number will be out of business within one year.[7] The state of Nebraska is now almost empty of people, but full of corporate farms. Corporate farms are a business investment, so environmental stewardship and the sustainability of rural communities become barriers to trade for the increasingly mobile agri-business corporations that have no commitment to place.

The restructuring of higher education has also resulted in a refocusing of the higher education curriculum. For example, integrated pest management and organic farming are management-intensive practices that involve few priced inputs but a great deal of skill. As such, they do not provide an efficient marketing site for transnational corporations to sell their products. Few, if any, agricultural colleges now provide courses involving these practices, but concentrate instead on input-heavy training involving pesticides and fertilizers. In addition, agriculture students are taught the skills demanded by corporate managers, not the skills to live sustainably on the planet or to critique the global market that is decimating the rural communities they live in. Adjusting to corporate globalization is the thrust of the new curriculum.

In addition, the restructuring of higher education has resulted in the promotion of land stewardship as voluntary compliance by private landowners. In the policy and enforcement vacuum left by the restructuring and downsizing of environment ministries, institutions of higher education promote the corporate agenda of voluntary compliance that frees transnational corporations from the "barriers" of national and provincial legislation. What effects will voluntary compliance have on the environment that rural communities depend on so closely?

And finally, the restructuring of higher education has also resulted in the promotion of economic development as the only legitimate kind of rural development, reproducing a micro version of globalized corporate values in rural communities. Ministries of agriculture and institutions of higher learning work together to support rural business projects, with little consideration of the overall place of business in the web of rural life.

One example of this promotion involves rural tourism. Corporate-friendly departments in institutions of higher education initiate business opportunities in tourism without considering their impact on the rural communities themselves. Imposing such top-down, outsider-driven projects on these communities does little to address the complex question of their long-term sustainability. In addition, injecting money for development or encouraging certain tourism projects can exacerbate already-existing gender and class divisions within rural society.

The future of higher education and rural communities

In an interview before his convocation speech at the University of Guelph, Noam Chomsky asked,

> Do we want universities to be places where people come to grips with human affairs, cultural tradition, and the problems that people face? Do we want it to be a place for advancing and understanding society? Do we want it to be a place for creative work? Or do we simply want students to be servants of private power?[8]

Chomsky's question cuts to the heart of the changing role of higher education in an increasingly globalized world, and the impacts of that changing role on society at large, including rural communities. Higher education, like government itself, is being remade in the image of the corporate agenda.

Vandana Shiva's[9] contention that institutions of the state are changing from being protectors of the health and rights of people to protectors of the property and profits of corporations applies just as accurately to higher education. No longer able to "afford" to support learning for its own sake, institutions of higher education increasingly promote marketing opportunities for transnational corporations, while molding compliant consumers. Rural communities experience the impact of this change on a daily basis, along with other changes brought about by corporate globalization, such as school, hospital and factory closures, environmental despoliation and depopulation. As one Canadian farmer asked: "Are we willing to let hundreds of communities fade away, taking their grain elevators, family stores and heritage with them?"[10]

What rural communities need is a policy change within both government and higher education that favours life over money, the public sector over the private sector, and community sustainability over corporate profits. Without such a change, rural communities in Canada face a bleak and uncertain future. In this globalized economy we can either follow the lead of countries such as the United States and demand no protections for rural communities, or we can follow the lead of countries such as Europe and Japan and stress the multi-functionality of agriculture as protecting diversity, the environment and the rural way of life[11].

As rural communities struggle to survive in the face of the kind of restructuring that has affected higher education, they provide a biopsy of Canadian society today. Within the social immune system they are an indicator of a deep structural sickness, a sickness that values money over people, communities and the environment[12]. To counter such a sickness, we need policy that values life first and foremost, the kind of policy that allows rural communities to survive and flourish.

In our globalized world, only the state has the power to protect us from the impacts of corporate globalization. No supranational institutions have taken on that role, and local governments are too powerless to demand compliance. And while the corporate agenda calls for less government, and many jurisdictions are conforming by downsizing, underfunding and restructuring the public sector, "there is still such a thing as society, with its own public interest, which can only be safeguarded by public institutions such as governments, to which private profit-seekers must be subordinated."[13]

We need a policy framework that protects the public interest and promotes a kind of sustainable globalization—a globalization that is life based and community friendly, one that includes a place for everyone, not just those decreasing few who can still afford to buy their way into the global market.

(Jennifer Sumner teaches the Rural Extension Studies course at the University of Guelph, Ont.)

Endnotes

[1] Lauzon, Allan C. and Danielle Leahy. 2000. "Educational Reform and the Rural Community: An Ontario Perspective." A report prepared for the SRC Research Program, Ontario Ministry of Agriculture, Food and Rural Affairs (Project 023450).

[2] Johnstone, D. Bruce, Alka Arora and William Experton. 1998. "The Financing and Management of Higher Education: A Status Report on Worldwide Reforms." Paper given at the UNESCO World Conference on Higher Education, Paris, October.

[3] E. Ann Clark. 1999. "Academia in the Service of Industry: The Ag Biotech Model." Paper presented at the Canadian Association of University Teachers conference, Universities and Colleges in the Public Interest: Stopping the Commercial Takeover of Post-Secondary Education, Ottawa, October.

[4] Chomsky, Noam. 1999. Convocation Address to Graduates of the College of Arts, University of Guelph, February 17, reproduced in *At Guelph*, March 30, p. 4.

[5] Nikiforuk, Andrew. "National Water Crisis Forecast." *The Globe and Mail*, June 7, 2000, p. 1, 5.

[6] *OAC at 125!* 1999. Ontario Agricultural College, University of Guelph, March.

[7] Canadian Broadcasting Corporation. 2000. *CBC Radio News*, January 30 at 8 am.

[8] Wicary, Stephen. 1999. "Are Students Servants to a Private Power?" *Id Magazine*, February 25 - March 3, p. 8.

[9] Shiva, Vandana. 1997. "Economic Globalization, Ecological Feminism, and Sustainable Development." *Canadian Woman Studies*, Vol. 17, No. 2, Spring, pp. 22-27.

[10] Canadian Press. 1998. "Rural Way of Life at Stake, Farmers Say." *The Globe and Mail*, December 5, p. A13.

[11] George, Susan. 1999. "Trade Before Freedom." *Le Monde Diplomatique*, November, p. 1, 2.

[12] See McMurtry, John. 1999. *The Cancer Stage of Capitalism*. London: Pluto Press.

[13] Salutin, Rick. 2000. "Walkerton and the Great Transformation." *The Globe and Mail*, June 9, p. A15.

Access in jeopardy? Social class, finances and university attendance
By Linda Quirke

Attending university has become much more expensive in recent years. As a result, students and their families are feeling the pinch. One out of every three university students say that they are very concerned about not having enough money to complete their education (Canadian Undergraduate Survey Consortium, 1998).

For some Canadians, paying more to go to university is not an issue. However, for most students, especially those from low-income families, the cost of going to university is a serious problem. Are rising costs having an effect on access? In other words, as university becomes more expensive, are students from low-income families less likely to attend? A University of Guelph study explored these questions, and found that students are increasingly being drawn from higher-income backgrounds. The results of this study are described below.

Context: Students paying more

Throughout the 1990s, university students paid more for their education than those who attended in the 1970s and 1980s. For the 1999-2000 academic year, "the average undergraduate arts student in Canada will pay $3,379 in tuition...more than double the tuition fees of about $1,500 in 1990-91" (Statistics Canada, 1999, p. 55).

Canadian families do not have enough money to cover the rising cost of attending university. Statistics Canada reports that: "By the mid-1990s, student fees were therefore less affordable for an average family than at any time during the previous 20 years" (Little, Statistics Canada, 1997, p. 18). Since 1980, tuition fees in Canada have risen by 115%, while average family income has grown by only 1% after adjusting for inflation (Clark, Statistics Canada, 1998).

In the face of rising costs, Canadian students are taking out larger loans, and taking on more debt (Clark, Statistics Canada, 1998). In Ontario, for example, where tuition is at the second-highest level in Canada, the changes over time are striking. When Ontario's Study Grant Program was eliminated in 1992/93, assistance shifted from bursaries to loans. Since then, average student debt levels in Ontario have doubled (Council of Ontario Universities, 1999).

Ontario's story 1960-2000: From universal access to user-fees

In 1960, one in 10 young people aged 18-21 attended university in Ontario. These students were primarily wealthy white males. To remedy this élite system, universities were created and expanded to be more accessible. The onus in the 1960s was firmly placed on government bodies to clear a path for students to attend university. Universities perceived it as the government's responsibility to provide funding for bursaries and grants to enable students to attend university (Association of Colleges and Universities, 1965).

1960s - Policy of universal accessibility

A policy of universal accessibility was seen as the best way to involve as many young people as possible in post-secondary education. Loans were seen as barriers to access. There was fear that, if students had to rely on loans, accessibility would be threatened. Ontario university officials felt that "loans should be used only for emergencies" (Fleming, 1971, p. 412). Women in particular, it was argued, should be protected from student debt, which constituted a "negative dowry," making females less attractive to prospective marriage partners (Pike, 1970 p. 111; Fleming, 1971, p. 409).

Universities saw themselves as responsible for providing education at the lowest cost to the student (Fleming, 1971). Ensuring access was given primacy over universities' own financial returns. For instance, universities absorbed rising costs resulting from shrinking government funding, rather than passing along financial hardship to students (Council of Ontario Universities, 1976).

1980s - Governments paying less; students paying more

Things changed in the 1980s. Rising participation rates were interpreted by the Ontario government as evidence that universities were now accessible. Students were now to bear a greater financial responsibility for their education. Loans were seen as a viable route by which all students could attend university. Governments were contributing less to universities, which made up for this deficit by increasing tuition fees (Little, Statistics Canada, 1997). In the 1990s, government grants have not kept pace with increased operating costs, leaving universities with shortfalls. "...Even after allowing for higher university operating costs...students are now paying more for their university education, primarily because governments are paying less" (Little, Statistics Canada, 1997, p. 14).

1990s - User-fee mentality

In the 1990s, the provision of university education to Ontario students is no longer seen as the responsibility of governments. Instead, the prevailing perception is a "user-fee" one, whereby individual students should pay a greater share of their education, rather than relying on the public purse. Higher tuition fees and rising student debt are thus seen as students' financial investment in their future (Stager, 1994), rather than an assault on access.

While the proportion of young people in the population has been declining for years, an increasing proportion of young people have been attending university. After decades of steady growth, full-time enrolments levelled off in the early 1990s (Statistics Canada, 1998). Nevertheless, rather than looking to enrolment rates, or interpreting rising participation rates overall as evidence that a system is more open, we need instead to look at how representative an institution is. To determine whether an institution is becoming more or less accessible, it is necessary to measure how well the composition of a student body reflects the diversity of larger society.

More than sex or ethnicity, attainment linked to social class

The financial burden of attending university is most grave for students from low-income families. Compared to affluent students, "those in the middle and lower SES [socio-economic status] groups must make a relatively greater financial sacrifice to attend university" (Statistics Canada, 2000, p. 105). Students from low-income families are more sensitive than higher-income students to tuition increases and the cost of attending university (Heller, 1997; Cameron, 1997). This is not a new phenomenon. The relationship between parents' social class and their children's educational attainment has been described as an "enduring link":

> ...fathers' occupation has a significant bearing on the likelihood of his children studying at the university level. These differences far outweigh any effects of sex or ethnicity (Guppy and Davies, 1998, p. 119).

Students' social class has traditionally been found to be related to both their educational expectations and achievements. For instance, children whose parents have low levels of education are not as likely as other children to attend university (Guppy and Davies, 1998; de Broucker and Underwood, 1998). Since the late 1980s, accessibility to university has diminished as the gap between the attainment of students from higher and lower income families widened considerably (Statistics Canada 2000).

Where the boys are: Male students are under-represented

The Guelph data show that male students are becoming more and more scarce: in 1987, only 4 in 10 incoming Guelph students were male. This under-representation doubled in 10 years; by 1997, only 30% of entering students were male. These results are not unique to Guelph. Men are less likely to be enrolled full-time in university, at 45%, compared to women. Women earn nearly 6 out of every 10 undergraduate degrees awarded in Canada; in 1998, men earned only 42% of undergraduate degrees (Statistics Canada, CANSIM, Cross-classified tables 00580701, 00580702; 00580602, 1998). Women have been earning at least half of undergraduate degrees awarded in Canada since 1980 (Statistics Canada 81-229).

Increases in the numbers of people who attend university say nothing about the composition of incoming cohorts of students. For instance, Canada may see increasing enrolment numbers, but these students may be primarily drawn from the highest income bracket, which results in a more exclusive, less accessible system. Any deviation of the composition of incoming university students from the general population should make us suspect that the institution in question is not accessible. Any deviation of the composition of factors such as gender, race and social class, of incoming student cohorts in Canadian universities suggests that a problem exists. In other words, equality of opportunity can only be achieved if the composition, in terms of the social background of incoming groups, matches the general population.

The following results come from a study conducted at the University of Guelph in 1999. This study relied on surveys filled out by incoming first-year students from the late 1980s to the late 1990s.

Findings: Low SES students cost-sensitive, taking loans, worrying

The study found a significant decline in the numbers of students from modest backgrounds attending university. In the late 1980s, students from modest backgrounds were slightly under-represented at the University of Guelph, compared with the class composition of Ontario families at that time. The social class composition of Guelph students has changed dramatically since then. Students are increasingly being drawn from relatively affluent homes where their parents are university-educated themselves. In the late 1990s, Guelph students were less representative of the general population in terms of their parents' education and income than they were in the late 1980s:

Regardless of how socio-economic background is measured, the SES composition of entering students diverged even further from the class composition of Ontario families between 1986 and 1997 (Gilbert, McMillan, Quirke and Duncan-Robinson, 1999, p. 11).

Guelph students were less likely to come from working class families in the late 1990s, compared to a decade earlier. Compared to the Ontario population, low-SES students at the University of Guelph went from being slightly under-represented in the late 1980s to being substantially under-represented in the late 1990s. Students from low-SES backgrounds were roughly half as likely to be attending the University of Guelph in the late 1990s compared with a decade earlier.

- Low-income students are considerably more sensitive than their high-income counterparts to the cost of attending university.

- Students from low-SES families taking on more in student loans: Between 1992 and 1997, students from low-SES families were not as likely to receive financial help from their parents, compared to students from more affluent families, and more likely to rely on student loans.

- Students from modest families more likely to worry about paying for their education: Low-SES students twice as likely, compared to high-SES students, to have "major" concerns about financing their education: For this study, personal interviews were conducted with six Guelph undergraduate students from modest backgrounds. While this small sample does not allow for generalizations, the results are telling.

"When I got here, all the prices went up": Students underestimate costs

Generally, university cost more than students were expecting. Students under-estimated the cost of things such as books, on-campus meal plans, athletic fees, and the like. One student did not realize that the university's meal plan only covered half of the academic year, and that he would have to pay again for a new meal plan half-way through the year. Some students applied for emergency loans part-way through the school year in order to make ends meet.

Taking on debt, stress, worrying about money "all the time"

Unable to rely on their parents, the respondents primarily relied on loans: "If I didn't get OSAP, I couldn't go to school." However, they were uneasy about taking on large student loans: "It really scares me that I have a debt to pay with money I don't have."

Students' concern about paying back their debt was a constant source of stress. Respondents felt that, in addition to feeling anxious about student debt specifically, their general financial situation was a constant source of stress.

"Scrimping and saving" – students learning to get by with less

Students used various methods of coping with their limited finances. One student purchased the smallest meal plan available, as a way to save money, saying that, if she had more money, she would have chosen a larger meal plan. When asked if her eating habits would be different if she had more meal plan points, she replied: "Oh yeah, I'd eat more fruits and vegetables." To cope, she was "selective," choosing side dishes, such as rice and vegetables, as substitutes for a main, more expensive dish. Students also employed more hidden ways to save money, such as having family bring them food, or having meals with friends or family in order to save money.

Students also took on part-time jobs during the school year in order to raise money. These students related that, if they did not have to work, they would rather devote that time to their schoolwork, on-campus sports, or other activities, or volunteering in the community. One student expressed frustration at how working part-time had curtailed her ability to become involved in other on-campus activities: "There's tons of stuff I wish I could be doing if I didn't have to work."

Finances and academic performance: "Working has definitely put a crunch on school work"

Students who worked part-time during the school year expressed difficulties in balancing their studies with working for pay. For instance, one student felt tired after working for pay, and found it difficult to motivate herself to work on school work: "When I come home after a day of class and work, I'm exhausted." Another student remarked: "No matter how many students say that having a job doesn't affect your homework, it does."

The students interviewed for this study were in a difficult position; while they were apprehensive about taking on debt, loans seemed to be a necessary evil that they must face to complete their education. Scholarships and needs-based bursaries given by the University of Guelph did help to ameliorate this situation.

The University of Guelph data suggest that access is being threatened, as the proportion of students from modest backgrounds has diminished considerably in recent years. There does seem to be a negative correlation between students' socioeconomic status and their concern about and sensitivity to the cost of university. In recent years, this pattern has become more entrenched.

Conclusion: Implications for post-secondary education

Overall, existing educational inequalities are being reinforced. Over the past decade, access to university has been threatened. The Guelph data show that students from low-SES families are coming to university in fewer numbers. Low-SES students are clearly at a disadvantage when it comes to financing their education; compared with their higher-SES counterparts, they cannot turn as readily to their parents for money, and as a result must rely more heavily on student loans. As a consequence, they seem more worried over time about being able to pay for the cost of university.

Low-income students appear to be more sensitive than higher-income students to the cost of attending university. Of students from modest backgrounds, those who opt not to attend the University of Guelph seem to be more sensitive to the cost of attending university, compared with those who enrol at the University of Guelph.

Tuition and other costs of attending university have surpassed Canadian families' ability to pay them. Students who cannot turn to their families for financial assistance face accumulating debt in order to attend university. The convergence of these factors creates a climate in which it may be increasingly difficult for many students from modest backgrounds to attend university. Access to university for students from modest backgrounds is being threatened.

The data outlined above are limited to one Ontario university. The availability of these data and the investigation of this issue is a testament to the University of Guelph's interest in addressing the problem of accessibility. Guelph is admittedly a higher-cost institution, as most students need to relocate in order to attend. Students who cannot rely on their parents for financial help are in a particularly precarious position, as are students living in communities without a university. These students may not be able to afford to attend university. On a positive note, the University of Guelph has shown a clear commitment to providing needs-based financial assistance to students. Our findings show that needs-based financial assistance can mitigate the effect of increased costs on enrolment composition.

While this study has not been able to establish a causal relationship between tuition increases and reduced access, it is clear that students from modest backgrounds are less likely to be found at the University of Guelph than they were a decade ago. These results may be indicative of a generalized accessibility problem. For example, across Canada, young people from the lowest socioeconomic quartile are lagging behind middle-class youth in terms of university attendance, causing concern about Canadian universities' ability to "ensure that domestic access to education is not compromised" (Statistics Canada, 2000, p. 45). If the Guelph data are an indication, we are slipping further from the ideal of equality of educational opportunity, or a truly open, accessible university system.

The information in this necessarily limited study provides educational policy-makers with compelling evidence of the negative implications on accessibility of public disinvestment in post-secondary education. As we have suggested elsewhere, restoring public funding to the post-secondary sector is essential. It is necessary to communicate results like those found in this study to the general public and to the public servants who have responsibility for resolving this issue.

(Linda Quirke is a Ph.D. student in the Sociology of Education at McMaster University. She completed the data outlined here for her M.A. in Sociology at the University of Guelph.)

Works Cited:

Association of Universities and Colleges. (1965). Financing Higher Education in Canada.

Cameron, D. Maritime Provinces Higher Education Commission (1997). MPHEC: Accessibility to Post-Secondary Education. Angus Reid Group, Inc..

Canadian Undergraduate Survey Consortium (1998). 1998 Survey of First-Year University Students. University of Manitoba Housing and Student Life Department.

Clark, W. (1998, Winter) Paying Off Student Loans. Canadian Social Trends. Statistics Canada.

Council of Ontario Universities (1999). Ontario's Students, Ontario's Future.

(1976). Statement on the Principles Which Should Govern the Setting of Tuition Fees. Toronto, ON.

de Broucker, P. and K. Underwood (1998). Intergenerational Educational Mobility: An International Comparison with a Focus on Postsecondary Education. Education Quarterly Review, 5(2). Statistics Canada.

Fleming, W.G. (1971). Ontario's Educative Society. Vol. IV: Post-Secondary and Adult Education. Toronto, ON: University of Toronto Press.

Gilbert, S., I. McMillan, L. Quirke, and J. Duncan-Robinson (1999). Accessibility and Affordability of University Education. Report to the Senate Committee on University Planning, University of Guelph.

Guppy, N. and S. Davies (1998). Education in Canada: Recent Trends and Future Challenges: No. 3. Statistics Canada.

Heller, D.E. (1997). Student Price Response in Higher Education: An Update to Leslie and Brinkman. Journal of Higher Education, 68(6).

Little, D. (1997, Summer). Financing Universities: Why are Students Paying More? Education Quarterly Review, 4(2). Statistics Canada.

Pike, Robert M. (1970) Who Doesn't Get to University—and Why: A Study on Accessibility to Higher Education in Canada. Ottawa. ON.

Stager, D. (1994). Returns to Investment in Ontario University Education, 1960-1990, and Implications for Tuition Fee Policy. Discussion Series Issue 5. Toronto, ON: Council of Ontario Universities.

Statistics Canada, Education in Canada: A Statistical Review. Cat. # 81-229

__ (1999). Education Quarterly Review, 6(1).

__ (1998). Education Quarterly Review, 5(2).

__ (1988) CANSIM, Cross-classified tables 00580701, 00580702; 00580602

__ (2000). Education Indicators in Canada 1999, Report of the Pan-Canadian Education Indicators Program. Council of Ministers of Education, Canadian Education Statistics Council.

The face of the faculty is still mainly white
By Karl Flecker

Strolling on the university campus in historic Kingston provides an opportunity to appreciate beautiful limestone buildings covered in ivy and tradition. It is an image of burnished copper and aged slate roofs, covering small castles.

For more than 150 years, this idyllic stereotype of the university has changed little, save the advance of creeping ivy, and pale limestone weathered by the years.

Maintaining the traditional face that accompanies the campus has a long history. Take, for instance, the case of Principal Grant, who in 1912 had no difficulty publicly advocating for the exclusion of Jews, Hindus or atheists from the professoriate. To accomplish this, he advocated for a religious test clause that would give only Christian scholars access to paying jobs.

Grant of course meant no ill-will toward these groups; he simply wanted to respect the wishes of the Christian founders of Queen's[1] who entrusted him to provide a higher education for some while purposely dismissing the perspectives of more than half of the rest of world.

But we speak of times long ago, and the current crush of students, darting between classes, indicates change is afoot. No longer is the face of the place, like a studio shoot of "Friends." It is now common to see many different shades of the world majority's people, aka people of colour, crossing campus.

Such change is expected, given dramatic changes in our population profiles. Generation X 18-34-year-olds represent 7 million Canadians, of which 20% are visible minorities. Generation Y, the 5-15 year-old band following the nexus generation, is the most racially diverse youth demographic Canada has ever seen, with one in three persons not white.[2]

Equity practitioners at Queen's are now taking steps to research more closely the application, admission and graduation and retention patterns for equity-seeking students like women, Aboriginal peoples, persons with disabilities, and people of colour. A pilot project initiated in 1999 requested applicants to voluntarily complete a census survey indicating if they are members of any of the aforementioned equity-seeking groups. The collected information is not used in any admission criteria, but rather is for planning purposes relevant to the pursuit of equity.

In the first year of implementation, many results surfaced, the most predictable of which was the backlash. Some argued the exercise would be futile, anticipating poor response rates, but the opposite was recorded. Nearly 6,000 students volunteered their status; considering that fewer than 3,000 first-year students are accepted by Queen's, this is quite remarkable.

Despite the passing of more than three-quarters of a century, shades of Principal Grant's era persist. It was not uncommon for the project handlers to learn of handwritten notes sent to senior officers of the University from members of Canada's prestigious élite questioning the "purpose" of the survey, despite a clear explanatory paragraph that accompanied the census form. Perhaps these parents were frustrated about their progeny's inability to tick off of any boxes that affirmed their child's powerful identity.

Backlash is no surprise to equity advocates—despite nearly two decades of institutionally sanctioned efforts in most universities to address the face of the workforce within academe. Workplace equality regulations like the Federal Contractors Program and collective agreement clauses that support workplace equity practices have been the prime motivators for changing traditional practices, but these initiatives often fall short of having the teeth to cut through years of the collegial self-governing, decentralized ethos that can persist inside a university.

Queen's employment equity action plans have been in place for a decade and, although some structural achievements for advancing workplace equality can be applauded (Queen's has twice received meritorious awards), the faculty makeup of designated groups has for the most part been unable to meet the representation levels of these groups in the workforce at large or meet the comparable level of "university teachers" found in Statistics Canada census surveys.[3] (**See table**)

An examination of other measures of equity, such as comparisons of remuneration rates, occupational segregation, distribution of authority and responsibility, provide additional evidence of the relative progress for designated group members

Designated group	Cdn population	Workforce	University Teacher's nationally	1993	1994	1995	1996	1997	1998
Women	50.8%	46.4%	34.4%	24.8%	26.5%	28.6%	29.2%	29.7%	31.0%
Aboriginal persons	2.8	2.1	0.5%	0.4%	0.4%	0.4%	0.4%	0.5%	0.6%
Persons with disabilities	7	6.5	3.7%	3.9%	3.6%	3.6%	3.6%	3.4%	3.2%
Visible minorities	11.2	10.3	12.0%	6.9%	6.8%	7.5%	8.1%	8.0%	7.9%

Notes:
Cdn population data is from the 1996 Census of Canada
Workforce population data for designated groups is compromised of persons aged 15 and over who worked sometime in 1995 or 96.
The workforce pop for PWD is comprised of persons 15-65 who worked anytime between 1986 and 1991
University Teachers national data is from the 1996 Census of Canada
1993-1998 columns are the representation levels of Faculty at Queen's, Source: Achieving Equity-Employment Equity Action Plan, Appendix 1: Designated Group staff profile 1993-1998
PWD, University Teachers data relies on Professional Occupation categories used by Census Canada as data on PWD University teachers is unavailable

within a workforce—but, with habitually low representational levels to start with, these additional equity comparators are somewhat mute.

How long will it take for our institutions to change their academic face? Dr. Shah, an award-winning professor at the University of Toronto, pondered that question after realizing that there were only two visible minority group members within his own department out of 28 professors. In three years, these two will both have retired. Shah realized that his department was a microcosm of the university, and, despite how diverse the face of the student body may be, in the classroom the professors are still mostly white men or white women.

Shah set out to determine how long it would take for the university to have a faculty with minorities representing a modest 15%. Using a mathematical model of probability that assumes the university fills an average of 15% of all job openings with a visible minority candidate, a faculty population of 1,710 and an annual rate of new hires of 5% or 85 job openings, Shah's study concluded that it could take anywhere from 25 years to an extreme of 119 years to reach a goal of just 15% minority staff, with the average being 54.5 years. The large variance takes into account that some years the university may fill more than 15% of jobs with minorities.[4]

Shah's conclusions are indicative of the situation for many universities. Clearly it is systemic discrimination that creates such an unreasonable timeline. Considering that visible minorities have a higher level of post-secondary education levels—19% vs. 13% in the rest of the population—this group still occupies the lowest four occupational levels in our workforce.[5]

The opportunity to make demonstrable changes is now. The pending arrival of the "double cohort" in Ontario—high rates of retirement due to attrition of the professoriate—translates into more than 12,000 job openings in academe at universities in Ontario alone. But are universities planning to use this opportunity to bring on board a new academic crew that looks like and can relate to the rest of the world? It is not easy to find evidence that employment equity has been integrated into these major change plans.

For example, neither of the two reports commissioned by the Council of Ontario Universities to address the enrolment crisis and faculty renewal issues address equity considerations.[6]

The federal government's April 2000 creation and $900 million dollar funding of the Research Chairs Program at Canadian universities for the next three years is another missed opportunity to strategically introduce a more representative face of diversity within academe. Alongside flaws in the program like larger universities benefiting disproportionately at the expense of smaller schools, the program is being implemented with such haste that equity considerations are barely an afterthought.

In the words of one academic involved in the process, "We pre-select our stars and then go a courting." An arranged marriage among families that know each other all to well often leads to less than desirable results. When the institutional processes to advance workplace equity are measured against the weight of traditional practices within the collegial system of universities, or against poorly designed faculty renewal initiatives, it appears that substantive change will be too little too late, in the face of the diversity that is already at the door.

(Karl is a policy analyst in the equity field at Queen's University.)

Endnotes

1. From Ph.D dissertation, G. Dueck. Source: Montreal Daily Witness, "Queen's University Bill" February, 24, 1912.
2. Bani Dheer & Robert Barnard, "Canada's First Generation of Visible Minorities Comes of Age," Horizons Volume 2 #3, September, 1999 Government of Canada Policy Research Secretariat.
3. Queen's Employment Equity Action plan: EE data appendices and 1996 Employment Equity Data report, release #2 Human Resources Development Canada-Labour Standards and Workplace Equity.
4. Kristin Rushowy, **Toronto Star** Jan. 10.20005. 1996 Employment Equity Data report, release #2 Human Resources Development Canada-Labour Standards and Workplace Equity.
5. "Will there be enough excellent profs?" Report on prospective demand and supply conditions for university faculty in Ontario-D.Smith for Council of Ontario Universities, March 2000.
6. "How will I know if there is quality?" Report on quality indicators and quality enhancements in universities: issues and experiences. D. Smith for Council of Ontario Universities, March 2000.

Free Money!...
(For those who already have it)

By Jim Stanford

The social policy legacy of the federal Liberal government is dubious, indeed. During its first term in office, the Chrétien government oversaw the most dramatic and painful retrenchment of federal funding for public programs in Canada's history. Federal program spending fell by one-quarter, measured as a share of Canada's GDP, between 1993 and 1997. Incredibly, federal restraint then continued right through the government's second term in office. Adjusted for inflation and population growth, federal program budgets did not increase at all between 1997 and 2000—despite bulging fiscal surpluses (which reached over $12 billion in 1999 alone), and contrary to the Liberals' solemn promise in the 1997 election to spend half of future surpluses on social reinvestments.

Amid this generally gloomy record of failing to support important public programs, one Liberal legacy stands out as particularly scandalous. During a time in which federal transfers to support provincially-run higher education programs were dramatically scaled back, the government managed to find billions of dollars for a bizarre scheme to subsidize university education through stock-market investments. The vehicle is called a "registered education savings plan," and it promises to be the next great step in the stock-marketization of Canadian social programs.

The RESP system was first implemented as a modest scheme to allow the parents and other relatives of young children to gradually accumulate savings to pay for the kids' future university education. Contributors could pay up to $1,500 per year per child into a savings plan held at a bank or other institution. Unlike RRSPs, contributors do not get to deduct the value of their RESP payments from their taxable income. But the income that is generated on the RESP investments is sheltered from taxes, until such time as the future students cash in their plans to cover their (extravagantly inflated) tuition fees. Since the student would not likely be in a taxable income bracket (since most students pay little or no income tax), the investment income accumulated while the child was growing up would probably be tax-free.

The initial scheme thus constituted a relatively modest tax-deferral or tax-avoidance measure. For those parents with both spare investible funds and a long personal time horizon, investing in an RESP was a smart thing to do—but the payoff was not especially lucrative. Since few Canadians with small children have neither the spare cash nor the mental energy to think about far-off university tuition fees, few Canadians participated in the scheme. By 1997, the whole tax loophole was costing the federal government a relatively paltry $30 million in foregone revenue.

All this changed after the Liberals began slashing their support for higher education. Paul Martin's 1996 and 1997 budgets expanded the maximum annual RESP contribution to $4,000 per child, from $1,500. This reflected the acknowledged impact that government cutbacks at all levels—and the corresponding escalation of tuition fees—was having on the cost of future higher education. Indeed, the program helped to justify those cuts: sure, it's going to cost you a fortune to go to school, but at least we'll give you a tax break to help you save for it!

With the 1998 budget, the government threw in an attractive sweetener. Ottawa would kick in an annual cash grant, equal to 20% of the RESP amount paid in by a child's parents or other relatives, up to a maximum of $400 per child per year. The money must be paid to an authorized financial dealer, who then invests it; the government is thus ensuring that the money managers of Bay Street get their share of this new action.

Ultimately, the government is giving away free money—but it is available only to those parents who already have the spare cash to sock away for future education costs. The grant is ostentatiously titled the Canada Education Savings Grant, but its philosophical foundation can be summed up more bluntly: to them that has, have some more. For those unfortunates whose parents didn't happen to have a few thousand extra dollars sitting around each year to pile into their RESP plans, the government offers nothing.

With this juicy sweetener of free cash, popular interest in the RESP scheme has exploded (at least among those who like to play the markets—preferably with a little government subsidy). And that growing interest translates into a steadily-rising cost of running the program. The government's cash CESG payouts have ballooned far above Paul Martin's own estimates when he introduced the plan in 1998. At that time, Martin guessed the federal government would be paying out $275 million in CESG grants by fiscal 2000; now he thinks the true figure will be more like $750 million, growing to $1.2 billion by 2002.

In principle, the RESP boondoggle should be the "fast ferry scandal" of federal politics: the government is spending hundreds of millions of dollars above budget each year, for a program that was dubious to begin with. But, because the program essentially involves the payment of public money to rich people, it attracts no critical media or political attention.

At the same time, the more people who pay into the system to get the CESG grants, the bigger becomes the pool of tax-free capital invested in RRSP plans, and hence the larger is the forgone revenue cost of the tax-sheltering component of the program. Finance officials expect to lose about $300 million in foregone taxes in fiscal 2002, pushing up the total federal bill for the RESP scheme to an incredible $1.5 billion—and this figure will grow with each passing year.

RESPs are wrapped up in an image of prudent self-reliance. In the words of the 1998 budget,

> The government believes RESPs will soon come to be considered as essential for future planning as RRSPs are now. With the new Canada Education Savings Grant, RESPs represent one of the best things that parents can do for their children.

In other words, forget about loving, caring, and nurturing your children. What's important is to start up their own personal stock market account to pay for their future education costs—and the sooner, the better. Parents who don't contribute to RRSPs are implicitly portrayed as uncaring or even neglectful. The fact that few families with small children can afford to make thousands of dollars of investments on their children's behalf (after all, a million children live in poverty in Canada, and that means their parents are not likely to be playing the stock market on their behalf) is conveniently ignored.

The RESP program also represents yet another gigantic handout to the financial industry. The money managers will love to have another large pool of government-subsidized capital to play with—charging, of course, the usual 2-or-3% annual administration fees. RRSPs represented the financial industry's first big foot in the door of Canadian social policy. But now the ways in which the government relies on tax-assisted financial investments to address important social policy issues is growing. Soon there will be a tax break (and a corresponding registered fund) to assist Canadians with all of life's little inconveniences: education, health care, retirement, even death. This approach to policy is incredibly inequitable: the pressure for personal financial investing effectively shuts out a great many Canadians from the relevant program.

We do not have data on how many Canadians are paying into RESPs, and—more importantly—their income and family characteristics. When the data become available, they will almost certainly replicate the same trends already visible with RRSP investments. The top 13% of Canadian taxpayers (those who earned over $50,000 in 1997) accounted for well over half of all RRSP contributions, and they received more like two-thirds of all RRSP subsidies (since RRSPs perversely subsidize the savings of high-income taxpayers at a higher rate than the rest of us). It's an expensive program, it transfers money from poor people to rich people, and it is used deliberately by the financial industry to undermine faith in the public pension system.

The RESP program replicates these mistakes. For the same $1.5 billion which the RESP program will cost Ottawa in 2002, the government could deliver $7,500 annual cash grants to 200,000 needy students in Canada—about half of the full-time post-secondary student population. Together with pumping some badly-needed money back into university and college funding, that would represent a far more just and effective means of addressing the problem of post-secondary accessibility. But no money manager gets a commission from a no-strings-attached government grant.

(Jim Stanford is an economist with the Canadian Auto Workers [www.caw.ca] and a CCPA research associate.)

Accessibility, affordability and accountability

Canada Student Loan Program: 1995-2000

Introduction

The Canada Student Loan Program (CSLP), which began in 1964, was intended to ensure that all Canadians have equal opportunity and access to the benefits of post-secondary education. Until recently, eligibility for the program was determined solely by financial need.

The Government of Canada guaranteed loans, dispersed to students through banks and credit unions. For nearly 30 years, the program remained largely unchanged.

In August 1995, the government significantly altered the previous student loan program when it entered into risk-sharing agreements with two of Canada's chartered banks (Royal Bank and Canadian Imperial Bank of Commerce). Under this agreement, the banks finance the CSLP in exchange for a 5% risk-sharing premium for a five-year period. In essence, the premium acts as insurance against those loans the bank is unable to collect over the life of the agreement. The agreement covered a five-year period, beginning August 1995. Since 1995, over $300 million has been transferred to the banks to insulate them from fiscal risk on the delivery of the CSLP.

Renegotiating the deal: A $100 million bailout

As the 1995 agreement neared expiration, the federal government entered into negotiations with the banks to strike a new five-year deal.

In January 2000, details of the negotiations were leaked to the media, and it was reported that the federal government had offered to increase the risk premium to 7% and 23% for loans to students at public and private institutions, respectively.

The most controversial aspect of the federal government's offer was the provision that these premiums would reach back to existing loans disbursed under the agreement signed in 1995.

Though the 1995 agreement was supposed to cover all loans negotiated between August 1, 1995, and August 1, 2000, the government's proposal would extend the new premiums to loans negotiated after August 1, 1995, but not yet in repayment.

This clause amounted to a further payment of $100 million to the banks for the 1995-2000 period, in addition to an offer that would nearly double the amount they would receive as a risk-sharing premium under a new contract.

The *Globe and Mail* broke the story of the proposed terms with a front page story on January 25, 2000 that featured comment from the Federation of Students. In the wake of this publicity, the banks became more strident about their continued involvement in the program.

It now appears that at least one of the banks rejected the aforementioned offer to extend the contract and proposed a counter-offer that was even more lucrative.

Late in February, negotiations broke off and, on March 9, the banks held a press conference to announce that they were withdrawing from the CSLP when the contract expired on July 31, 2000.

Bank profit vs. access to higher education

In detailing the chronology of events, government officials from the Canada Student Loan Program confirmed this analysis by admitting that the program could not be delivered economically by a for-profit enterprise.

In a meeting with the Federation of Students, federal government officials made abundantly clear the extent to which our assessment was correct by noting the role that the banks' 'hurdle rate' played in the negotiations. In financial parlance, the hurdle rate represents the rate of return on investment deemed acceptable to a bank's shareholders.

In essence, this reference casts doubt on the banks' claims that they were losing $200 million a year on the student loan portfolio. In reality, the reference to the hurdle rate likely means that the banks' claim of $200-million-dollar losses is actually the opportunity cost of the money disbursed under the CSLP.

In short, the banks left the program because the profit margin was not sufficient.

Ensuring accountability

In addition to the fiscal pressures the banks put on the CSLP, they were also able to leverage several very regressive policy measures from the federal government. These included credit checks on student loans and the 10-year prohibition on declaring bankruptcy on student loans.

Determining the exact nature of the federal government relationship with the banks, however, remains impossible since both Human Resources Development Canada and the banks refuse to release data on the program. Moreover, the banks have consistently refused to release the methodology they use to account for the program.

The current landscape

For the academic year beginning September 2000, the CSLP will be financed by the federal government and administered by a private service bureau. This new model of funding will introduce a third type of federal student loan. It is possible that some students will have a CSL under the pre-1995 system of guaranteed loans, a loan under the risk-sharing agreements covering 1995-2000, and finally a new direct finance loan in 2000.

In terms of repayment, students will, in essence, be paying back three separate federal student loans if they find themselves in the anomalous situation outlined above. The Government of Canada will hold and collect the pre-1995 loans, as well as the new direct finance loan. As per the risk-sharing agreements, the banks are responsible for collecting and administering loans disbursed between August 1, 1995 and August 1, 2000.

What will students see?

In the short term, the transition to the new direct finance system will mean some logistical changes in the CSLP. Full-time and part-time students will continue to undergo a similar process of applying for loans, but face two very different situations for cashing them.

For full-time students, cashing a loan should be very similar to previous years. Students pick up the certificate of eligibility at the student financial aid office and cash it at a chartered bank. The federal government has an agreement with CIBC, Royal Bank, and Bank of Nova Scotia to deposit loans.

Because the federal government was unable to secure an agreement from the banks to deposit loans for part-time students, these students will see the most change in the way loans are negotiated. Part-time students will be negotiating their loans at Canada Post outlets.

Students will pick up their loan at the student financial aid office and then phone a toll-free number (1-800-O-CANADA) to fill in the terms of their loan (i.e., period of study, interest rate, etc.). The paperwork must then be brought to a Canada Post outlet and funds will be transferred electronically to the student's account within three to seven working days.

Students will be advised of the nearest full-service Canada Post location when they pick up their loan. In the case where the postal outlet is too remote, the student can negotiate the loan by mail, which will, of course, delay the process. Students will also confirm their 'in school' status when they call the 1-800 number.

Verifying student status

Students who have risk-shared loans (August 1, 1995 to Aug 1, 2000) who are not taking out a loan this year will still file the same paperwork to confirm full-time enrolled status.

If a student is remaining in part-time studies but not taking out a new loan as of September, they obtain the same form from the student financial aid office and file it with the bank that holds their loan. As

MILLENNIUM SCHOLARSHIP SHUFFLE
~Performed by Paul Martin, Mike Harris and an unsuspecting student~

GSAÉD © 2000
by J.Étudiante

usual, if students do not file this paperwork, the bank will automatically assume they have graduated and put their loans into repayment after six months.

There will be new paperwork to confirm full-time status for those who are taking out a loan this fall.

The Federation has official assurances from HRDC that this year they will be very lenient about technical defaults —that is, those loans that go into default because of paperwork and logistical confusion caused by the transition to a new system. We have secured this commitment and we will hold them to it.

The future of the Canada Student Loan Program

To publicize the changes, Human Resources Development Canada ran a radio campaign in August and has produced 500,000 posters for distribution across the country. In addition, a toll-free number (1-800-O-CANADA) and a web-site (www.canlearn.ca) are in place to provide further information.

Beyond the 2000-2001 year, the federal government intends to contract out student loan administration. To that end, they have begun the process of securing an agreement with a private service contractor. The service provider will be responsible for the collection of data and administration of the loan while the student is in school, and collection of the loan when the student leaves school.

On May 5, those firms that showed serious interest were invited to appear in Toronto to make a presentation and participate in a series of interviews with stakeholders, including the Federation.

Twelve potential providers made presentations and took questions in the day-long meeting. Of the twelve, three were collection agents and two were American companies. American firms are entitled to bid on the program as a result of provisions in the North American Free Trade Agreement (NAFTA) that prohibit "monopoly" bidding practices.

The official 'Statement of Work' for this process has now been prepared. HRDC hopes to have an agreement in place by mid-October. The service provider will not officially take over administering the program until February 28, 2001; in the interim, the federal government will administer the program.

(Michael Conolon is the National Chairperson of the Canadian Federation of Students— www.cfs-fcee.ca)

Registered Education Savings Plans: A national grant program for the wealthy

By Michael Temelini

The federal government's existing system of national grants: public subsidies for private savings

To address the growing problem of the soaring cost of education, the federal government has recently introduced two national grant programs: one is in the form of indirect grants—a Registered Education Saving Plan (RESP); the other is in the form of direct grants —the Canada Education Savings Grant (CESG).

The Registered Education Savings Plan (RESP)

The RESP is an investment vehicle that allows a contributor to save for a child's post-secondary education. Unlike Registered Retirement Savings Plans (RSPs), the RESP contributions are not tax deductible. However, the savings grow tax-free until the beneficiary is ready to go full-time to college, university, or any other eligible post-secondary educational institution. Under the current rules you can contribute a maximum of $4,000 per year for a lifetime limit of $42,000. Contributions can be made for 21 years and the plan must be collapsed after 25 years.

The RESP is in fact a national system of indirect grants: the income generated by the RESP has accumulated tax-free. The foregone tax revenue is tantamount to a grant payable only to RESP investors.

The Canada Education Savings Grant (CESG)

With the 1998 Federal budget, RESPs became more attractive because in addition to an indirect grant in the form of foregone tax revenue, the federal government said it would offer a direct grant – the Canada Education Savings Grant (CESG)– to any parent who had sufficient income to purchase an RESP. The Government of Canada pays directly into a beneficiary 's RESP 20 percent of the first $2,000 in contributions made into an RESP on behalf of an eligible beneficiary each year. This means the Grant can be as much as $400 each year per beneficiary until the end of the beneficiary 's 17th year, which means a total lifetime maximum grant of $7,200 per child In other words, if you 're wealthy enough to put aside $2000 per year, from the time your child is born until the end of the year in which your child turns 17, the government of Canada will give you a tax-free grant of $7,200 towards your child's education. That's a tax-free gift of $400 every year for 18 years. With the 1998 federal budget legislation, if none of the parent's children take advantage of the RESP, the grants must be repaid, but not the income generated by the grant money, which has accumulated tax-free. Under certain circumstances, where no child pursues post-secondary education, the money can be rolled over into the parent's RRSP. Before the 1998 budget changes, you risked losing all of the investment income in the plan if your child did not pursue post-secondary education. Depending on the plan, the investment growth would go to a pool to finance the education of other children or be donated to an educational institution.

How much has the federal government disbursed so far?

Because the CESG is a statutory expenditure, there is no predetermined budget for the program: if every single eligible Canadian invested in an RESP, the federal government would have to pay as demanded.

Between 1998 and May 2000 the government of Canada spent over $454,069,661 in grants. It expects to spend another $70,418,244 by the end of this year and the forecast for 2000-2001 is $435,000,000.[1] In other words the federal government's projected accumulated expenditure for the Canada Education Savings Grant Program is expected to be some $959,487,905 by the end of 2001—almost $1-billion. If every eligible parent participated in the CESG, and invested the maximum $2,000 per year the federal government would spend every year $2,885,617,200.[2]

The Inequity of the CESG: A national System of Direct Grants for the wealthy This national system of indirect and direct grants that is currently in place is unfair and should be scrapped. Both the Registered Education Savings Plan and the Canada Education Savings Grant reward those who need the least help: the children or grandchildren of those who are wealthy enough to save. There are four 'wealth-care' rewards to the RESP/CESG: First, the RESP savings generate income that is tax-free-earnings grow tax-sheltered until taken out by the student for educational purposes. Second, the federal government guarantees an annual 20% return on investment for those who have enough disposable income to invest in an RESP. Third, public funds could subsidise private universities outside Canada. The beneficiary may be eligible even if she attends an educational institution outside Canada that offers post-secondary schooling and at which the beneficiary is enrolled on a full-time basis.

An "almost perfect tax deferral" Fourth, when the student begins to use the RESP for education, both the RESP income[3] and the grant income are effectively tax-free. Technically the income accumulated on the subscriber contributions and the grant as well as the grant itself become taxable. However, because the student typically has little other income, he or she effectively pays little or no tax on RESP income. Because the income is taxable to the student instead of the high-income parent, the RESP has been called an "almost perfect tax deferral."[4]

Scrap the RESP/CESG and establish The Canada Student Grants Program Where does the Canada Education Saving Grant leave low-income parents and their children? Absolutely nowhere, and the inequity here is clear: tax dollars and tax breaks are subsidising those who are already in a position to save instead of ensuring access for those most likely to be denied entry in the system of post-secondary education for economic reasons. Because of the inherent unfairness and elitism of these federal programs, the Canadian Federation of Students demands that they be scrapped. The existing national system of indirect grants, the RESP program, should be terminated and the existing national system of direct grants, the CESG program, should be cancelled. In place of the elitist RESP/CESG we propose the establishment of an equitable needs-based system of national direct grants – the Canada Student Grants Program. The national grants program proposed by the Canadian Federation of Students will be equitable, will cost no more than the current elitist system, and will provide greater access to post-secondary education.

(Michael Temelini is the Government Relations Officer at the Canadian Federation of Students.)

Endnotes

1. Canada Education Savings Grant, Quarterly Statistical Review, May 2000.
2. The sum cited is derived as follows: in 1998 the number of children aged 0-17 was 7,214,043. This number is multiplied by the maximum grant of $400. Canada Education Savings Grant, Quarterly Statistical Review, May 2000. Based on Statistics Canada, Annual Demographic Statistics 1998, Catalogue #91-213-XPB.
3. A fact actually cited on the web site of the Registered Education Savings Plan program: http://www.hrdc-drhc.gc.ca/hrib/learnlit/cesg/resp/resp.shtml
4. Geoff Kirbyson "Pro: Why Open an RESP "IE: Money, August 1999, page 20, August 1999.

Underemployment and life-long learning: Canadian views

By David W. Livingstone

The existence of extensive underemployment in the Canadian workforce, and particularly among younger workers, has now been carefully documented (see Livingstone, 1999). As Jackson et al (2000, p. 48) state: "The real story in Canada is not one of 'skill shortages,' but of an ever more highly educated workforce chasing fewer and fewer jobs that actually demand high levels of qualifications." If workers experience discrepancies between their formal education and their job requirements, and especially underuse of their previously achieved knowledge and skills, what are their general responses in terms of further learning practices? I will look first at participation in adult education courses, and then at involvement in informal learning activities.

Underemployment and adult education

It was often suggested in the early studies in the underemployment tradition that workers might tend to become disenchanted both with further employment-related learning and established society in general (e.g., O'Toole 1975). But more recent empirical studies have found that the underemployed have been at least as likely as other employees to be planning further education.

A case study of underemployed male college graduates in British Columbia in the late 1980s (Borgen, Amundson and Harder 1988) documented a complex array of responses to the general condition of underemployment, including anger, frustration and sadness; but this study discovered frequent efforts at retraining for job change, or further education that "I can always use...in other aspects of my life" (156). Similarly, on the basis of a 1989 Canadian national survey, Lowe (1992, 58-59) concludes that:

> Ironically, many individuals possessing higher credentials than required for their particular job believed that they must obtain even more education to compete effectively for a better job.

As for the underqualified, who have lower formal educational attainments and are frequently school dropouts, the prevailing assumption has been that they typically have even lower learning motivation and capacity for continuing education than the underemployed.[1] But, again, empirical studies have uncovered little evidence to support this assumption. The underqualified, just like everybody else, now believe that obtaining a post-secondary formal education is becoming increasingly important to getting along in this society and to qualifying for a future job (Lowe 1992, 89-107; Livingstone, Hart and Davie 1995, 32). Faith in the power of more education to close the education-jobs gap, or at least compensate for it, appears to be strong on both sides of the gap.

According to the 1989 national survey, further education *plans* were most common in sales and service jobs where people were most likely to feel overqualified (Lowe 1992, 53-59). OISE Survey data indicate that the underemployed in Ontario were slightly more likely than others to have such plans, but that the majority of those who were underqualified also expected to take further courses in the mid 1980s (Livingstone, Hart and Davie 1987).

Our preliminary analyses of *actual* participation rates in organized adult education courses, as reported in our series of general Ontario surveys between 1986 and 1992, have found no significant differences in participation rates between credentially underemployed, matched and underqualified workers (Livingstone 1992). Analysis of the 1994 and 1996 surveys confirms these findings. The credential gap has little effect on participation in further education courses.

However, further analyses of participation by *performance gap status* provides a somewhat different picture. As Table 1 summarizes, those whose educational qualifications exceed the actual performance requirements of their jobs are just as likely as those with matched statuses to participate in further education courses. The highly underemployed remain at least as likely as those with matched statuses to have enrolled in a course during the prior year. The participation of young underemployed post-secondary graduates in further education increased especially quickly during the early part of this period (Livingstone 1992). But those who are underqualified for their jobs on performance criteria had lower participation rates than other workers in the mid 1980s. Their participation increased to parity levels by the early 1990s, but appears to have declined again more recently.

There has been a reduction of government provision of general adult education courses during the mid-1990s (Livingstone 2000); the highly underqualified, who are also typically the lowest income workers as well as the least schooled and oldest, have probably borne the brunt of these reductions.

It should be noted here, as Table 1 also documents, that the officially unemployed have increased their participation rates in further education programs quite dramatically over the past decade, from less than 10% in the mid-1980s to around a third in the 1990s. This may reflect increased government efforts to reallocate social welfare funds, such as unemployment insurance, to provide increased retraining programs for the unemployed, as well as the increased difficulty of qualifying to be counted as officially unemployed and eligible to enter such programs. In any case, the officially

Table 1
Participation in adult education courses by performance gap status,
Ontario labour force, 1986-1996

Performance Gap Status	Annual Participation Rates						
	86 (%)	88 (%)	90 (%)	92 (%)	94 (%)	96 (%)	Avg.
Highly underemployed	32	34	45	38	32	33	36
Underemployed	25	30	34	40	33	32	33
Matched	31	30	34	39	33	36	34
Underqualified	12	22	25	34	32	22	22
Highly underqualified	12	19	24	34	11	11	16
Unemployed	7	16	28	40	32	39	30
Totals	26	30	34	37	32	31	32
N	590	559	581	526	715	610	3580

Source: OISE Survey of Educational Issues Data Archive.

unemployed are now participating in further education courses with as high a frequency as any other social group.

While many of these courses may be very useful to unemployed workers, a vicious downward spiral of training courses appears to now have been established among the unemployed and marginally employed, whereby previously secure workers take such a course when laid off, then bump other lower-level workers from their temporary jobs and into similar courses, only to be bumped themselves in the next round by more highly certified applicants.[2]

So, at both extremes of the education-jobs gap, among highly underemployed post-secondary graduates and unemployed underqualified high school dropouts, the participation rates in adult education courses are now comparable to or higher than the general population rates. With the lone exception of the small minority of the older working poor with very little schooling, there is no sign in these voluntary participation rates of any growing disenchantment with educational institutions among either the underemployed or any other discernible social group.

Our in-depth interviewees' responses to questions about their future plans and aspirations concerning education and jobs provide further insights into the extent of belief, on both sides of the education-jobs gap, in the power of education to improve future life chances.

For the underemployed, the equation between more education and better jobs is far from certain in light of the underuse of education in their present jobs. But the apparent necessity to respond to this uncertainty by pursuing yet more formal education also remains largely unquestioned:

I don't have anything I would call a plan at this point...There is certainly a thought at the back of my mind that more education would be a goal at some point. Certainly it would be a potential goal at least...If I am to remain in the field that I am in, I need to learn a lot more about computers, accounting and other things specific to the field, basically improving my qualifications. In today's economy, the employer expects you to have it when you walk in the door. But, to be honest, I've no idea what I want to do with the rest of my life. (Underemployed middle-aged male waiter with a B.A.)

I think I will be going back for my doctorate, it seems, the way jobs are...I'd like to be a professor or open a small business. I'm pretty sure I can get these jobs. It will take a while, but I need more education. It's just one last hurdle! (Underemployed young male part-time cook with a Master's degree)

If a student loan comes through, I'm going to broadcasting school. And I've got to get computer training...After all my education, I should have an answer, but I just want a job. There's a huge gap between the dream and most of this stuff. It's so far away for me. (Unemployed middle-aged male civil servant with multiple degrees)

It is very important for people to get a good education. Some people can't, but there should still be an emphasis on continuing education, because nobody wants to work at MacDonalds' all your life. (Underemployed older female service worker with a college certificate)

Among the underqualified interviewees, there is a virtually unanimous equation between further educational credentials and either a better job or a fuller life:

I'm discouraged because I didn't pass the math test to get into the program I wanted. It takes so long to go through all the upgrading courses and I'm afraid I'll be too old to find a job. But education is so very important. I don't mind going to school the rest of my life because I enjoy learning...I want to get enough training to open my own business—and get a high school diploma with math when I retire. (Unemployed older female service worker with no formal schooling)

I'd love to get my Grade 11, that's my dream...I'd really like to be an auto mechanic but I'm not able to get it—don't have enough skills in my head, too little education. Education is still my dream. I feel I've been deprived of something. If I had the education, I wouldn't be here today. Education gives you power...I'm not a smart person, but I'm not a stupid person. (Unemployed middle-aged female factory worker with some elementary schooling)

After upgrading, I'm going to an adult high school to get some training credits—unless I score a job, and then training's kaput. I don't think that will happen. I've looked for any kind of a job—not hiring, too much experience, not enough experience, just hired somebody else, et cetera. It gets very depressing. I'm trying hard. That's all you can do. You've got to try somewhere. (Unemployed middle-aged factory worker with some high school)

I'd like to do an advanced credit course and take a skill. I've got to get some education. I don't know exactly what now, but I have to see if I can get a better job. Want to learn more about my hobbies, too. I hope I'll be able to get a job if I get some school in—looks like a lot of people hope so! (Underqualified young male factory worker with some high school)

The entire concept of the economy is downsizing. Computers run our operations. It's all changing. What I used to do on a 12-hour shift can be done in two hours. Some might say why spend the money to educate more people. But in 10 years we will all need more education because everything is so sophisticated. (Underqualified older male industrial worker with some high school)

You shouldn't tell a person they can't learn. Can't say, hey, you go to high school and that's it. That is wrong. A mind is a terrible thing to waste. (Underqualified older male supervisor with some high school)

So, in spite of their common experience of a superficial connection between their formal educational attainments and the requirements of their current or recent jobs, both underqualified school dropouts and underemployed university graduates continue to believe and act as if more education is the personal solution to living in the education-jobs gap. There are undoubtedly many motives associated with the popular demand for and engagement in adult education. But whether the major motivation is seen to be competition for scarce jobs, the desire to be an effective consumer or citizen, assertion of the democratic right to equal educational opportunity, or a more generic quest for knowledge to cope with uncertain times, there is now an almost universal general perception that more education is a fundamental imperative in contemporary society.

Underemployment and informal learning

Informal learning outside of organized courses is at least as extensive as course-based learning in current societies, and also appears to have increased in recent years (see Livingstone 1999). However, the now well-established tradition of research on self-directed learning has paid virtually no attention to the informal learning practices of the underemployed, and very little attention to the informal learning of the underqualified, however these respective groups may be defined.[3]

The very limited amount of prior research on the learning practices of economically disadvantaged adults with low formal educational attainments suggests that the vast majority do a significant amount of informal learning (see Leean and Sisco 1981). Studies of economically disadvantaged urban adults, high school dropouts, functional illiterates and the unemployed have all found similar patterns (Livingstone 1999). The 1996 OISE Survey asked all respondents to estimate the amount of time they typically devoted to informal learning activities outside organized coursework. We have analyzed these estimates by underemployment statuses. As with most other prior comparative studies of informal learning activities, the variations within underemployment statuses are far greater than between statuses.

Analyses of the incidence of informal learning by the credential gap have found no significant differences in either the amount of work-related or general interest learning between the underemployed, the matched and the underqualified. Regardless of one's credential gap status, the amount of informal learning people engage in appears to be very similar.

But once again, relations between the *performance gap* and informal learning activities is a bit different. The results in relation to the performance gap are summarized in Table 2. Those who are moderately underqualified on performance criteria average more time in work-related informal learning that anybody else, about 400 hours a year. This may reflect their greater need to upgrade their skills for adequate job performance. But the small number who are highly underqualified for their jobs tend to spend less time in both work-related and general interest informal learning activities

Table 2
Estimated Informal Learning Activities by Performance Gap Status, Ontario Labor Force, 1996

Performance Gap Status	Average Hours per Year*		
	Work-related[1]	General interest[2]	Total Gap
Highly underemployed	350	325	675
Underemployed	300	275	575
Matched	300	325	625
Underqualified	400	300	700
Highly Underqualified	225	200	425
Unemployed	300	325	625
Total (N=691)	325	300	625

*Weekly estimates have been multiplied by 52 weeks and rounded to the nearest 25 hours.
[1] "Not counting coursework, about how many hours in a typical week do you spend trying to learn anything related to your paid or household work, or work you do as a volunteer? Just give your best guess."
[2] "Not counting coursework, about how many hours in a typical week do you spend trying to learn anything of general interest to you? Just give your best guess."

than any other group; this pattern is very similar to their participation in adult education courses.

This group represents only about 5% of the labour force and includes mainly people who are older with very little schooling; they typically have very limited income to support learning activities learning beyond their low-wage jobs. But even these folks with little schooling and little money to afford further courses estimate that they devote an average of over 400 hours a year to informal learning.

In the follow-up interviews to the 1994 OISE Survey, conducted in 1995 with credentially mismatched respondents to the initial survey, we pursued extensive questioning about all their organized and informal learning practices over the prior year. The basic findings are summarized in Table 3. Underemployed university/college graduates and underqualified people with high school or less were spending an average of about 13 hours per week, or 680 hours per year, on their various deliberate learning activities. The average amount of time spent on work-related and other general interest courses by both groups was quite similar, as was the amount of time devoted to informal work-related learning. The main difference was that underemployed university/college graduates claimed to be spending more time in informal learning related to their general interests.

This finding might be taken to suggest that underqualified people with less schooling have less predisposition or capacity to engage in informal learning activities beyond their work than underemployed university and college graduates do. But this would be to ignore the fact that self-directed learning is often underestimated among working class people because of a tendency to deny a major learning component in some manual activities,[4] just as many professional and managerial class people find it difficult to recognize important manual components in their activities.

For example, one of our respondents, who would be classified as functionally illiterate by most standards, spent a good deal of time in the interview resisting the notion that any of her personal activities could constitute a learning project. But she also added that:

I like meeting people and learning about things and I do a lot of sports and practical things like crocheting. But it's all old stuff, not real learning. (Underqualified middle-aged female factory worker with less than four years of elementary schooling)

More fundamentally, the entire tradition of research on self-directed learning projects is based on a conceptual model of an individually-realized intentional learning process. Particularly in many working class households and communities, a significant amount of important learning occurs without planning, in collective learning processes.[5] Such learning is beyond the scope of conventional measures of learning activities, again serving to underestimate the scale of working class learning. The current study is subject to the same limitations in this regard.[6]

However, at least these results are consistent with and shed a little further light on the general population survey findings that underemployed and underqualified people are spending substantial amounts of time in continuing learning activities in relation to their work and more generally. Both underemployed university/college graduates and underqualified non-college workers spend at least as much time on informal work-related learning as people whose credentials match their jobs. They also spend much more time in informal learning projects than they do in organized course-based learning, generally about *ten times as much time*. Neither underemployment nor underqualification serves to shrink the iceberg of informal learning.

As in prior studies that have compared patterns of informal learning across social groupings, variations in learning time *within* the underemployed college and underqualified school groups is much greater than the differences between them. In particular, there is no systemic difference between the credentially underemployed or underqualified and the rest of the workforce in their work-related continuing learning capacities and interests.[7] Regardless of their work status and in spite of various institutional and material barriers, most folks living in the education-jobs gap continue to engage in quite substantial informal learning activities.

In terms of the more specific content of their learning activities, both underemployed college graduates and underqualified non-college respondents participate in a wide array of work-related courses. School upgrading courses are most common among the credentially underqualified, while the underemployed are frequently involved in courses to develop additional vocational skills such as business administration. But the most common course participation in both groups now is in computer training.

Some of the flavour of the kinds of informal learning that underemployed and underqualified people engage in around their paid workplaces is conveyed by our in-depth respondents' comments:

Our products are constantly changing. We're reading blueprints, drafting all kinds of new things. I learn something new almost every day. We're learning all the time, but it's not job retraining. (Underemployed middle-aged male industrial worker with a community college certificate)

Once you get into a job, you realize how you start to learn more about business and what goes on. Formal education only has a minor role in the picture. There's a lot more learning to do once you finish school. You learn everyday at work. (Underemployed middle-aged female service worker with a university degree)

Much of my learning in the last year has been in response to the downsizing of our whole plant. They're reorganizing the entire work structure, giving us more accountability. We have to learn new concepts of team participation. But I've also been taking the time to read up about my rights and options if the next layoff hits me. (Underqualified middle-aged male factory worker with some high school)

I've spent a lot of time in internal cross-training, with someone else to cover a different job. We always do lots of on-the-job training with new techniques. And I've spent a fair amount of time in learning new computer programs. (Underqualified young male technician with a high school diploma)

Overall, these recent surveys and follow-up interviews indicate that there are no significant differences between matched and mismatched employees in their increased general participation rates in organized adult education courses. The general population survey of informal learning activities and the follow-up interviews with credentially mismatched employees demonstrate that there are also no major differences between underemployed and underqualified employees in the total amount of time they now devote to employment-related learning activities. It appears that these mismatched employees are spending at least as much time in informal learning as other adult learners.

The condition of underemployment has evidently not discouraged people from continuing both their employment-related and general learning activities. As for objectively underqualified workers, most of whom deny they are actually underqualified for their jobs, the evidence suggests that most of them are devoting at least as much effort to continuing employment-related learning activities as matched and underemployed workers. The learning efforts of both the underemployed and the underqualified are clearly much more extensive than the dominant rhetoric of cor-

Table 3
All Estimated Learning Activities of Credentially Underemployed College Graduates and Underqualified Non-college, Ontario Labor Force, 1994

	Work-related courses	Other Courses	Informal work-related	Informal other interests	Total
Credential Gap					
Underemployed college	50	30	310	370	760
Underqualified œh.s.	30	30	240	240	600
Total (N=136)	40	30	310	310	680

*Course time has been estimated by respondents in terms of total contact hours and related homework assignments. Weekly estimates for informal learning activities have been multiplied by 52. All averages have been rounded to nearest 10 hours.
Source: Follow-up interview of credentially mismatched respondents to Tenth OISE Survey of Educational Issues, February-March, 1995.

porate and government leaders about the pressing need for those in the education-jobs gap to get more training would suggest.

Those living in the education-jobs gap give no serious indication of giving up on the faith that more education should get them a better job. Indeed, their current situation seems to have provoked in many at least a quiet sense of desperation that somehow they must continue to get more and still more education, training or knowledge in order to achieve any economic security. The conviction of underemployed people that our current economic system can produce the jobs to which they continue to feel entitled has definitely been shaken. But, in the absence of any economic alternative that seems plausible, most of those living on both sides of the education-jobs gap are actively engaged in trying to revise rather than reject this conviction. The promise and pursuit of further education are now playing a similar role to the "make-work" programs of the Dirty Thirties in preoccupying the swelling number of outcasts and misfits of the labor market.

(David W. Livingstone is Chair, Department of Sociology and Equity Studies in Education, Ontario Institute for Studies in Education, University of Toronto. This article was adapted from David Livingstone's **The Education-Jobs Gap: Underemployment or Economic Democracy.** *Toronto: Garamond Press, 1999.)*

References

Adams, M. et al. (1997). *Preliminary Bibliography of the Research Network for New Approaches to Lifelong Learning.* Toronto: Centre for the Study of Education and Work, OISE/UT.

Borgen, W., N. Amundson and H. Harder. (1988). "The Experience of Underemployment," *Journal of Employment Counselling* 25: 149-59.

Bates, I. Et al. (1984). *Schooling for the Dole: :The New Vocationalism.* London: Macmillan.
Candy, P. (1993). *Self-Direction for Lifelong Learning: A Comprehensive Guide to Theory and Practice.* San Francisco: Jossey-Bass.

Curtis, B. et al. (1992). *Stacking the Deck: The Streaming of Working Class Kids in Ontario Schools.* Toronto: OurSchools/OurSelves.

deRoche, J., B. Riley, and G. Smith. (1994). "Job Dislocation and Retraining: The Case of Sydney Steel," *Making Waves* 5, 4 (Winter): 12-3.

Foley, G. (1987). "Adult Education for the Long Haul." Paper presented at the 27th National Conference of the Australian Association of Adult Education, Sydney (September).

Jackson, A et al. (2000). *Falling Behind: The State of Working Canada, 2000.* Ottawa: CCPA.

Leean, C. and B. Sisco. (1981). *Learning Projects and Self-Planned Learning Efforts among Undereducated Adults in Rural Vermont.* Washington, D.C.: National Institute of Education.

Livingstone, D.W. (1992). Lifelong Learning and Chronic Underemployment: Exploring the Contradiction. In P. Anisef and P. Axelrod (eds.), *Transitions: Schooling and Employment in Canadian Society.* Toronto: Thompson Educational Publishing, 113-125.

Livingstone, D.W., D. Hart and L.E. Davie. (1987). *Public Attitudes Toward Education in Ontario; Sixth OISE Survey.* Toronto: OISE Press.

Livingstone, D.W., D. Hart and L.E. Davie. (1995). *Public Attitudes Toward Education in Ontario (1994): Tenth OISE Survey.* Toronto: OISE Press.

Livingstone, D.W., D. Hart and L.E. Davie. (1997). *Public Attitudes Toward Education in Ontario (1996): The Eleventh OISE/UT Survey.* Toronto: University of Toronto Press.

Livingstone, D.W. (1999). *The Education-Jobs Gap: Underemployment or Economic Democracy.* Toronto: Garamond Press.

Livingstone, D.W. (2000). *Working and Learning in the Information Age:: A Canadian Profile.* Ottawa: Canadian Policy Research Networks.

Livingstone, D. W. and P. Sawchuk. (2000). "Beyond Cultural Capital Theory: Hidden Dimensions of Working Class Learning". *Review of Education/Pedagogy/Cultural Studies,* 22,2: 203-217.

Lowe, G. (1992). *Human Resource Challenges of Education, Computers and Retirement.* Ottawa: Statistics Canada.

O'Toole, J. (1975). "The Reserve Army of the Underemployed: I-The World of Work, and II-The Role of Education" *Change,* (May/June): 26-33, 60-3.

Willis, P. (1977). *Learning to Labour: How Working Class Kids Get Working Class Jobs.* Farnborough: Saxon House.

Endnotes

[1] For a critical analysis of such claims, see Curtis, Livingstone and Smaller (1992).

[2] See, for example, deRoche, Riley and Smith (1994). Consider also the cycling of young people between short-term training courses and temporary jobs, which has been more extensive to date in countries such as Great Britain where the normal school leaving age has been much lower than in the U.S. and Canada (Bates et. al. 1984).

[3] For a critical overview of this field of research, see Candy (1993). An extensive bibliography of current research on informal learning has been produced by Adams et al. (1997). This bibliography is accessible online at the Website of the National Research Network for New Approaches to Lifelong Learning (NALL): www.nall.oise.utoronto.ca.

[4] Willis' (1977) classic ethnographic study of this tendency traces the presumptive denial of mental aspects of manual labour among working class lads involved in rejecting an academic school culture and headed for manual jobs.

[5] For a provocative discussion, see Foley (1987).

[6] In an attempt to address this limitation, we have recently conducted a research project in cooperation with several labor educators and trade unions in the Toronto region. The project uses participatory action research methods, engaging with workers and members of their households to identify the scope and content of working class informal learning activities and develop more effective educational resource centers. See Livingstone and Sawchuk (2000).

[7] It should be noted here that further analysis of the follow-up subsample of underqualified non- college respondents has found that the small minority of the credentially underqualified who identify themselves as actually underqualified are spending much more time in work-related course studies than any other group, an average of about 150 hours per year.

The tax cut context
By Robert Chernomas

"The budget is the skeleton of the state stripped of all its ideologies."
—R. Goldscheid.

Canadians experienced in the 1990s the lowest per capita Gross Domestic Product (GDP) growth in 50 years, and the lowest among the G-7 countries—10% unemployment, growing inequality, and serious problems in the health and education systems.

The federal Liberals analyzed the situation and concluded that the problems with Canada's economic performance are rooted in a non-competitive productivity performance due to inadequate investment in research and development (R&D) and manufacturing, especially in machinery and electronic equipment, and an associated brain drain to the United States.

Implicitly, the measures previously introduced at the behest of the business community, including the right-wing Business Council on National Issues, the **National Post, Globe and Mail**, and the Chamber's of Commerce, to revitalize the economy such as free trade, deregulation, privatization, the attack on deficits and the debt, anti-inflation measures and massive cuts to government social spending, 25% in the four years between 1993-1997, have failed to deliver in the key areas. At the end of the decade some significant economic growth and a reduction in unemployment, much of it the result of growth in the U.S., has occurred, but this has had little if any effect on the underlying structural problem.

The business community's remaining agenda items include tax cuts and the further privatization of public services.

The right-wing rationale for tax cuts

According to the business community and their advocates, tax cuts improve savings and therefore increase investment and productivity, promote an incentive to work, and reduce the brain drain by providing employees with more retained earnings. They assert that taxes crowd-out savings and therefore reduce investment and productivity, reduce work incentives, and thereby increase business costs, all of which affects the business community's ability to compete globally.

The inevitable conclusion is that the government surplus should be used almost exclusively for tax cuts. In other words, in spite of the promises, free trade, deficit fighting and anti-inflation battles have not provided enough help with respect to competitiveness, productivity, and the brain drain. The solution, apparently, after decades of conservative economics by parties of all stripes, is more of the conservative agenda.

The 1999 federal budget included a reduction in corporate and personal tax rates (disproportionally for the already wealthy) in hopes that the lower cost for businesses would increases incentives to invest, and the cuts to personal income taxes would increase savings and work incentives. Further cuts to capital gains taxes were introduced, purportedly to retain profit for investment and lower the risk for venture capital.

The rationale behind these tax cuts is that Canada's manufacturing productivity is falling relative to the United States and the other G-7 countries. Yet, when analyzed, the productivity gap with the U.S. is limited to two industries: machinery and electrical products; otherwise Canada is doing just fine.

Currently, Sweden and the Netherlands are doing better with respect to productivity growth than the U.S., while paying much higher corporate taxes. The likely results of these tax cuts are a reduction in federal revenues, which will force the continuation of the social spending restraint.

Federal spending cuts under the Liberals have reduced social program spending down to 1940s levels, when measured as a percentage of GDP. The further loss of tax revenue could delay reinvestment in social infrastructures of hospitals, universities and colleges, public housing, etc.

Tax cuts are a weak instrument for promoting growth and higher productivity. Well-targeted public investments would do more than across-the-board tax cuts. Declining public capital spending has been linked to declining private sector productivity. Government-sponsored R&D provides very high rates of return. The federal spending used to fund R&D tax expenditures should be turned into targeted public investments.

If a productivity gap is the problem with the Canadian economy, what should be done?

The Canadian private sector has a dismal record on research and development, despite Canada's having the most generous tax support in the industrialized world. About half of Canada's R&D expenditures are made by businesses, the other half by government and non-profit institutions. Of the eight leading economies of the Organization for Economic Co-operation and Development (OECD), Canada had the lowest private R&D outlays to national income.

Canada already has lower overall business costs than do the Americans, and taxes are only a fraction of overall business costs. Taxes are more likely—if collected and used by the public sector appropriately—to do more to improve innovation, productivity and investment than tax cuts, in part by helping to pay for an better-educated citizenry. The Canadian corporate sector is among the least likely to provide on-the-job training or perform any R&D, in spite of the best tax incentives in the world.

The real question is: if corporate taxes are not paid and therefore not collected by the federal government, who will then provide the funds for education, training of skilled workers, communications and transportation infrastructures that are necessary for business to be able to function and be innovative? Cutting corporate taxes may actually end up raising overall business costs. The monies freed up from tax cuts are more likely to be used for speculation (paper profits), foreign investment (capital flight), and dividend payouts than they are to be used for R&D and training.

The biggest effects will be public revenue loss and inequality, and the possibility of some disproportional small increase in socially useful real investment and marginally small effects on productivity. Social spending on post-secondary education and publicly-funded research will likely do more to improve productivity in this country then will untargeted corporate tax cuts.

Where does Canada stand with respect to overall taxes? In the middle—17th out of 29 OECD countries, many of which have better productivity growth than Canada does. If health and education spending is included, the average U.S. tax is the same as the Canadian. Disposable income for those at the average industrial wage is slightly larger than for their U.S. counterparts. At upper-income levels, U.S. taxes are lower.

Is our tax rate too high?

Our manufacturing tax is relatively low, while our service taxes were proportionally higher before Paul Martin reduced them. However, it is important to point out that taxes usually rank 5th-7th in importance when investment decisions are being made. What really matters is the cost of doing business, of which taxes are only one element. Skills, modernization of plant and equipment, new technology, research, physical and social infrastructure, education and training are all-important factors. As discussed above, there are high-tax countries with high productivity and low-tax countries with low productivity.

What is the evidence for and against tax cuts as a means of improving the economic well-being of Canadians?

Government spending vs. tax cuts

First of all, a dollar spent by government has a larger impact on the economy than a dollar in tax deduction. Why? Because tax cuts may lead to savings, imports buying, or investments outside Canada. Government spending means more spending on Canadian goods and more labour-intensive work in health and education.

The evidence shows that lower or higher taxes seem to have little or no impact on hours worked, except for women in high-income families. Higher-paid workers tend to work the most hours, and if workers did work fewer hours in an economy with less than full employment, this would mean more jobs.

Furthermore, access to skilled workers, good public infrastructure, access to energy, resources, and other inputs at favourable prices are all potentially more important in terms of providing a competitive business environment then are tax cuts.

Capital gains taxes

The last time the federal government cut the capital gains taxes under Prime Minister Brian Mulroney, it cost the Canadian treasury billion of dollars in lost revenue, and failed to stimulate investment in any way. The tax savings went for real estate speculation and paper profits, as opposed to real investment.

The result was a revenue loss and increased inequality, and little or no effect on the problems of innovation, investment or productivity.

Personal income taxes

Personal tax cuts are not effective at promoting a savings effect or work effort. The U.S. has low personal tax rates and consistently has had one of the lowest savings rates in the OECD. The U.S. savings rate is approximately zero, with no apparent effect on innovation, investment or productivity. Taxes have no important effect on savings, and the cuts required to have any effect would generate enormous inequality.

Personal savings have little to do with investment. In both the U.S. and Canada, 90% of investment is funded out of corporate profits.

Brain drain

Anecdotal evidence, provided in the daily newspapers, is that some Canadian high-tech firms are losing their best and brightest to their American counterparts, and include complaints from these corporations about high government taxes and the effects of these on the corporate sectors' ability to compete. Who have moved to the United States? Laid-off nurses and university researchers who have had their research funds cut and their labs run down.

But one thing is very clear: taxes are not the issue. Nurses and researchers are casualties of the war on the deficit and the debt, which has and will cost this country dearly for years to come.

Half of the emigrated graduates who have left would like to come back. In reality, there is a net brain **gain** for Canada of highly educated people from around the world, and emigration to the U.S. is less now than it was in the 1950s and 1960s.

There are structural and cyclical factors that explain this emigration of some of our best and brightest who do migrate to the U.S. One important cyclical factor is that at present the exceptionally tight U.S. labour market is drawing people in from all over the world, not just Canada.

The structural response to the brain drain issue was that it is the private sector's lack of dynamism that is at the root of the problem. The Canadian private sector fails to invest enough in capital and research and development, in spite of some of the best tax incentives in the world.

The big issue is the job opportunities that exist in the U.S., where the private sector is more committed to R&D. These opportunities are particularly attractive to the top half of university graduates. Even if the personal income tax rate were cut by one-third, the evidence suggests that this would not affect the brain drain.

Canadian corporations don't invest as much as their competitors, so their productivity is lower and in turn they can't/don't provide sufficient salary levels in order to compete for skilled labour with the Americans. The starting salary differential offered by Canadian high-tech firms are significantly lower than for their U.S. counterparts, and the salary differentials increase over time. The wages of high-tech workers are higher in the U.S. and the opportunities are better, and, until this changes, Canadians will continue to emigrate to the U.S.

Trade and globalization

It would be hard to exaggerate the degree to which the concept of globalization has penetrated North American culture. It is treated at once as an economic tidal wave and as a paralyzer of the state.

It has been used to justify deregulation, privatization, environmental degradation, free trade, deficit/debt mania, high interest rates, zero inflation targets, anti-labour legislation, cuts to social spending, and upper-income and corporate tax cuts.

These policies are of course executed by individual nation states. The rationale in defense of these policy changes is that the rules established by the now dominant transnational corporations and the uncontrollable high-speed market highway they travel on must be obeyed lest you be run over and/or left behind.

The trouble with the concept of globalization is that, objectively, it is largely a myth, while the consequences of its power to organize our thoughts as to how the world works has real effects. It is the capitalist class attempting to use the threat of capital flight to free themselves of taxes, labour and environmental regulations, on the one hand, and on the other for them to turn everything from education to health care into a for-profit enterprise.

Research

The federal government is concerned about the innovation gap in Canada, relative to its competitors in the OECD, arguing that Canada can no longer survive as a resource or commodity or branch plant supplier for its trading partners, in particular the Americans. This is the age where human capital is replacing fixed capital and resources as the prime growth engine, and, if Canada cannot create and hold on to its own human capital, it will fall behind in the intense global competition to dominate the evolving growth sectors. From the Liberal government's perspective, an industrial productivity strategy was needed.

The federal government has made major cuts to public research though decreases in transfer payments to the provinces and decreases in the budgets of the three research-granting councils. The Liberals now proclaim that they are reinvesting in the knowledge-based economy, but they do not believe they should simply fill in the old holes again. They believe that university-based research should be the catalyst for the private sector, given that it is an underutilized source of research capacity and highly qualified personnel.

The government, however, is expecting some payoff in the form of improving the commercialization of university research. The model to be implemented is a partnership model by the Liberals in exchange for a fraction of the money lost to the spending cuts of the early 1990s. The costs and the results must be shared, they argue, because partnership produces better results.

The Liberals, scrambling to catch up to the U.S. in the so-called new growth industries, have discovered the need to reinvest in research. But the years of federal cutbacks means that it is going to take them years to make up for the damage to the infrastructure (buildings and laboratories) and loss of a knowledge pool and talented researchers.

Of even greater concern is the structure of the new plan. The plan for billions of dollars of taxpayer money to be spent on the Canadian Foundation for Innovation (CFI) and 21st Century Research Chairs is structured so as to provide more control over post-secondary education and research by the business sector—putting the relatively successful university research program increasingly under the control of a private sector that has proven itself incapable of keeping up with its counterparts in other countries in innovation, investment and productivity.

What should be done?

What exists at present in Canada is a short-run perspective, a business class that historically has had a branch-plant and resource business mind-set, and that by experience is not likely to spend these untargeted handouts and tax cuts in a socially useful way. Decreased corporate taxes are not likely to result in the desired outcome—i.e., investment in manufacturing, research and development.

Precisely because the corporate sector has failed to invest in these initiatives, what is needed now is long-term reinvestment in public programs, services and research.

Tax cuts and deductions must meet the test of transparency and accountability, and they must serve the public interest. Corporate tax loopholes should be closed so that corporations and their stockholders are not paid out of tax revenues to increase their non-productive speculative investments, consume more luxuries, and invest outside of Canada.

Tax giveaways that are not targeted to meet the public interest must be reversed. Capital gains, dividend and corporate income taxes that do not meet the needs of increasing productivity, innovation and investment should be increased. Foreign tax investment subsidies should be eliminated. Real research and development investments and real investment should receive favourable tax treatment. Taxes on profits that are used by the corporations for investment in machinery, equipment, and R&D should be reduced: taxes on profits that are paid out as dividends or used for foreign investments should be taxed at a steeper rate.

It is the Canadian corporate sector that has failed to generate competitive investment rates and that has manufactured the illusion of a brain drain crisis blamed on tax rates. The companies that have not invested enough in R&D and therefore cannot and/or will not pay their workers competitive wages should not be rewarded with more control over public money.

Funds allocated to the CFI and the 21st Century Research Chairs should be transferred back to the granting councils and core funding through transfer payments so that universities might provide the service to Canadian society that make our graduates supposedly so attractive to the Americans. In this way, the universities can continue to provide the basic research and scrutiny of private sector products that help to ensure a productive and safe society.

An example of public investment in university research is the Synchrotron at the University of Saskatchewan. This was an investment of $173 million in capital cost, and not a cent came from the private sector. Why? The Canadian corporate community seems to have a particularly short-run investment time frame. California, the high-tech centre of the known universe, has discovered that the more the public sector spends on research, the more the private sector spends.

What is true for the U.S. is certainly true for Japan and Sweden, and the business community's current poster child, Ireland: free university tuition, subsidies from the European Union, large public expenditures for infrastructure, and social contracts for labour and capital. Lower taxes were largely the **result** of success, not the cause.

Policy alternatives have been provided for several years now through the Alternative Federal Budget (AFB) which promotes using "Martin's surplus" for social reinvestment in order to lower unemployment, increase investment and productivity, raise personal income, improve the environment, and reduce inequality.

They call themselves by different names—liberals, neoliberals, conservatives, neoconservatives—but there is only one perspective out there being driven by the interests of the business community to constrain everyone but themselves. There are lots of good progressive ideas; it is our job to make it impossible for those ideas to be ignored.

(Robert Chernomas is a professor of economics at the University of Manitoba and president of the Manitoba Organization of Faculty Associations.)

Quality

University finance in Canada: 1972-the present
Ron Melchers

This report takes a historical look at the finances of Canadian universities. Certainly, we see again how government funding of universities since the early seventies has failed to keep up with enrolments and has fallen behind most other areas of social spending. We will also see again how students, through tuition fees, have been forced to shoulder a larger share of the cost of university education and how faculty have been increasingly charged with raising funds for their universities through the pursuit of external research funding. These changes have made the university more dependent on their own sources of revenues and less so on public funding, making the university more "private".

However, this report will also look at a less-often-told story – that of how those charged with the financial management of the university have, not merely coped, but also contributed to the impacts of these financial pressures in their own decisions. It shows how these decision-makers, through their own financial decisions, have played a key role in reshaping the purpose of universities and show what vision of the future of the university emerges from the choices they have made.

Decisions that shape the university are made in good times and in bad. Whether taken under constraint or in pursuit of specific aims, decisions over the resources of institutions are among the most important forces that shape their roles and directions. Awareness of these forces is a prerequisite to accountability in decision-making and it is with this intent that I have examined the record of university financial allocations since 1972. It is my hope that this discussion will stimulate discussion about where the decisions of university Boards and executive officers are taking the institution.

Trend in university revenues

General Trends
University revenues recover in 1998

After several years of "real" (adjusted for inflation) declines, revenues from all sources for all Canadian universities increased in fiscal years ending in 1998 to reach an all-time high of $12 billion. Continued increases in revenues from student fees and income from private sources have accounted for almost all the improvement in university revenues. Universities have also improved their financial positions due to increased investment income flowing from growing fund balances and trusts.

Everywhere, revenues from non-government sources helped universities improve financial pictures.

Revenues from government
Has the decline of government funding for universities "bottomed-out" in 1998?

Dwindling government financial support for universities showed the first signs of "bottoming out" in fiscal years 1997-1998 and total university revenues from public sources even showed some slight (0.2%) recovery. As a share of university revenues, government grants and contracts have declined steadily since 1978, when they represented 74.5% of total university revenues. They represented only 55.6% of university revenues in fiscal years ending 1998.

Government funding for general operations continued to decline (-0.3%) in 1997-1998 from their previous year level, as did capital grants (-0.2%). The only real increases after inflation in government funding were for Special Purpose and Trust (2.5%) and for Sponsored Research (2.0%).

Revenues from student fees and charges for ancillary services
University's reliance on student fees increases dramatically

The transfer of financial responsibility for university education from governments to students is the most significant change in the financial situation of Canadian universities in the past 25 years. Student fees are the largest source of non-government revenues for universities and the most rapidly growing source of revenue from any source.

Growth of university revenues from student fees is most significant after 1990. Revenues from student fees grew from $388.7 million in 1981 to $2.3 billion in 1998, a change in real (or constant) dollars of 224%. Student fees represented 9.4% of total university revenues across Canada in 1981. By 1998, this proportion had climbed to 19.5% nationally and as high as 28.2% in Nova Scotia.

Per full-time equivalent enrolment, real revenues from student fees more than doubled from a low of $1,584 in 1981 to $3,271 per full-time equivalent in 1998.

Private sources of revenue
Universities increasingly reliant on private sources of revenue

Private funding of universities from bequests, donations and from non-government grants has grown from a little over $54 million in 1972 (3% of total income) to more than one billion dollars (8.9% of university revenues) in 1998. In current dollars, this is an eighteen-fold increase and a real increase of 365%.

Nearly one-half of all private income of universities in 1998 came from corporate business enterprises.

Almost two-thirds of university revenues from private sources are as private research grants and contracts. Other revenues collected by universities from private sources (22.2%) were reported as Special Purpose and Trust revenues.

Sponsored Research
Universities have doubled their reliance upon sponsored research for revenues

The fastest growing source of university revenues after student fees has been grants and contracts for sponsored research activities. Sponsored research contributed $167 million dollars (9%) to total university revenues in 1972 of $1.8 billion. By the end of fiscal year 1997-98, revenues for sponsored research had reached nearly $2 billion dollars (17%) out of $11.9 billion of total university revenues.

As in other areas, public financial support for university sponsored research accounts for a smaller share today than in the past.

More than one-half of sponsored research revenues from private source come from corporations, with private foundations and non-profit organisations each contributing less than a quarter of sponsored research revenues.

Special purpose and trust revenues and flows
Universities increasingly flow revenues into their trusts and endowments

Revenues categorised under Special Purpose and Trust have grown from less than 1% of total university revenues in 1972 to over 6% in 1998. These funds have increasingly reported revenues from private sources. In 1998, Canadian universities collected Special Purpose and Trust revenues totalling $791 million and reported expenditures of $553 million, representing respectively 7% and 4.7% of total university revenues and expenditures. Another $159 million of revenue in Special Purpose and Trust was transferred to plant funds for capital additions (53% of net transfers) and to endowment funds (47%). Unexpended Special Purpose and Trust revenues stood at the end of fiscal 1998 at $823 million for all universities.

Endowment funds
Canadian universities' endowments reach $3.8 billion in 1998

In 1983, the first year such information was collected, the total principal of university trust and endowment funds for all Canadian universities stood at $625 million. By the end of fiscal 1998, the total combined principal of trust and endowment for all Canadian universities had risen more than five-fold to nearly $3.8 billion dollars, a real increase after inflation of 285%.

Growing endowment funds, increasing revenues from privately-funded sponsored research, higher tuition and fees for ancillary operations are all strategies designed to reduce reliance on government operating support and make universities increasingly "private".

Total fund balances
Canadian universities are increasingly accumulating unexpended revenues: charging the present to pay the future

Fund balances have risen at a faster rate than the total expenditures of universities has risen, rising from just over 12% of total expenditures in 1983 to nearly 20% in 1998. The net surplus, excluding capital, of all universities ($1.3 billion) represents over 11% of total non-capital (plant) revenues received by all reporting universities in 1998.

Nearly half of reported fund balances are held in capital funds[1]. When capital funds are included, reported fund balances of

Canadian universities reached a new record high of $2.3 billion in 1998.

Capital fund balances
Universities are building funds for capital depreciation

One explanation for rising fund balances is that universities are accumulating funds for renewal of capital stocks in anticipation that capital grants from public sources will not be forthcoming. Universities are now required to capitalise and amortise capital assets. The consequence is that, to fund depreciation of capital assets and collections, universities are now reducing other areas of expenditures, including shrinking their financial allocations to core business operations – teaching and non-sponsored research.

Trends in university expenditures

General trends

Total university expenditures have risen from $1.8 billion in 1974, after the end of the university construction boom, to $11.7 billion in 1998, a real increase (adjusted for inflation) of 84%.

Salaries, wages and benefits
Universities decrease their reliance on human resources

Salaries, wages and benefits are the largest single class of university expenditures, representing 63.1% of total expenditures for all funds in 1998. For more than two decades, salaries, wages and benefits have been declining as a share of total university expenditures; from a high of 74.2% of non-capital expenditure in 1976 to their now lowest level of 66.8% in 1998.

Academic rank salaries now represent only 27% of total non-capital university expenditure and this proportion has dropped each year since 1973, when 34% of university non-capital expenditures went to academic rank salaries. The number of full-time faculty in Canadian universities declined from 37,422 in 1991 to 33,327 in 1998.

Average earnings of both full- and part-time faculty declined by 3.8% after inflation between 1994 and 1998.

Employee benefit costs rose at a higher rate than other expenditures for most of the period examined and increased rapidly from 1990 to 1993. Since then they levelled off and have now been declining since 1996. In 1998, benefits were 12% of total compensation costs for all universities.

Expenditures for non-academic rank instruction and research salaries, often integrated into student financial assistance measures, or a part of sponsored research, also increased at a faster rate than expenditures as a whole, but levelled off after 1994.

Non-compensation expenditures
What expenditures have driven the increase in university costs?

Most of the contribution to growth in expenditures occurred in the costs of insurance, institutional membership fees, travel and the cost of goods sold which together accounted for 10% of total university expenditures in 1998, $1.16 billion.

Operational supplies and expenses, furniture and equipment are the second fastest growing expenditures for universities, accounting for 15% of total expenditures. Sponsored research, representing 17% of total university spending, accounts for 36% of the expenses for operational supplies and equipment.

The most rapidly growing expenditure, although it represented only 2.6% of 1998 university expenditures, has been for scholarships, bursaries and prizes.

Interest paid on debt, representing 2% of total university expenditures in 1998, also grew at a rate faster than expenditures as a whole.

Buildings, land and site services, utilities, renovations and alterations, space rental and property taxes grew at the slowest rate, once the university capital expansion boom ended by 1974.

Instruction and non-sponsored research
Teaching and non-sponsored research occupy an ever-shrinking share of the "business" of the university

General operating expenditures have risen at a slower rate than other areas of university activities. Universities are spending less on their core functions and more elsewhere. While general operating expenditures rose 57% from 1972 to 1998, expenditures for Special Purpose and Trust funds rose by 663%. In the same period, expenditures for sponsored research rose 182%. Expenditures of ancillary enterprises increased 122%. Only capital expenditures have risen at a slower rate than general operating expenditures, 21% since the end of the university construction boom in 1974.

The traditional functions of the university, those services performed by academic staff in the main, appear thus to have declined in priority for university decision-makers. As a consequence, the ratio of students per full-time faculty member has increased continuously over the past decades, from 13:1 in 1979 to a ratio of 19:1 in 1998.

Expenditure on instruction and non-sponsored research per student (FTE) fell from $8,369 in 1979 to $7,078 in 1997. This decline of service to students has occurred at the same time that students have been paying more for university education. Per full-time equivalent enrolment, real revenues from student fees more than doubled from a low of $1,584 in 1981 to $3,271 per full-time equivalent in 1998.

1998-99[2]

According to the most recent release of financial statistics of universities and colleges, covering fiscal years ending in 1999, current trends identified from the previous year's data have continued at the same pace. Total university revenues from all sources combined continued to recover slowly from the real stagnation and decline of the years 1992 to 1997, and are now growing 4.5% annually. The greatest year-over-year 1998-1999 recovery was experienced in Saskatchewan (8%) and Nova Scotia (7%), whereas university revenues declined in both British Columbia (-1.4%) and Newfoundland (-1.3%).

Unlike in the previous year, some small part of this recovery finally appears to be shared by general operations, which supports the teaching mission of universities. In 1998, only sponsored research and special purpose and trust funds showed any real recovery. In 1999, although these continue to be the fastest growing areas, there is some evidence of recovery spilling over into teaching as well. In 1999, operating revenues increased at the same pace as total revenues (4.5%). The increase in operating revenues was strongest in Nova Scotia (7.4%) and Ontario (6.7%), the two provinces where reductions in public support in the 1992 to 1997 period had been the deepest. Operating revenues of British Columbia universities, which had been spared some of the deepest cuts in previous years, declined (-1.2%) in 1999.

Except for the province of Québec, increases in university revenue from tuition (6.8%) outstripped growth of revenues from provincial operating grants (2.7%) in fiscal years ending in 1999. Revenues from tuition, which reflect changes in both tuition costs and enrollment, increased most rapidly in Alberta (14.2%), Prince Edward Island (8.6%) and Ontario (8.5%). Tuition revenues of Québec universities declined (-0.4%). Provincial Operating grants increased most rapidly in Alberta (6.3%), Québec (5.4%) and Nova Scotia (5.3%). Provincial support of education, which also reflects changes both in the size of transfers per student and in enrollment, declined in Newfoundland (-2.7%), New Brunswick (-1%) and British Columbia (-.01%).

The greatest relative growth in university revenues once again was for sponsored research. This reflects a rapid and fundamental change in the role of at least some universities in Canada. Canada's largest and most research-intensive universities are thus experiencing growth not shared by universities with a primarily undergraduate teaching mission. This shift from teaching to sponsored or "science shop" research is being led by significant increases in federal funding for sponsored research (+16% in 1999) and is increasingly being supported as well from private sources. Québec universities received the largest share (37.4%) of the $250 million in new money from all sources for sponsored research in fiscal years ending in 1999, followed by Ontario (32.1%) and Alberta (17.5%). This reflects a specific public policy thrust in Québec and a more economy-driven trend in Ontario and Alberta. British Columbia universities, despite a strong research tradition, received only 4.5% of new money from all sources for sponsored research. All other provinces together accounted for only 8.5% of new money. There continues to be evidence supporting the emergence of a two-tier university system, in which teaching occupies a lower priority for growth and investment than sponsored research.

University revenues for capital stock additions and replacement continued to decline in 1999, reaching a real twenty-year low of $310 million. Capital funding decline most dramatically in Québec and in British Columbia. The latter change may partly reflect the winding up in 1999 of the B.C Educational Institutions Capital Financing Authority and the transfer of its balance to the Province. The only increases in university capital funding were modest increases in Manitoba and Saskatchewan. The capital assets of Canadian universities continue to decline at an alarming rate. Canadian universities transferred $84 million out of operating revenues, principally to prop up crumbing capital infrastructure.

The only area to have experienced greater erosion in university spending is the academic payroll. Academic salaries remained in 1999 at a thirty-year low of 30% of non-capital spending. The number of full-time academic rank faculty increased for the first time since the start of the 1990's, but by only 200 new faculty, an increase of only 0.8%. However, academic salaries for instruction and non-sponsored research declined once again to a new record low of 25.7%. Academic salaries for sponsored research accounted for two-thirds of new investment in academic labour by Canadian universities in 1999. As previously indicated, this growth has only occurred at a small handful of universities. Elsewhere, investment in academic labour engaged in teaching is continuing to decline and is declining at a even faster rate than that for capital infrastructure.

Conclusion

Universities have become more "private" and diverse corporations as public financial support declines and universities increasingly orient their activities to pursue other revenues, student fees, privately source research contracts, as well as bequests, donations or endowments. In this pursuit, the traditional core resources of the university have been reduced both as a proportion of total allocations and in relation to enrolments. The financial surpluses universities now enjoy have created deficits in teaching and in capital stocks.

The teaching deficit is one familiar to any university student or faculty member who has recently spent time in a Canadian university. Students are certainly aware that they are paying more tuition for less and less contact with dwindling numbers of overworked faculty. Faculty is certainly aware of swelling class sizes and graduate supervision loads and of shrinking resources to cope with the additional demands they are expected to meet. These are now the common experience of most university students and faculty.

The financial pressures under which the university is placed are most felt, if not exclusively felt, in the classroom and in all areas of teaching. To survive, many teachers have been forced to reduce their teaching ambitions and lower their expectations to those that can be manageably assessed in a mass teaching context. Students' aspirations, parents' hopes and future employers' needs are the first losers in this race to the bottom. But, ultimately it is society that loses when successive generations of university students are not supported.

Nor is the capital deficit of Canada's universities unfamiliar to anyone who has recently walked the halls of academe. The physical deterioration of university facilities is made all the more acute by their unsuitability for today's mass teaching environment. Buildings, rooms, hallways built to accommodate hundreds of students are now called upon to accommodate thousands. Time required simply emptying out and refilling classrooms between classes now uses up an inordinate portion of scheduled class time.

The increasingly "private" character of universities is also evident, even without a careful analysis. Faculty comes under increasing pressure to obtain research funding for their universities through career advancement criteria that privilege this activity to the exclusion of all other tasks, including service to students and non-revenue producing services to society. Often the most basic operational supplies and equipment, even those required for teaching and service tasks, may only be acquired through external source research grants and contracts. Areas of specialisation within the university particularly suited to the procurement of sponsored research contracts from corporate business enterprises often receive more support at the expense of less commercially viable areas of scholarship. Increasingly, it is the impression of many that the business of universities has become fund-raising in place of service to society.

The prime responsibility for this situation lies with governments. Since the early seventies, government funding has failed to keep up with the growth of enrolments in universities. University operating grants have fallen in relation to other areas of public expenditure through this time. Since the early 1990's, government financial support for universities has fallen in absolute terms while a levelling off in enrolments limited universities' efforts to replace lost revenues with increased tuition fees.

Nonetheless, declining government funding has not alone led to the erosion of the core functions of universities. This erosion commenced long before the most acute period of cuts and has continued good year and bad year for most of the past few decades. Whether by retreat in the face of financial exigency or by advance in the pursuit of another vision of their institutions, university decision-makers have contributed to and, in many cases, purposefully created the changes this document has described. Whether it has occurred by inaction or by action of its leadership, the university has become a fundamentally different place today than it was thirty years ago – one less focussed on serving students and society and one more focussed on raising funds to ensure future autonomy.

Whether these changes serve or disserve society is a question that is not being asked in the appropriate venues today. It may or may not be mused upon by university presidents when they gather. Who is to know? It may be raised in discussions at governing councils of universities, members of which are often drawn from among close relations of university presidents and representatives of corporate "clients" which contract with universities for sponsored research. Experience suggests however that such thoughts take a back seat to the real business of universities today, that of amassing sufficient funds –often at any expense – to avoid having to answer any such questions ever again.

University autonomy, the prime driving force behind the changes we are seeing made today in the university, is first and foremost a defense against accountability. A fully autonomous university renders accounts to no one but itself. Ultimately, this is the greatest casualty in the race to the bottom in government financial support of universities, the loss of public power to ensure that they serve the public good. In this sense, at least, those making the institutional decisions today reshaping the university and governments hostile to public spending have a common goal, to make universities less accountable to the public interest. The question which remains is what are the interests driving this change?

(Ron Melchers is a Professor of Criminology at the University of Ottawa)

This article is based on a much longer report by Ron Melchers (*University Finance in Canada: 1972-1998*), who was the CAUT Visiting Scholar in Post-Secondary Studies when this report was completed in October 1999. The entire report is available from the Canadian Centre for Policy Alternatives.

Endnotes

[1] An unknown number of institutions appear to have erroneously reported plant equity in capital balances in 1998. This may inflate capital fund balances by an amount that is impossible to estimate.

[2] This section has been added since the completion of the original report in October 1999.

Research, innovation and prosperity
By Denise Doherty-Delorme

Canadian research and development is performed by universities (and to some extent the community colleges), government agencies and projects, such as the National Research Council and Genome Canada, as well as by private enterprise. University research is separate and distinct from the other two areas because the university itself serves as the centre for three inseparably linked functions—research, teaching and community service—and the three functions are carried out free and independent of any external authority.

University researchers, especially tenured faculty, given the funding, space and academic freedom to set their own parameters, have shown great success in providing a wide body of knowledge, which in turn has ensured the success of explorations done by government agencies and private corporations.

The government of Canada funds all three sectors through a variety of measures such as grants for graduate students, transfer payments for universities, direct funding of granting councils and government research facilities, and loans and tax credits for the private sector.

The refrain coming from both government and private enterprise is for the need for even more innovative innovation, and quicker rates of applicability and commercialization. But, instead of acknowledging past accomplishments, respecting the particular role of each of the three research sectors, and of building on this foundation, the government is set on dismantling it all and allowing the private sector to set the country's research agenda.

Funding for universities, the granting councils and government agencies is being diverted to the private sector through new funding agencies, research and development tax credits, and the private universities.

Scientific research, when governed by private for-profit interest, is seen only as an input to innovation or as a unit serving public policy. As J. Lomas of the Canadian Health Services and Research Foundation, in his article *Connecting Research and Policy* (Isuma V.1 N.1 Spring 2000), suggests, "… the "abuse" of research findings often occurs because a single study within one stage of the process… is taken as the product of the entire process and used as if was a synthesis of all stages and applicable in far or complex "real world" conditions."

This is true for all disciplines, social sciences as well as bio-medical, and the humanities along with engineering. Single projects or distinct research findings are not to be considered consumable knowledge, products or services. University research has both intrinsic and utility value that puts it at odds with the mandate of corporations, which is to find the most profitable results in the shortest term possible.

That is not to say that research and development done by the private sector has no value. As part of a triple- tiered approach, it has served both its shareholders and the society well. But much of the research done by corporations depends on a foundation of knowledge that is the result of university research. By underfunding university research or by putting it under the control of the private sector, the very base upon which prosperity is built will be removed.

As Neil Tudiver declares in his book **Universities for Sale** (CAUT 1999), under the corporate influence "Universities eventually lose their balance." Corporate influence hampers the free flow of information and expects exclusive rights to the results; commercialism affects the university by transforming it into a training school for students to serve corporate clients; and privatization threatens social analysis, creative expression, and critical thinking, and robs society of creativity and innovation.

Public support for core funding of universities and renewed support for university research is crucial to the economic prosperity, innovation, and cultural sustainability of Canada. This has been the message from students, faculty, support staff, and university administrators alike.

"As Canada anticipates its future prospects, it needs to look upon university research as a powerful stimulant for economic growth and social development. In the final analysis, the issue for society is not whether we can afford to invest in university research, but whether we can hope to prosper without it." (AUCC Research File, V.2 N.3 1998).

To ensure social and economic prosperity and innovation, research must be done by universities and government agencies, as well as the private sector.

Role of university research

For university research to retain its quality, it must be tied to both teaching and community service, and have the freedom to carry out research in all domains of inquiry. Research is not a single event, nor does it 'produce' a single measurable product. Good research develops an idea and adds to the body of knowledge—not just in one narrowly defined field of inquiry, but in many inter-disciplinary areas. The outcome of research—successful research—can even be proof that something does not work; or it may assess new areas of applicability or methodology.

Production produces products, while research is a process that teaches, adds knowledge, and maybe even raises more questions than answers. University research, if the space and funding are provided, can develop new methods of research and advance new areas of inquiry.

Genuine creativity and innovation depend on defining the questions to be explored, and is aided by the knowledge of what areas have previously been attempted—both successfully and unsuccessfully.

In an Association of Universities and Colleges Canada Research File (V2N3) titled *"The Economic Impact of University Research"* it is estimated that expenditures on university research surpass the spending on research of the top 15 private sector and Crown corporations combined. University research is unequalled in its ability to produce not only an end product, but also the knowledge to understand it: showing the researchers how to put the knowledge to work and to ask the questions on how new products and advances will affect present and future societies. University research provides the means for people to make improvements in labour and resources, and helps develop new knowledge and expertise.

Constraining university research capacity through faculty shortages, budget cuts, or calls to produce commercial results reduces universities' ability to foster this kind of economic and social development. There is a move in some of the provinces—Ontario being the prime example—towards separating the universities by their functions: major research university, teaching university, and private university. This will in turn separate research and teaching by classifying universities and faculty as either—as Stanley Aronowitz calls them in his book *The Knowledge Factory*—knowledge producers or knowledge transmitters (2000, pg32).

Universities perform their community service in a assortment of ways. They carry out research in wide variety of areas. The results of the research are reviewed by a jury of peers and then disseminated by publication in academic journals, in the media, and in public presentations.

Role of Faculty

Universities that fully respect academic freedom, provided most solidly through tenure, provide faculty members with the right environment for them to carry out the three functions of scholarship, teaching research, and community service. Community service is accomplished through research, reviews of colleagues' work, and the free dissemination of the results of their own work.

Faculty also teach and mentor graduate students and engage them in ongoing research studies, thereby providing a continuous supply of future researchers. These future researchers are employed by the universities themselves as well as by government agencies and the private sector. Much of the success of university research and future researchers depends on the involvement of faculty.

As observed by the late Dr. David C. Smith in his report, *Will there be enough excellent profs?*, "Many factors affect the contribution universities can make to education and research—factors such as the learning environment, the abilities and motivation of students, and the physical infrastructure... But no factor exceeds in importance the quality of faculty. It is faculty who help guide students' thinking through the relevant bodies of knowledge—challenging them to deepen their understanding of the world within and about them—and who provide evaluations of students' progress in chosen subjects." (as cited in COU Fall 2000)

In *Access to Excellence* (Fall 2000), the Council of Ontario Universities outlines the importance of the role of faculty and what is necessary to guarantee the connection between student and teacher. "The most direct route to an "innovation culture" is to place students in an environment that nurtures innovation. Research, creativity and scholarly activity—the wellspring of innovation—pervade every aspect of university teaching and learning, pushing the boundaries of knowledge and encouraging free inquiry. Faculty are the catalyst in this dynamic interchange. Universities must be able to compete successfully for quality faculty by offering a vibrant culture and tangible support that, together, provide the tools for success in both teaching and research. This is what attracts and retains excellent faculty."

Evidently, adequate funding is a key element in providing for quality faculty and an innovative culture.

The role of public funding

In 1999-2000, the federal government used public dollars to provide more than $6 billion in support for research and development. As awesome as this dollar figure may sound, graduate students, university researchers and facilities and the granting councils have had to be content with less and less.

As the Council of Ontario Universities reports, "Canada depends on the higher education sector for almost one-quarter of its national research and development effort. No other G-7 country relies so heavily on its universities for R&D. In spite of this impressive level of contribution, Canada lags behind its G-7 counterparts in expenditures on research... (COU, 2000). But, as a percentage of all R&D done in Canada, the share done by universities has declined from 27% in 1994 to 21% in 1997. During this period, the granting councils had their funding reduced by 15%.

The COU report goes on to show that Canadian universities are falling behind the American schools, and the disparity between provinces also continues to increase. Ranking all 50 states and 10 provinces in their spending for universities over the period of 1995-96 to 1999-2000, the COU found that Ontario ranked second last, with a decline of 8% in public funding. All other Canadian provinces underfunded their universities by approximately 4%. In comparison, the American states increased funding by an average of 28%.

Last summer, Statistics Canada released its annual Report on University Finances, which revealed that in 1998-99, for the first time in six years, federal and provincial government grants and contracts to universities had increased by 3.6% over the previous year. Government grants and contracts account for 55.2% of total university revenue.

As a share of the economy, however, federal cash transfers earmarked for post-secondary education are still at their lowest level in more than 30 years. University re-

Federal funding for post-secondary education and research

1916: The National Research Council (NRC) is created with a mandate to coordinate government research programs and provide graduate fellowships and grants for university research.

1957: The Canada Council is created to provide grants and fellowships to support university research in the humanities and social sciences.

1967: The Federal-Provincial Fiscal Arrangements Act establishes core funding for post-secondary education, to be shared equally between both levels of government.

1977: The Fiscal Arrangements Act is renamed Established Programs Financing (EPF).

1978: The Natural Sciences and Engineering Research Council (NSERC) and the Social Sciences and Humanities Research Council (SSHRC) are created to perform the research support functions of the NRC and Canada Council, respectively.

1978: The Medical Research Council is established to support university health care research.

1984, 1986 and 1990: Cuts administered to EPF decrease the federal cash transfers to the provinces.

1987: Prime Minister's Advisory Council on Science and Technology University Committee recommends greater support for university research through increased funding to the three Granting Councils.

1996: The Canada Health and Social Transfer (CHST) replaces EPF and further decreases the cash transfers.

1990 to 1997: Federal support for university research is reduced by 15%.

1997: The Canadian Foundation for Innovation is established.

1997: Networks of Centres of Excellence are made permanent.

1994-2000: Federal cash transfers (EPF + CHST) earmarked to post-secondary education are cut by $3 billion.

1998: NSERC and SSHRC budgets returned to 1994 levels.

1999: Liberals post a $12.3 billion federal surplus.

2000: Prime Minister's Advisory Council on Science and Technology releases report on the Commercialization of University Research, recommending that universities accept commercialization of knowledge as their fourth mandate.

2000: The Canada Institute for Health Research (CIHR) replaces the MRC to fund a broader definition of health care research, with the purpose of integrating the bio-medical with social sciences, humanities, natural sciences and engineering.

2000: 21st Century Canada Research Chairs (CRC) provides funding for 2,000 new chairs by 2004-05.

2000: $3.6 billion needed to repair crumbling universities, says Canadian Association of University Business Officers (CAUBO).

2000: February and fall federal budgets allocate only $0.20 in social spending for every dollar spent on tax cuts.

2000-2001: The Liberals expected to post a federal budgetary surplus between $20 to $30 billion.

search cannot be funded by starving the university because research funding alone does very little to help the teaching function of the universities.

Over the period 1993-94 to 1997-98, while total federal and provincial support declined approximately 10%, funding from private sources (not including tuition fees) increased 35% to over $1 billion dollars annually. This sum, however, carries with it the push to have universities perform the research that should be left in the private sector.

Public funding for university research is delivered by the federal government in a variety of measures:
- cash transfer payments to the provinces;
- grants to graduate students;
- funding of the Granting Councils: SSHRC, NERSC and CIHR;
- funding the CFI and the CRC;
- supporting government agencies and projects: National Research Council and its regional facilities, Genome Canada, Canadian Biotechnology Strategy, Climate Change Action Fund, the Tri-University Meson Facility;
- supporting a particle accelerator laboratory, and the Atlantic Investment Partnership; and
- research and development tax credits for private sector R&D.

One area that has been overlooked is university infrastructure: buildings, laboratories and libraries. Over the period of 1990-2000, all the provinces except for Quebec have decreased their capital expenditure allocations. It is estimated that an annual allowance of 2% to 4% of replacement value is needed, but no provincial government allots this amount. British Columbia earmarks 1.5% and Ontario only 1%.

A report sponsored by the Canadian Association of University Business Officers (CAUBO) titled *"A Point of No Return"* (2000) estimates that, in order to repair our crumbling universities, it will take an infusion of $3.6 billion, of which one-third is urgently needed for immediate repairs.

The four Atlantic provinces are far worse off then the rest of the country. Statistics Canada notes that, over the period of 1993-94 to 1998-99, the percentage of university expenditures spent on buildings declined from 4.3% to 2.9%. In 1998-99, spending increased by 8.9%, but spending is still 30% less than it was five years previously.

The provinces of Manitoba, Quebec, Nova Scotia, and Alberta spend more the 5% on buildings.

The CAUBO report goes on to enumerate the causes of the problem:
- Average age of university buildings is 32 years.
- Universities have had reduced or static funding since 1990.
- Private funding will not support general capital upkeep.
- Greater demand for new buildings due to increased enrolment and a greater demand for research.

These crumbling facilities will have a serious impact on university research.

An investigation done by University Affairs (Feb. 2000) titled *"Death By A Thousand Cuts"* finds that university researchers must contend with equipment that is over 20 years old; library budgets are half of what they were 15 years ago; student/faculty ratios are up over 30% in the last two decades; public funding has decreased by 30%; some universities are selling off buildings; other universities have tried cutting programs, others increasing tuition fees and enrolment, and still others accepting more money from private partners.

Students are paying more for less access to professors, less contact with teaching assistants, evaluations based on multiple-choice exams instead of longer essays, and less research equipment, be it in the laboratories or in the libraries.

Robert Giroux, president of the Association of Universities and Colleges of Canada (University Affairs FEB 2000) proclaims: "Governments have to show more vision and responsibility. The provinces and the federal government are using universities as the ball that they throw back and forth to each other in a game of political football."

From viewing the history of the funding of both universities and research in Canada, we can discern the trend towards privatization that is moving public money away from public universities and public programs in order to benefit the private sector. Increases to core funding are needed to repair the damage done by years of cutbacks. Yet funding provided through the Canadian Foundation for Innovation and the Canadian Research Chairs are less likely to be given to the social sciences and humanities or smaller schools, or allocated to general operating budgets, graduate students, or repairing old buildings.

"Innovation and growth takes place in society, and is deeply affected by cultural, moral, social, and of course linguistic conditions. An economy without a fundamental appreciation of social and cultural factors is an unbalanced economy. Investments in hard sciences should not be financed by counterproductive cuts in the humanities and social sciences." (B Svedberg)

Trading off more funding for private enterprise or allowing private interests to direct research dollars will inevitably lead to the demise of university research.

In a report titled *"The Canada Research Chairs: Doing Industry's Research,"* the Canadian Association of University Teachers (CAUT Ed. Review V.2N.2, www.caut.ca) explains the problem with the 21st Century Research Chairs. The CRC, it says, will broaden the disparity between the larger and smaller universities, as almost two-thirds of the Chairs will be allocated to only 10 of the 69 Canadian universities. And most of those will be concentrated in Vancouver, Toronto and Montreal, exacerbating existing regional disparities.

In the legislation establishing the CRCs, there is no comment on the division of the Chairs among the three research areas, though it has been stated that 20% of the Chairs will be allocated to the social sciences and humanities, where over 40% of the graduate students and faculty are researching. The funding for the Chairs does not include monies to cover indirect costs of doing research, such as the cost of buildings, laboratories and libraries. This funding is delivered through the CFI infrastructure grants, which require matching funds that most likely will be received from the private sector.

The CAUT points out that, "In such cases, CFI requirements will give private interest a **de facto** veto over which research chairs will receive infrastructure funding. This raises serious concerns that private economic interests, rather than scholarly interest, will determine much of the research content of the program. It is particularly alarming that the federal government is designing the Canada Research Chairs program to advance greater ties between university researchers and industry at the same time as conflicts between corporate interests and university policies are raising serious ethical and public interest issues."

What can be done

One example of a well-researched solution to the problem of underfunded research was presented in September 2000 at the Arctic Science Conference, where the Natural Sciences and Engineering Research Council and the Social Sciences and Humanities Research Council released a report Titled *"From Crisis to Opportunity - Rebuilding Canada's Role in Northern Research"* (www.nserc.ca).

Citing social, physical, health, educational and environment challenges in Canada's Far North, the report calls for new collaborations between universities and the peoples of the northern communities. In order to deal with the crisis, solutions must be found based on solid research. In part, says the report, the crisis has been due to a lack of government funding and the rising cost of research.

The report makes several recommendations to improve opportunities in the North: a) establish research chairs;

Total cost to eliminate accumulated differed maintenance
Canada = $3.6 Billion

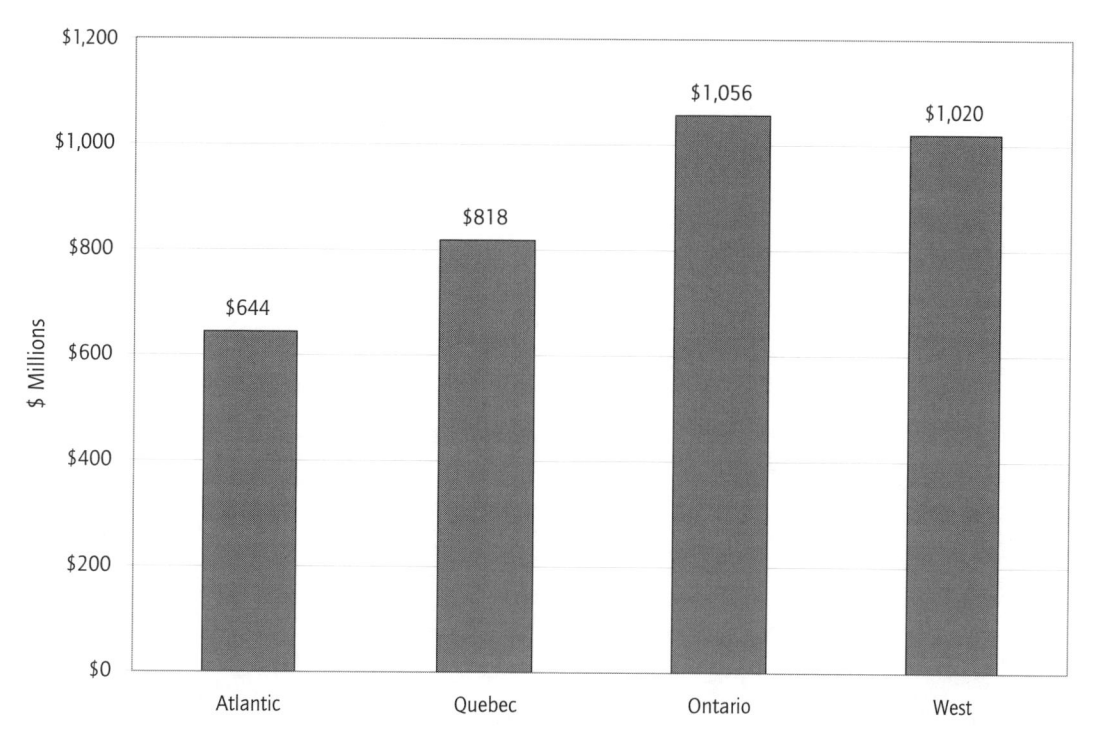

Region	$ Millions
Atlantic	$644
Quebec	$818
Ontario	$1,056
West	$1,020

b) create northern graduate scholarships and postdoctoral fellowships;
c) support strategic research projects;
d) build partnership between northern communities and university researchers; and
e) provide funding for critical equipment, infrastructure and logistical needs.

Prosperity and innovation depend on research, and the foundation of research done by government agencies and the private sector is university research. University research is needed precisely because it is different from research performed by the other two sectors. Universities must be funded by public dollars so as to allow research and inquiry to occur in all disciplines, from bio-medical and engineering to the social sciences and the humanities. Funding must be guaranteed to repair and rebuild the classrooms, offices, laboratories and libraries. The results of university research must be peer-reviewed and allowed to be shared with colleagues, government agencies, policy-makers, private enterprise, and the public at large.

Initiatives that tie university research to the needs of the private sector must be discontinued. The Granting Councils must have their funding increased so as to allow parity between the disciplines, between the larger and smaller schools, and between geographic regions.

Private sector research and development alone will not ensure prosperity and innovation, nor will allowing private sector-style research to be performed in the university. Leadership is needed, and Canadians are calling on the federal government to take the lead by establishing a secure and solid foundation built on core funding for universities, grants for graduate students, support for the Granting Councils and government research agencies, and for their initiatives.

(Denise Doherty Delorme is an education researcher and writer, and a Research Associate of the CCPA)

The state of university education and the liberal arts

By Dr Livio Di Matteo

I would like to discuss the state of university education and some of the serious issues that threaten its viability. I want to talk about how persistent funding shortfalls over the last decade have undermined the effectiveness of the university system by creating "crumbling campuses" and how this makes the case for direct federal transfers into the university system. I want to talk about how these funding shortfalls have provided an impetus for the "corporatization" of university campuses—both in terms of fund-raising as well as management procedures. Finally, I want to talk about how the shortage of funding ultimately threatens the university's orientation towards basic research and the liberal arts and sciences. The future of the liberal arts is linked to funding and attitudes towards basic research and knowledge.

Canada's university campuses are crumbling in five basic ways. First, with respect to teaching, the number of full-time faculty in Canada has dropped 11% over the last seven years. Enrolment is expected to increase by 20% over the next decade and one-third of faculty to retire. We will be trying to renew and expand our university faculties in a global talent market after a period of restraint that has allowed salaries and working conditions to erode.

Second, the physical infrastructure of universities is literally crumbling. Universities underwent significant expansion of their physical plant in the 1960s, and these buildings are now showing their age. There are millions of dollars of deferred maintenance at campuses across the country, and these expenditures cannot be met out of current operating budgets. The Canadian Association of University Business Officers and the Association of Universities and Colleges of Canada recently estimated that the tab for deferred maintenance at universities is now $3.6 billion, of which $1.2 billion is urgent.

Third, the rise of the Internet and information technology has brought an entirely new infrastructure problem. It is estimated that nearly $300 million per year over the next five years is required to effectively implement information technology and internet connectivity across Canada's university campuses. A computer is no longer a frill but an essential tool, but all too often researchers are left to their own devices when it comes to basic computer hardware and software. How can universities move forward and be on the cutting edge of the information highway if funding relegates them to the *information cow-path*?

Fourth, there is the escalating cost of books and journals, which is causing our university libraries to move away from being living cultural and intellectual complexes to simply museums where the dates of the books in the catalogue indicate when the funding ended. When libraries cease to grow, they become artifacts rather than effective research tools. Despite the talk that electronic access to books and journals on the Internet will be a substitute for printed volumes, it is merely rhetoric because even electronic access takes substantial resources. The Canadian Association of Research Libraries recently reported that, across Canada's regions, the purchasing power of 27 major academic research libraries over the last five years has fallen by a range of 22-to-33%, with libraries in Quebec the hardest hit. It is estimated that nearly $200 million per year is needed to help university collections in this country recover, and approximately $1 billion is needed to provide one-time access to electronic journals and collections in libraries.

Finally, there is the issue of graduate students. There is insufficient granting council support for graduate students and the next generation of scholars. Levels of financial support for graduate students are approximately where they were in the mid-1980s in terms of size of awards, and only a small fraction of graduate students are ever able to get support from the federal granting councils. Given the important role that graduate students play in teaching and research in universities, as well as the fact that they represent investment in the future, this is not an optimal situation.

Why are campuses crumbling? Essentially, it comes down to funding and resources—*money*. You get what you pay for, even in university education. Our system is mainly publicly-funded and the 1990s have seen steady erosion of university grant revenue from government, resulting in tuition increases in an effort to offset that decline.

Let me use Ontario as an example. Since the 1990/91 fiscal year, operating grants to Ontario universities have been cut by nearly 25% after adjusting for inflation. As the accompanying graph shows, real per capita grants in this province peaked in 1992/93 at about $205, and declined to about $140 where they have remained. Since 1996/97, universities in this province have only managed to stay afloat by increasing tuition substantially, but even with increases of over 10% per year, per capita revenue is still below what it was at the start of the decade. Tuition now accounts for close to 50% of university operating revenue, creating a situation where universities are *publicly-assisted* rather than *publicly-funded*.

Are public funding shortfalls because of tough economic times? No. Universities in Ontario are simply not a government priority. During the course of the 1990s, there has been in Ontario an 11% increase in population, a 20% increase in real GDP growth, and a 26% increase in real total provincial government spending. Yet, real operating grants to universities have fallen 24% and real per capita grants 31% (**See Table 1**).

Table 1
Selected Ontario statistics: 1990/91 to 1998/99

Population growth	11%
Real GDP growth	20%
Total provincial government spending	26%
Real operating grants to universities (1999/00 $)	-24%
Per capita real operating grants (1999/00 $)	-31%

Sources: Statistics Canada, Government of Ontario, Council of Ontario Universities
Data Source: Council of Ontario Universities

There is some good news on provincial operating grants recently. With the exception of New Brunswick, Nova Scotia and Ontario, operating grants to universities are being raised in provincial budgets. However, Ontario is the noticeable holdout, given its importance in Canada's economy. Moreover, it should be noted that recently the Ontario government capped tuition fee increases at 2%. It is inconsistent and ultimately destructive to have a policy that caps tuition fees without increasing government funding to cover the loss in revenue. While lower tuition fees will increase accessibility, funding decreases will diminish the quality of the education offered. Ontario, along with the other provinces, needs both an accessible and high quality system of post-secondary education.

Of course, the problem is not entirely provincial. Federal cash transfers have also declined substantially during the 1990s. Creation of the Canada Health and Social Transfer has hurt universities—first, because of the reduction in resources, and second, because there is no explicit mention of post-secondary education in the transfer. Block transfers of cash for universities are important because they allow for decision-making suited to local academic conditions and environments. When governments target funding, they distort the resource allocation decision by imposing centralized decisions.

Although education is a provincial responsibility, the cash component of federal transfers allows the federal government to show leadership in the research area of university education. There is a vital federal role in the construction and maintenance of a national research capacity (much like railroads in the 19th century, health and social welfare in post-WWII) and cash grants allow the federal government to commit itself to that priority while allowing universities the necessary operating flexibility.

In an effort to lobby the federal government, last year, the Humanities and Social Science Federation of Canada convened an expert panel to draft a report on university funding options. The panel consisted of a number of academics and academic administrators. They recommended five ways in which the federal government could inject resources into the university system. The call was for an additional $2 billion in federal transfer funding for post-secondary education.

First among the methods for boosting federal funding of post-secondary education is transferring $2 billion into the

Canada Health and Social Transfer (CHST) via either cash or tax points, subject to reaching an agreement with the provinces, or by creating a separate federal post-secondary transfer payment. Second, there could be direct federal support for students via the income tax or a voucher system— for example, a 100% tuition tax credit. Third, more funding could be directed to federal research granting councils (SSHRC, NSERC, CIHR) so that they could attach overhead and indirect research cost percentages to all grant awards as well as create more and larger graduate student fellowships. Fourth, new funding could be provided to the National Library of Canada to establish a national library infrastructure program. Finally, a program providing new funding for the electronic connection of campuses could be established.

The February 2000 federal budget was disappointing in that, while the CHST was increased by $2.5 billion dollars, it was to be spread out over four years, and no specific mention of universities was made. Given the clamor and urgency of the health situation, little if any of this money would find its way into post-secondary education. There was no direct money for granting councils (though, oddly enough, budgets were increased slightly via ministry allocations). There was also no specific commitment to increasing transfers to universities, suggesting that the federal government has rejected a strategic approach to post-secondary education.

One should not, however, be too hard on the federal government because, unlike the provinces, they have been demonstrating a strong commitment to university research via the Federal Research Chairs Program, the Canadian Foundation for Innovation, and the Canadian Institutes for Health Research. Their reluctance to hand over a blank cheque to the provinces on transfer funding, whether it is for post-secondary education or health care, is part of the *immeasurable majesty* of our federal system of government. One can only hope that eventually the federal commitment to university funding will percolate down to provincial government policy initiatives.

Over time, persistent public funding shortfalls have generated pressure for increased corporatization of universities across two dimensions. First, universities in Canada are becoming increasingly corporate in their management. Second, closer links to corporations and business for fundraising and research purposes are being established.

The corporatization of university governance is being partly driven by resource scarcity, which has created the pressure to manage what remains more intensively in an effort to get more for less. Many universities are now acquiring a slew of Vice-Presidents, Directors, and Coordinators in the belief that resources are scarce and that faculty and programs have to be managed both in terms of program direction and day-to-day contact. This approach is rooted in a technocratic approach to management that sees a technical solution to every problem and that operates in a milieu that is devoid of institutional history or the past resource environment. It is no longer fashionable to argue that management is more a leadership art with an empirical and judgment component, rather than a science of spreadsheet and flowchart applications.

Corporate models of governance are being applied that often clash with traditional notions of collegiality and academic governance. Deans, for example, now spend more of their time as academic managers and fund-raisers rather than academic leaders. When it comes to hiring, universities are "filling in lines" rather than hiring faculty with expertise in certain fields. In day-to-day operations, there is a growing emphasis on "serving your customers" which threatens to trickle down into aspects of the classroom that are not appropriate.

This is not to say that there is no room at all for the application of some corporate and management principles. For example, enrolment management is of importance. Having a database that links your student population to a wide variety of data characteristics is useful for recruiting, as well as fund-raising. Moreover, despite the usual academic reluctance to praise administrators, the fact is that good administrators *are vital* to the smooth running of a university, especially with respect to its fund raising, public relations and revenue enhancement efforts, campus infrastructure and general operating procedures. From a faculty perspective, good and capable administrators should be in the background, ensuring the infrastructure and resource needs of programs, rather than micro-managing day-to-day delivery of academic programs and content.

Nevertheless, the corporate "customer service paradigm" is one aspect of business-style management that should be approached with caution at a university, and not blindly applied. After all, *in education,* *the customer is not always right,* and paying your tuition does not entitle you to a certain grade or career. While it is a difficult concept to sell in our consumer-oriented society, what you want and are willing to pay for may not necessarily be right for you. Not everyone can be a great hockey player or rock star, and not everyone is going to be a good philosopher or computer software engineer. And sometimes, someone with an independent frame of mind and with no direct vested interest in the outcome needs to say that. The professor in a classroom ultimately must be a learned scholar and teacher, and not simply a cruise director for the course.

Another difficulty is that the core educational functions of a university become skewed when decisions are being made solely based on attracting tuition dollars, corporate donations, or targeted government funding. The autonomy of a university as a place of independent scholarship and research becomes compromised if decisions are made only to attract the academic flavour funding opportunity of the month. Just as government intervention in the economy needs to be approached with caution, government intervention in the marketplace for ideas is also dangerous. Government does not really know what the labour market or economy is going to be like 10 years from now, and sometimes taking direct action can be worse than leaving things alone. A case in point: the government of Ontario decided to reduce the intake of medical school students a number of years ago because they believed there were *too many doctors*. Now, half a decade later, there is a scramble to boost admissions to medical school as the realization dawns that this action was partly responsible for bringing about the current shortage of doctors.

Resource scarcity has also created the need to find alternate sources of funds, and corporations have been involved in funding universities, not just in terms of donations and grants to buy equipment and endow chairs, but also contract research and exclusive selling rights. Some campuses have given companies like Coca-Cola exclusive rights to sell their beverage on campus or to put up advertising in public areas. Universities, as pools of expertise, are interested in using the inventions of their faculty as revenue sources and links with corporations, especially in science, and technology can help to make that happen. There are a number of issues here, as the following examples illustrate.

The University of Montreal recently announced a unique $125 million campaign which proposed 150 projects of interest to business [example: Networks of e-commerce chairs, a science and technology complex]. The problem here is that only a handful of the projects are dedicated to the arts, culture and literature, because it is more difficult to find funds for this type of project from the private sector. Moreover, it does give the appearance of a "kept university" as it solicits funds from projects geared not to the interests of faculty and students, but to corporate customers.

In another example, it was recently reported that McGill wants to raise the university's "cut" of profitable inventions and innovations developed by its university-based researchers, with the inventor's share to drop from 50% to 35%. This is a typical example of interventionist management on the part of some university administrators and government bureaucrats who sometimes view faculty not as independent learned scholars and researchers, but simply as salaried civil servants. In the long term, this type of action may reduce the incentive to do research within the university. Moreover, it could actually speed up the brain drain as the traditionally more generous division of the proceeds from innovations in Canada relative to the United States may have compensated for the substantially lower salaries.

With respect to the relationship between universities and corporations, the concern is not with the commercial application of research arrived at via mutually beneficial agreements between faculty researchers, universities and corporations. There is nothing wrong with links arrived at via a process of voluntary negotiations between a faculty and a corporation where rights, responsibilities and benefits are openly discussed and arrived at. Concerns occur when it is automatically taken for granted that a researcher's work belongs to the university rather than to the researcher who performed it. Concerns occur when commercial application of research becomes a research evaluation criterion rather than scholarly publication in refereed academic journals. Concerns occur when links to corporate and government funding interfere with academic freedom. What if a university-based researcher discovers that a certain corporation's product is dangerous? Can or should the corporation be allowed to invoke contract rights that would prevent the study from being published? Finally, concerns arise regarding what happens to those research and scholarly areas without direct and immediate market applications, such as basic scientific research or the liberal arts.

A targeted funding-driven university system—whether those funds come from government agencies or corporations—neglects the importance of basic research and the liberal arts because there is no short-term cash pay-out or benefit to investing in them. Targeted funding induces universities to expand programs based solely on external priorities and incentives. In the case of government and corporations, they pick the winners and losers. A prime example is the current provincial government funding initiatives in Ontario that intend to stream students into science and technology because of the belief that that is where our economic future lies.

It is extremely important that there be public investment in basic scientific research and liberal arts, because they provide benefits not captured by the market process. Just because something does not have a market price does not mean it is without value. An example of successful basic research, the Internet, is today a largely private-sector-driven operation, but much of the seed money and ideas were provided in research- intensive university environments. The basic theoretical underpinnings of the Internet were not funded by corporations, but were arrived at by university-based researchers in the 1960s literally "playing" with new ideas. By the 1970s, the first applications were being done with government funding via the U.S. Defense Department and its DARPAnet, while the European Union supported CERN facility in Geneva. The commercial applications of all these innovations finally came to fruition in the 1990s.

The underfunding of basic research will have important ramifications 20 and 30 years from now when the supply of innovation dries up. Corporations generally do not want to fund basic research with benefits 20 years down the road; they like funding the commercial applications. For society to continue to benefit from the flow of innovation in the long term, public investment is required.

As for the liberal arts—the humanities and social sciences— they may not always create a product that can be immediately sold for profit, but they do create the fundamental foundations of a society of ideas and a literate and civil society of citizens. If you do not believe a civil and literate society is important to the conduct of everyday business life, you only need visit those countries around the globe where civil society has broken down. The liberal arts provide interpretive and communication skills that help build the human mind and provide critical thinking skills.

Even corporate CEOs realize the importance of balance in education and have issued very public statements regarding the need for education in the liberal arts and science to complement scientific and technical training. In a recent statement, high-tech CEOs write that many of their technology workers began their higher education in the humanities, and they are clearly the stronger for it. "This was time well spent, not squandered. They have increased their value to our companies by acquiring the level of cultural and civic literacy that the humanities offer."

Along with acquiring knowledge for its own sake—the hallmark of a traditional university education—individuals trained in the liberal arts can conduct research that deals with the implications of science technology. For example, what will the impact of genetically modified food and cloning be on our agricultural sector? What is the economic impact of an extended life span? Are not these important questions?

Corporate CEOs need people educated in the liberal arts with diverse academic backgrounds to interpret technological and financial data, to map broad societal trends, to strategically plan for their companies. As one director of a high-tech company recently put it with a reference to Star Trek, "We need more Captain Picard, less Scotty in the engine room." Technological change has dramatically increased the supply of information, and businesses must try to deal with the deluge of facts and figures. Liberal arts-educated graduates are well suited to this type of analysis, being able to see the forest for the trees. Corporate high-tech CEOs who realize the value of a liberal arts education include Jean Monty, at Bell Canada, Kevin Francis at Xerox Canada, and John Wetmore of IBM Canada.

Finally, we should lay to rest the belief that liberal arts degrees destine you for unemployment. Research has shown that people with liberal arts degrees do quite well. The recent Allen Report presents unemployment data for 25-29-year-old men and women by fields, and finds that arts and humanities graduates do find work and over the longer term earn very high incomes. Indeed, it might surprise you that some of the scientific fields have higher unemployment rates than arts, humanities and social sciences.

Finally, it is important to justify the liberal arts in non-economic as well as utilitarian terms. Fundamentally, the critical thinking skills fostered by the liberal arts are essential to civilized society and are worth doing for their own sake. As David Bentley, an English Professor at the University of Western Ontario, recently wrote: "The arts are the arts precisely because they do not entirely belong in the day-to-day world of jobs and business." Therefore, justifying their study entirely in utilitarian terms does them a dis-service.

There is a need for balance in university education, and the recent preoccupation with science and technology does a disservice to the future. We do need science and technology, and generous resources should be provided to those areas because good research and teaching in science and technology is capital and equipment intensive and requires a lot of money. However, *there must be balance*.

If we are to adequately meet the challenges of the future, universities must strive to provide balanced research and education that includes the liberal arts—in particular, the humanities and social sciences. With a few notable exceptions, research and degrees in these fields do not provide an immediate commercial product or application. Nevertheless, they are of value and importance, and, if the market fails to provide, then there is a role for government. Government needs to ensure that adequate and generous general funding is provided to universities so that they can provide a balanced education and research environment.

Governments, however, do not necessarily respond to rational arguments or logic. They do respond to voters and interest groups. If you are convinced that the liberal arts and basic research are important, then it is vital we make ourselves heard. We need to impress upon decision-makers the need for increased general public funding for universities so that a healthy and independent university environment can flourish. We need to argue the importance of the liberal arts, not only in terms of their benefits to society, but also *for their own sake*. It is fundamentally a flawed strategy to continually make the case for liberal arts only in terms of what it can do rather than what it is. Ignoring the inherent importance of the humanities and social sciences to civilization suggests that we are somehow embarrassed about what we do.

I believe that in the 21st century, in the wake of technological, social and economic change, there will be a demand for the benefits provided by education in the liberal arts. Moreover, the changes wrought by the economy and technology will spawn a search for deeper meaning in life and a demand for the intangibles provided by education in the humanities and social sciences. In the university environment, the challenge will be to combine the new technological and social environment with traditional cores of liberal arts education.

(Dr Livio Di Matteo is an Associate Professor of Economics at Lakehead University and Vice-President External Relations, Humanities and Social Sciences Federation of Canada—www.hssfc.ca)

Online learning: Compromising quality
By Michael Temelini

Introduction and background information

Canadian students support and encourage the use of new technologies for the advancement of learning both inside and outside the classroom. However, we would like to raise a number of concerns, both general and specific regarding the social and political implications of online learning.

Our critical remarks are as follows: first, we have serious concerns about the impartiality of the committee. Second, we have concerns about the fact that online learning will perpetuate the erosion of the quality of Canada's post-secondary education system. Finally, we have some critical comments about the underlying political economy of online learning.

1. Committee composition

The Canadian Federation of Students has serious doubts about the impartiality of the Advisory Committee for Online Learning. We notice that the committee has no representation from either university and college teachers' organisations or from students' unions, nor does it have representatives from the general public. Furthermore six voting members of nineteen (one-third) are senior corporate representatives from The Learning Partnership, AT&T, Bell Canada Enterprises, Bank of Montreal, Lucent Technologies and IBM Canada. Along with such noted supporters of online learning as University of Waterloo President David Johnston and Acadia President Kevin Ogilvie, the committee is entirely made up of representatives who clearly have an interest in promoting online learning.

For this reason, we share the concerns raised by the Canadian Association of University Teachers that the committee composition is unrepresentative and biased toward those who view education as a marketable commodity. Without fair and equal representation, that is to say 'democratic' representation, the committee cannot possibly be expected to provide a careful, balanced and broad-based consideration of the complex issues involved with online learning. Therefore the committees' final recommendations will be tainted by the composition of the committee.

2. Compromising quality

The second critical comment we would like to raise is that the current drive for online learning will do nothing to improve the quality of post-secondary education. In our view, it's more likely to exacerbate the ongoing erosion of quality. As David F. Noble has recently argued, the paradox or Achilles heel of online learning is that pedagogical promise and economic efficiency are in contradiction.[1] Quality education is labour-intensive. It requires a low student teacher ratio, and significant interaction between the teacher and student. Any effort to offer quality in education must therefore presuppose a substantial and sustained investment in educational labour whatever the medium of instruction. However, by definition, the commercial requirements of online learning undermine the labour-intensive foundation of quality education.

As Noble argues, the history of correspondence education provides a cautionary tale for those now promoting online learning. He argues that the rhetoric of the distance education movement (the correspondence course) a century ago was almost identical to that of the online education movement today. The promise of distance education was a genuinely progressive movement for democratic access to education, particularly adult education.

Distance educators have always insisted that they offer a kind of intimate and individualized instruction not possible in the crowded competitive environment of the campus, accessible to anyone from home or workplace. To make their enterprise profitable, however, they were and continue to be compelled to reduce their instructional costs to a minimum, thereby undermining their pedagogical promise. Since distance education was invented over a century ago, the central concern of the correspondence firms has been to keep instructional costs to a minimum. Instead of quality, students receive pre-packaged courses of instruction, 'delivered' by a casualised workforce of readers who work part-time and are paid on a piece work basis per lesson or exam.

In order to make a living, many correspondence instructors had to deliver a high volume of lessons and were unable to manage more than a perfunctory pedagogical performance. "Such conditions were of course not conducive to the kind of careful, individualised instruction promised in…promotional materials."[2] The result was not only a degraded labour force but a degraded product as well. And so the commercial effort at correspondence courses devolved into what became known as 'diploma mills'.

Noble's carefully researched analysis reveals the remarkable similarities with the current situation. For-profit enterprises are once again competing to provide vocational training to working people via computer-based distance education. Universities, although trying to distinguish themselves from their commercial rivals, are now collaborating with them and they are coming to resemble them—"this time as digital diploma mills."[3]

Are the federal and provincial governments committed to quality teaching and research, or are online studies simply destined to be digital diploma mills? The student movement sees no evidence at all that 'quality' is a priority. On the contrary, since 1985 there has been a sustained public divestment from post-secondary education. Between 1982-83 and 2000-2001, public funding to post-secondary institutions steadily decreased as a percentage of operating revenue from 74% to 55%.[4]

To compensate for this massive underfunding, university and college administrators adopted a number of related policies: they have passed off costs to students in the form of higher tuition and user fees; they have turned to private funds such as corporate donations and sponsorships; they have dramatically reduced the numbers of full-time faculty and they have reduced wages and degraded working conditions for other employees. Jobs and wages have been threatened as the work of Teaching Assistants and maintenance workers are contracted out and privatised. Students and their parents have been forced to mortgage their futures for a degree or diploma. Private colleges and universities have emerged, draining resources from the public system, and equity seeking groups have found that their fight for access is even more difficult as post-secondary education increasingly becomes a privilege for the rich.

According to Statistics Canada, between 1990 and 2000 university tuition fees have increased on average some 126%. Average tuition fees in undergraduate Arts programs have more than doubled across Canada. They are now over $3,378, up from about $1,500 in 1990.[5] The costs of other programs have increased even more dramatically. As students increasingly assume the financial burden of their education, so their debts have steadily increased. Average student debt is now at a historic high of between $25,000 to $28,000.

Moreover, universities are relying more on part-time faculty to deliver their educational programs. Between 1992-93 and 1997-98 the number of full-time faculty in Canada declined by nearly 10%. The number of full-time teaching staff fell in all provinces except Prince Edward Island and British Columbia. The number of part-time faculty increased 6% in the same five-year period. At the same time, the number of full-time and part-time university students decreased by less than 2%.[6]

The federal and provincial governments have made no indication that they are prepared to restore the billions of dollars cut from universities and public colleges to solve the problem of inaccessibility and degrading quality engendered by staff reductions and overcrowded classrooms. The enrolment explosion will be an even bigger concern in 2002 when the so-called 'double cohort'—the Ontario graduating classes of grades 12 and 13—will simultaneously enter the Canadian post-secondary system.

For their part, Canada's university and college administrators have made no indication that they are prepared to hire the thousands of full-time professors and teachers that are necessary to restore quality to Canada's education system. On the contrary, most university and college presidents have readily and all too uncritically implemented the draconian austerity measures decreed by provincial governments obsessed with economic expansion and tax cuts for the wealthy. Throughout the late 1980s and well into the 1990s, universities and colleges accelerated the degradation of quality. This accelerated decrease in quality occurred as a result of a number of policies: by promoting early retirement, by closing departments and faculties (euphemistically referred to as 'rationalisation'), by increasing workloads, by freezing and reducing the wages and benefits of Teaching Assistants and Sessionals, and by reducing the numbers of administrative support staff and maintenance workers.

This trend helps explains why most students are sceptical about the supposed benefits of online learning. The problems in post-secondary education are something that online technology cannot solve. Since at least the 1985 federal budget, the biggest problem faced by colleges and universities is the billions of dollars that have been cut from provincial transfers. The Advisory Committee is interested in learning how universities and colleges can 'reap the benefits' to online learning. But what federal or provincial committee is investigating the devastating effects of two decades funding cuts? What federal department is concerned about restoring faculty-student ratios to levels that truly advance the quality of post-secondary education? If the underlying aim of online learning is to ignore or undermine the labour-intensive foundation of quality education, then its pedagogical promise to quality contradicts its aim for economic efficiency. An online degree will cost the same as a regular one, only it will be of poorer quality.

3. The new ideology: Education as 'knowledge based industry'

The first two problems identified here are merely corollaries to a more fundamental issue that the student movement has with online learning. The assumption on which our movement was founded is that education is a fundamental right, not a privilege limited to the wealthy. When we say 'education is a right,' we do not make a distinction between primary, secondary and post-secondary education. We mean that a free and democratic society and a vibrant and socially just economy depend upon universal access to post-secondary education. Long gone are the days when a high school education is enough. Post-secondary education is essential.

The system of education we defend is one that is based on the five principles of the Canada Health Act: public administration, comprehensiveness, universality, portability and accessibility. To preserve this public system, Canada's post-secondary education system requires a complex and comprehensive framework of federal, provincial and territorial policies, laws and funding arrangements that restrict the rights of private investors and service providers. We believe that the Canadian as well as provincial and territorial governments must have the power to enact laws to protect the public system of education, laws that reflect and enhance the regional, cultural, linguistic and political complexities of Canada.

The trade liberalization objectives of Industry Canada, in cooperation with the various international financial institutions, fundamentally conflict with these principles. International finance and trade agreements exist to reduce the common good to just another commodity or product that can be bought and sold on the market. This new

Unexus University at-a-glance
By Sarah Dopp

Unexus University opened for business in October 1999 in Fredericton, N.B. (New Brunswick allows schools to call themselves "universities" and grant degrees without provincial accreditation.) Not only is it the first private, on-line university in Canada, but it is also a for-profit university as part of a publicly-traded company.

Unexus U. is owned by the Ontario-based Learnsoft Corporation, which spent $1.5 million[1]— of which $600,000 came from the Human Resources Development Canada jobs fund and the Atlantic Canada Opportunities Agency[2]—to establish the school.

"Get your degree without ever leaving your house or office...any time, anywhere: there's a university on your desktop."[3] Unexus markets itself to any adult who wants to pursue a business degree but "is travelling, has a family, is too busy to attend a university."

The two-and-a-half year Executive Master of Business Administration (eMBA) program, launched in January 2000 with 12 students, costs $28,000. The eMBA program will be customized to meet the needs of particular industries. A second regular MBA program was introduced this fall for students interested in business and management, but who do not qualify for the eMBA program because they lack experience.

Unexus U.'s Advisory Board for both programs includes Michael Gaffney, Unexus U. president and president and CEO of Learnsoft Corp., and senior executives and managers from CICSO, Nortel, Telexis, KPMG, Rennaissance Worldwide, Lucent Technologies, Tele-education New Brunswick, and Connections Nova Scotia.

Dual degrees in the MBA program and a Master of Science in Management can be attained through Unexus U.'s partnership with the Arthur D. Little School of Management of New England, the world's first accredited corporate university.[4] Students can pursue the regular MBA at Unexus and a Master of Science in Management through Arthur D. Little.

Unexus U. has also partnered with karROX Technologies Ltd., a computer training and education company based in India. The arrangement allows Unexus to offer its eMBA and regular MBA to students in India while karROX markets and sells the programs, and provides them with Internet service through its education centres. As part of the latest agreement, karROX will deliver 1,350 students to Unexus' regular MBA program over the next three years.[5]

"India has a very large, well-educated middle class, and professionals are demanding effective on-line education, especially business education, from a reputable North American institution," said Gaffney.

As for the quality of education, Gaffney boasted in the **Globe and Mail** that Unexus could provide higher quality education than other business schools because Unexus could attract the best professors without having to worry about a unionized staff with tenure.[6]

Endnotes

[1] Susan Taylor. Canadian Firm to Open Internet University. Reuters, November 14, 1999.

[2] CUPE Report on Privatization 2000.

[3] Unexus University Website www.unexusu.com

[4] Unexus University Website www.unexusu.com Partnerships

[5] Unexus University Press Release. World's first private Internet university expands agreement with major Indian training company. August 18, 2000.

[6] Keith McArthur. Internet MBA program shakes Ivory Towers Traditional business schools sound the alarm over no track record or provincial accreditation. The Globe and Mail, January 14, 2000.

The classroom vs. the boardroom
By James Clancy

One of this country's most valuable resources is a workforce that's skilled and has access to high quality education and training. This has come from having one of the most effective and comprehensive systems of post-secondary education in the industrialized world.

What has made this system so successful are the principles which Canadians insist must guide it: accessibility, accountability and affordability. It's on this foundation that Canada's network of public universities, colleges and community colleges has grown and contributed to the nation's prosperity.

Over the last decade, as the information highway has grown, we've witnessed the unbridled, unchecked and unregulated proliferation of so-called on-line learning opportunities. While there's no question that the Internet holds vast potential for providing learning opportunities to tens of thousands of Canadians who may otherwise not have access to them, this breakneck burgeoning of on-line educators calls for special vigilance on the part of governments.

In order to ensure that Canadians continue to receive the high standard of education that has served this country so well, the same values and principles that have made our post-secondary system so effective must be applied to these new learning opportunities.

If there was ever a situation which called out for leadership from the federal government, this is certainly it. After all, the potential to provide quality education across the country is at stake. Sadly, the federal government has failed to take up this challenge.

In the July announcement of the creation of an Advisory Committee for On-line Learning, federal Industry Minister John Manley made it clear that the government is content to let the whims of the marketplace drive the future of on-line education in this country. Instead of appointing educators to the committee, the minister has created an officially-sanctioned corporate cheering section, made up entirely of administrators and representatives of such vested interests as IBM, AT&T, Bell Canada, Lucent Technologies, and the Bank of Montreal.

There's no voice on the committee for the university and college teachers who know what works in education. There's no voice for the students or working people for whom on-line learning holds potential. Instead, there are companies whose bottom lines will be affected directly by the decisions they make; companies that will be providing the "education" opportunities for a profit.

Before the government and its corporate advisory committee run headlong into commandeering on-line education, they would be well-advised to take a long and serious look at the long-term ramifications of corporatizing learning. They would be well-advised to work with educators, students, and the people who know and understand education to develop a set of standards for on-line learning.

It's essential that we hold on-line programs to a high standard of academic rigor and that we ensure proper interaction between faculty and students. Our post-secondary system has succeeded because it is accountable. These same standards must be applied to on-line learning in order to safeguard against fraud, waste and abuse.

The time for a comprehensive look at on-line learning is certainly now. But instead of creating a corporate committee to study how to "reap the benefits," Minister Manley and provincial education ministers should be guided by the principles of quality, affordability and accountability, which have proven so effective in post-secondary education.

If that were the case, the voices of many more knowledgeable Canadians would be heard, and the future of on-line learning for all Canadians could be secured.

(James Clancy is National President of the National Union of Provincial and General Employees.)

globalization ideology and its goal of 'commodification' of education is not a hidden agenda. To the contrary, Industry Canada has wholeheartedly endorsed and promoted the strategy of turning 'rights' into 'products'. Promoting the commercial trade of education is the self-described mandate of most federal and provincial governments. In his letter of August 2000, to Michael Conolon, Chairperson of the Canadian Federation of Students, the chairman of the Advisory Committee for Online Learning, David Johnston, offers evidence of the new philosophy of public policy:

The Council of Ministers of Education, Canada (CMEC) is committed to assisting jurisdictions across Canada in developing vibrant post-secondary education systems. For its part, Industry Canada recognises the potential for expanding domestic and international markets for a Canadian learnware sector. Both recognize the interdependence of the economic and educational policy agendas.[7]

In the same letter, Johnston uses a similar language to describe online learning. The justification for online learning is not to improve the quality of or accessibility to post-secondary education. The reason given to embrace this new technology is that "Canadian institutions face severe competition in their local markets from foreign public and private training enterprises." He adds, "We are concerned that the majority of our universities and colleges are not in a good position to take advantage of online learning opportunities and benefit from the transformative potential of online learning."

The great symbol, or rather 'showcase' of this new ideology of education was scheduled to occur Nov. 26-30, 2000 in Halifax at the 14th Conference of Commonwealth Ministers of Education. In a concerted effort to promote the trade of education, a parallel event was to be held: an International Trade Fair, with the theme "Shopping for Solutions." According to the June 2000 Operational Management Plan, the goals and objectives of the trade fair were as follows:

1.3.1. Goal:

The International Trade Fair will place an emphasis on putting on show a range of systems, packages, projects and approaches, from traditional to technology-based, that offer proven solutions to many of the challenges that the Ministers will be deliberating on.

1.3.2. Objectives:

The International trade Fair is not simply about putting a range of products on display. It is expected to enable delegates from a wide range of Commonwealth countries to have a one-stop appreciation of possibilities for tackling the many issues and problems that they are grappling with in education. It is also expected that, where there are packages on display, it should be possible for countries to make the kind of contact that can promote rapid transfer, adaptation and sharing of these, in the best tradition of the Commonwealth, and in keeping with mutually beneficial commercial transactions.[8]

1.5. Incentives (Expected Results/Outcomes)

As we know, the domestic/international education and training markets are evolving quickly and the education sector is one of the important integral elements of Canada's knowledge-based industry. Canadian educational "savoir-faire" and products are in great demand in all parts of the world and the need for expertise in the development of educational and instructional products requiring different delivery models and infrastructures are increasing in all countries. A number of Canadian organisations are currently investing considerable resources to the marketing and export of Canadian educational products and services. Participation at the International Trade Fair will be seen and managed as such, an investment in showcasing products and services, and potentially an opportunity to expand our market share internationally.[9]

Stripped clean of any pretence to equity, fairness, quality and accessibility, herein lies the new public policy, or ideology, of post-secondary education. Education is now a business opportunity, a 'sector' of the economy like any other. Under the market-obsessed direction of Industry Canada, education has now become perversely redefined as a "knowledge-based industry" that offers "training services" and "instructional products" requiring different "delivery models". Even more troubling is that such an ideology is being promoted by ministers of education.

Canadians reject this vocabulary entirely. Education is a universal right, not a business opportunity. It is something inherent to the self, to our very notion of what it means to be a person. Because education is not an optional but an essential part of being a full and equal citizen, it is simply a mistake to redefine it as a commodity—as something that can be traded, or bought and sold in the 'global market.' Education is part of what the ancients called the *res publica*—the public's thing—the common good. Education must therefore be publicly funded and administered for all to enjoy and benefit equally. Like Canada's cherished health care system, education must be protected from any attempts to reduce it to a personal privilege, or any effort to subject it to the profit-driven logic of supply and demand.

It is the resistance to the very idea that education is an industry, a business, a product, a commodity, a 'sector,' that has compelled the student movement to organize in historic numbers. On Jan. 25, 1995, and in succeeding peaceful public demonstrations (Feb. 7, 1997, Jan.28, 1998, Nov. 5, 1999, and Feb. 2, 2000) hundreds of thousands of students and their supporters demonstrated against home-grown structural adjustment economic policies and international structural adjustment economic policies promoted by various international financial institutions and trade regimes, such as the Asia Pacific Economic Cooperation

(APEC) organization and the World Trade Organization (WTO).

Students marched, rallied, organized forums, leafleted, camped out, and even conducted strikes to highlight the crisis in post-secondary education. Part of the criticism raised in these student protests was to call into question the subordination of human rights (the right to education and health care, for example) to the rules of trade and commerce and the dictates of private corporations.

The stated goals of trade and investment regimes like APEC and the WTO and international financial institutions such as the International Monetary Fund (IMF) undermine the integrity of basic social, economic and environmental standards. Their basic principles clash head-on with the principle of high quality and accessible education. To reduce or compare education—our shared and contested understandings of the world—to a collection of commercial transactions, is simply ridiculous. To turn what is a right into a consumer product is simply absurd.

The 'student' cannot be reduced to a utility maximizer in a great marketplace of learning. The student is an apprentice, scholar, researcher, pupil, disciple, fellow, and novitiate. The student is someone who is taught not just to understand but also to challenge traditions and conventions. Rather than 'consuming' knowledge, students are researching, investigating, questioning, probing, receiving collective wisdom, and in the words of Milton, "beholding the bright countenance of truth in the quiet and still air of delightful studies."[10]

The government of Canada and the Council of Ministers have a duty to abandon the growing commercialization of education and support instead publicly-funded and publicly-administered post-secondary institutions, and the non-profit sharing of science and technology.

To promote the right to education is also a global strategy, and it is not a new one. In fact, it was a Canadian who helped to co-author *The United Nations Universal Declaration of Human Rights* of which Article 27 (1) provides:

> Everyone has the right to education. Education shall be free, at least in the elementary and fundamental stages. Elementary education shall be compulsory. Technical and professional education shall be made generally available and higher education shall be equally accessible on the basis of merit.

Furthermore, in 1976, Canada recognized the right to education by signing the *International Covenant on Economic, Social and Cultural Rights*. Article 13 (1) (2) (c) obliges signatory states to achieve the full realization of the right to equally accessible higher education, "in particular by the progressive introduction of free education."

By voting in favour of the *Universal Declaration* and then ratifying the *International Covenant on Economic, Social and Cultural Rights*, Canada has not tacitly but expressly recognized that higher education must be free in order to be "equally accessible." We would like to note for emphasis that the *Declaration*, one of the most sacredly held and influential human rights charters of the

20th century, lists education as a universal right, not a universal product or a universal service. Therefore, to treat education as a 'sector' and a 'product' is to expressly violate both the spirit and letter of the *Universal Declaration* and the *International Covenant*.

To keep these international promises, the federal and provincial governments must adopt another global strategy than the one currently promoted by Industry Canada. That is, Canada must create and support democratically accountable institutions whose focus is not just finance and trade, but also the advancement and protection of human rights, social justice, and the environment. We must promote institutions in which knowledge (the humanities, science and technology) is shared equally, not sold to the highest bidders or those more technologically advanced.

The government of Canada has a duty to discuss *access to education,* not access to 'learnware' markets. The government of Canada has a duty to discuss the barriers to that access: the cost of education, racism, sexism, homophobia, and linguistic and cultural barriers. The government has a duty to discuss what it should be doing to reduce the terrible legacy of debt it has inflicted on an entire generation of young Canadians. It should be putting on the table options for making our education system open to students all over the world, regardless of their financial means, not through a computer terminal but on campus and in the classroom with other students.

In this way, high quality will be achieved the way it always has been: through interaction with others who have similar and different cultural perspectives, in discussion and debate, in agreement and conflict, by making mistakes and working with others for solutions, by being encouraged by a professor who serves as an inspiration and mentor. This kind of education imparts not just 'knowledge' in the technical sense, but what Aristotle called *phronesis*: understanding of ourselves and others who live in our society and our world.

Conclusion: What is a quality education?

One of the mistakes of the new globalization ethos is to reduce all human practices to commercial transactions, but also to assume that it is through commercial transactions alone that technology is shared and produced. Yet history does not support this view. Since the first university was founded in Bologna in the 11th century, scholars around the world have shared their understanding of nature and the human condition without the goal of profit. Furthermore, it is only a recent phenomenon that we would conflate 'education' with the technical means to promulgate it.

To equate education with technology is to miss the point entirely. As professor Noble writes, education is a human relationship. It is a process that necessarily entails an interpersonal relationship between people that aims at individual and collective knowledge.

Whenever people recall their educational experiences, they tend to remember, above all, not courses or subjects or the information imparted, but people, people who changed their minds or their lives, people who made a difference in their developing sense of themselves. It is a sign of the current confusion about education that we must be reminded of this obvious fact: that the relationship between people is central to the educational experience. Education is a process of becoming for all parties, based upon mutual recognition and validation and centring upon the formation and evolution of identity. The actual content of the educational experience is defined by this relationship between people and the chief determinant of quality education is the establishment and enrichment of this relationship.[11]

We cannot dispute that there are potential benefits to 'online' learning. However, they cannot possibly replace the benefits of 'offline' learning. The students of Canada will not accept the premise that machines can or should replace people. Until the provinces and federal government commit to more public funding to hire more people—faculty members, teaching assistants, administrative support staff and maintenance staff—the quality and accessibility of education will not improve, regardless of the latest technological discoveries.

(Michael Temelini is the Government Relations Officer at the Canadian Federation of Students. This article was adapted from a brief submitted to the Advisory Committee for Online Learning.)

Endnotes

[1] David F. Noble "Digital Diploma Mills: Rehearsal for the Revolution" in James L. Turk (ed.) *The Corporate Campus: Commercialization and the Dangers to Canada's Colleges and Universities* James Lorimer And Company Limited, Toronto, 2000, pages 103-104.

[2] Digital Diploma Mills, pages 106-107.

[3] Digital Diploma Mills, page 104.

[4] Statistics Canada and Council of Ministers of Education, *Canada Education Indicators in Canada: Report of the Pan-Canadian Education Indicators Program 1999*, Canadian Education Statistics Council, 2000, page 62; and Statistics Canada "University tuition fees", *The Daily*, Monday August 28, 2000.

[5] Statistics Canada, "University Tuition fees", *The Daily*, Monday August 28, 2000.

[6] Statistics Canada, "Part-time university faculty", *The Daily*, Wednesday August 30, 2000.

[7] David Johnston, Chairman, Advisory Committee for Online Learning, Letter to Michael Conlon, August, 2000.

[8] "Building a Showcase: The Canadian Presence at the International Trade Fair 14th Conference of Commonwealth Ministers (CCEM) An Operational Management Plan", June 2000, page 3.

[9] "Building a Showcase", pages 5-6.

[10] John Milton, *Reason of Church Government: Introduction*, book ii.

[11] Digital Diploma Mills, 101-102.

Harnessing university research to business needs
By Neil Tudiver

Over their history, universities have served business at arm's length, supplying trained graduates, independent studies, expert advisers, and contract research, while maintaining a degree of autonomy from commercial influence. University autonomy began to falter in the 1980s. Government had scaled back core funding and was striving to tie university research to business needs. Lack of public support for core programs made universities vulnerable to the enticements of private sector money.

Government now acts as matchmaker to marry business and university interests in seamless research enterprises. Targeted funding requires researchers to follow granting agencies' priorities. National initiatives through the granting councils routinely require commercialization. Researchers are expected to direct the flow of ideas and resources from the university to the market via partnerships with businesses, product licencing, and spin-off companies.

Commercialization policies

Intense efforts to commercialize the university began with public policy of the latter 1970s and 1980s. Government programs encouraged partnerships aimed at enabling business to exploit the full market potential of findings from university research. These partnerships marked a significant turning point in business approaches to universities. A business executive member of NSERC explained it in 1985:

> Industry can no longer afford to do all of the long-term research it needs to survive; thus it is no longer looking at universities simply as an inexpensive source of trained people, but also as a vast reservoir of expertise which can perform that urgently needed long-term effort (NSERC 1985, 74).

At the time Canada's industrial research was weak. OECD studies showed Canada lagging behind other member countries in encouraging university-industry ties (OECD 1984). Despite government efforts through the Science Council of Canada and NSERC, industrial research and dev elopment in Canada was just one percent of GNP, compared to an average 2.5 percent for other OECD countries. Part of the problem was industry's poor research record. Corporations carried out just 48% of the Canadian total, concentrated among a few very large firms, compared to between 60% and 70% in other OECD countries. Federal government research consisted of regulation and provision of in-house information.

University research was thus a vital part of the Canadian mix. In 1981 universities accounted for about 26% of total R&D expenditures in Canada, as compared to 14% for the United States (Doutriaux and Baker 1995). Ottawa attempted to redirect the priorities of university research towards the needs of industry. The Science Council played a lead role: its chair, Geraldine A. Kenney-Wallace, issued a "call to intellectual arms," imploring Canada's universities to transfer their knowledge and findings to corporations (Science Council of Canada 1988, x).

During the mid-1980s, the Science Council promoted the concept of the *service university*—one that would directly provide scientific benefits to industry and government through entrepreneurial, technical, research, training, investment, and management services. The Council even stepped beyond the boundaries of its science mandate to prescribe service roles for social scientists and humanists: market research, personnel management, and study of the social impact of corporate actions.

Slow response from university scientists displeased the Council, which criticized universities for underplaying the transfer of knowledge and technology to industry. It urged university presidents and administrators to encourage faculty and student commitment to this mission (Science Council of Canada 1988, Davidson 1988).

Business responded favourably to government's support for partnerships. In 1983, university and corporate presidents established the Corporate-Higher Education Forum to advocate a new model of partnership over the old one of corporate patronage. Forum members exhorted university researchers to define projects according to the needs of business, and corporations to seek profitable returns from closer partnerships with universities. Placing corporate interests on the research agenda drew favourable nods from university officials who saw opportunities for new income (Corporate-Higher Education Forum 1987).

Giant corporations like IBM already sought concrete benefits from their donations. The company had traditionally given small arms-length donations to a large number of universities. Now IBM replaced them with a smaller number of negotiated arrangements with greater visibility and closer relationships with university staff for training, hardware, and software development. IBM committed close to $50 million of in-kind contributions over the first three years of the program. Recipient universities were required to put up an equal amount of money (Maxwell & Currie 1984).

The federal government took up the partnership cause with a host of new but ill-defined granting programs that required university researchers to demonstrate how outcomes would benefit business with new products, expanded markets, or more efficient production. Academics could hardly ignore these programs as other sources of money disappeared. Government poured public money into private companies on the assumption that recipients would make good use of it. It also offered money to researchers prepared to meet industry's requirements. There was no comprehensive planning other than emphasizing research for business. Promises for grants and subsidies were supposed to motivate potential applicants.

Program requirements were confusing, and delivery poorly organized through an ad hoc mixture of agencies. One review in the latter 1980s identified no less than eight separate special programs promoting university-industry linkage in the National Research Council alone. It located another six in the federal Department of Industry, Trade and Commerce, and numerous initiatives in other departments. The federal Department of Supply and Services gave preference to private industry in its annual $2 billion for engineering services contracts. Contracts with universities had to show how the resultant technology would be transferred to industry. Provincial research councils and programs also targeted support for home industries (MacAulay & Dufour 1984).

Although these initiatives followed the huge withdrawals of money from university core budgets, they did not replace the lost money or repair damage from cuts. They merely redirected some of the lost money to targeted programs benefiting the private sector.

Programs for commercial research

We can get a flavour of changing priorities by looking at a few of these programs. Many were in the Department of Industry, Trade and Commerce. Industrial Innovation Centres focused university resources on aiding small and medium-size technology-based firms. The centres were supposed to develop products, processes, and businesses; provide courses; conduct research on entrepreneurship, management, and innovation; and develop spin-off companies.

Between 1970 and 1982, Centres of Advanced Technology sponsored 15 centres to apply university teaching and institutional research to higher-risk industrial technologies. Most centres were on university campuses, but the more successful ones had additional support through parent provincial research organizations, where facilities were already established for specialized industrial technology, technical information services and active industrial networks (MacAulay & Dufour 1984).

Another departmental program, Industrial Research Institutes, set up institutes on 11 campuses between 1967 and 1980 to market university research to industrial firms. After initial grants, these Institutes were expected to be self-supporting from fees for overhead and program management. At least four achieved this objective. In his summary of a departmental review of the program, James MacAulay (1984) notes that, except for a successful program at the University of Waterloo, the other 10 had limited accomplishments.

Industrial Research Associations was a multi-year, multi-million-dollar program for companies in an industry to contract with universities for academic expertise. Associations were established for sulphur, welding, gas, masonry, and plastics. The Welding Institute of Canada sponsored a Masters of Science degree in welding engineering with the Universities of Toronto and Waterloo that became part of Waterloo's cooperative on-the-job training program. Associations had minimal appeal for researchers because competing companies protected proprietary information on products and production processes (MacAulay & Dufour 1984).

In early 1980, Industry, Trade and Commerce set up a special electronics fund which received $93 million by 1982 for major projects in proven firms. The fund supported a university centre in every province, at $1 million each, to develop microelectronics applications for manufacturing and processing industries in its region. Centres were run jointly by representatives from industry, government, and university.

The provinces also supported technology transfer. Ontario's Board of Industrial Leadership and Development (BILD) matched grants for university-based, corporate-sponsored research. BILD started in 1981, with $5 million over two years for projects in the natural sciences and engineering. Each project required a contract between the host university and a corporation to "facilitate the successful transfer of research results from the university laboratory to industrial production in the future, and thereby contribute to the continuing development of the province" (Bell 1990).

BILD matched corporate contributions to a maximum of $50,000 per contract. More than 85% of $4.27 million spent on 167 projects went to large universities: Queen's received 8.6%; McMaster 15.9%, University of Toronto 28.3%, and University of Waterloo 32.5%. Seven universities shared the remainder.

BILD program findings reveal the notorious weakness of using matching grants to influence business investment. A survey of corporations whose research contracts at Ontario universities were awarded BILD matching grants suggested that the majority would have participated in university research without government support. Nonetheless, BILD was followed by more ambitious initiatives. The University Research Incentive Fund, set up in 1984, paid out $3.3 million to 29 projects in its first year and another $17.8 million on 215 corporate projects between 1986 and 1988 (Bell 1990).

Federal experience shows similar patterns. The national granting councils spent close to $400 million in 1987–88 to match cash or in-kind contributions from corporations, foundations, trusts, non-profit organizations, and Crown corporations, provided the money went to a council or university. A 1988 review by the Senate Committee on National Finance deemed the program unnecessary, since most of the projects it supported would have proceeded without the matching funds. The program did little more than subsidize private companies for contributions they were already prepared to make (Cameron 1991).

Ottawa also reorganized government agencies to focus more directly on research assistance to industry. In 1990, the federal government created the department of Industry, Science and Technology by absorbing the more science-focussed Ministry of State for Science and Technology and the Industry, Trade and Commerce Department, which had been relegated to a branch of the Department of Regional Industrial Expansion. The new department's mandate was to direct science policy towards the concerns of industry.

Research councils were reorganized. Between 1976, when it was spun off from the NRC, and 1981, NSERC paid out $1.2 billion in grants to encourage closer ties between corporations and universities. NSERC became a leading player in Ottawa's drive to shape university research to the needs of industry. By 1984–85, annual grants of $656 million accounted for 36.1% of all money received by Canadian universities for research in the natural sciences, engineering, and medicine. The Medical Research Council was second at 21.8% (NSERC 1985).

NSERC paid sizable sums to university researchers for serving industry interests. Corporations contributed very little new money. NSERC's second five-year plan noted that "university-industry interaction existed long before the specific targeted programs and would exist today without those programs." Universities attract corporations because they offer profitable investment, regardless of whether government adds money. Matching grants do not improve the level of corporate contributions (NSERC 1985, 1991).

The federal Networks of Centres of Excellence program (NCE) took commercialization further. In the first competition in 1988, each application had a 20% weight for demonstrating linkages among industry, university, and government, and 20% for showing that results would lead to new products or processes for commercial exploitation. Quality of the proposed research program counted for 50%, and 10% was reserved for proof that an adequate management structure was in place.

The first 15 projects, funded in 1989–90 for $240 million over five years, involved 32 universities and 168 corporations. One centre was in the social sciences, a network on aging based at the University of Toronto. The other 14 were scientific. An interim review of the program noted increased collaboration between scientists in universities and industries, and called for more of the same (Canada 1989). Most of the network involvement went to large universities that assembled the myriad required participants and prepared the complex applications. The bias towards major universities reflects the extensive resources necessary for preparing costly time-consuming proposals.

A favourable review of Phase I by the House of Commons Standing Committee on Industry, Science and Technology, Regional and Northern Development recommended retaining the criteria and weights (House of Commons 1993). Phase II, for three-year projects starting in 1994/95, increased emphasis on commercialization, explained in five equally weighted criteria. *Excellence of the Research Program* stressed "areas of research with high economic and social impact." The criterion for *Highly Qualified Personnel* required expertise "in research areas and technologies that are critical to Canadian productivity and economic growth." *Networking and Partnerships* expected "links among academic institutions and public and private sector participants." *Knowledge Exchange and Technology Exploitation* required developing "new products, processes or services for commercial exploitation," and transferring technology to private and public sector partners. The final criterion required evidence of sound *Network Management* (Networks of Centres of Excellence 1995).

A report prepared for the NCE suggested the changes were designed

> to increase private sector involvement in all network activities, *including the establishment of research priorities*. One premise of the program is that strengthening the linkages between university, government, and private sectors will facilitate the exchange of information and technology, stimulating the private sector's ability to capitalize on frontier research and accelerating the commercialization of research results from the network (ARA Consulting Group 1997, 12, emphasis added).

Corporate university

Within a short period of time, eligible academics have put considerable effort into working with industry and designing projects for commercial outcomes. Some—in fields such as engineering and computer science—are already amenable to working with business. Others—in medical and social sciences or humanities—do not have the business orientation necessary for commercial applications, spin-off firms, and equity fund-raising. This may be the most significant impact of the networks: shifting the focus in these fields away from research for teaching and professional development towards commercial research for corporations.

Universities in the forefront of commercialization offer elaborate schemes to induce faculty to work for business. MIT's Industrial Liaison Program (ILP) serves hundreds of corporate members that pay annual fees in the tens of thousands of dollars. Faculty earn points for serving ILP members. In 1997 they received one point for each unpublished article that was given to an ILP member, two points for a phone conversation or brief campus meeting, and 12 points for visiting a company's headquarters or laboratory. Each point was worth about $35 that could be exchanged for prizes such as office furniture, computer equipment, or travel to professional conferences (Soley 1997).

Canadian policies are driving universities in a similar direction. In May 1999, a committee of the Prime Minister's Advisory Council on Science and Technology released a report urging that universities receiving money from the federal government adopt "innovation" as a fourth mission. The committee defined innovation as "the process of bringing new goods and services to the market, or the result of that process" (Expert Panel on Commercialization of University Research 1999).

The committee recommended a national IP policy fashioned after the 1980 Bayh-Dole Act in the United States. The Canadian version would require universities to hold the rights to commercialize all IP that results from federally funded research, and to make their best efforts to commercialize the IP, by either doing it themselves or assigning it to industrial partners. The committee proposed that universities should provide incentives for faculty to create intellectual property. This would include making commercialization a factor in tenure and promotion policies. Ottawa would monitor their progress by requiring universities to file annual performance reports on commercialization strategies.

Implementing these recommendations would establish unprecedented government interference in universities. Until this development, Ottawa's requirements of grant recipients were mainly to abide by federal policies for ethics reviews or affirmative action. This initiative threatens to alter the university's core priorities by adding commercialization to teaching, research, and community service.

Over the course of about 25 years, government has replaced university grants with programs targeted for commercialization of research. The result is a considerably transformed university system in Canada. Reduced core money from government has meant that universities can less easily set their own priorities, but must instead meet the requirements of targeted funding programs. In the process, their priorities are driven more by external markets and less by internal academic criteria. Research is being run like a business, with projects designed to take advantage of commercial opportunities. This is one of the essential elements of the expanding corporate university.

(Neil Tudiver taught at the University of Manitoba for 23 years. He is currently Chief Negotiations Officer at the Canadian Association of University Teachers—www.caut.ca)

This article is based on excerpts from Neil Tudiver's book, *Universities for Sale: Resisting Corporate Control over Canadian Higher Education*, (Lorimer, 1999). The book is available from Formac Distributing for $19.95. Orders are accepted by phone (1 800 565 1975), Fax (902 425 0166) or mail (5502 Atlantic Street, Halifax, NS B3H 1G4.

References

ARA Consulting Group Inc. (1997), *Evaluation of the Networks of Centres of Excellence Program*, prepared for the NCE Program Evaluation Committee, Ottawa: January.

Bell, Stephen (1990), "Using Matching Grants to Facilitate Corporate-University Research Linkages: A Preliminary Examination of Outcomes From One Initiative," *The Canadian Journal of Higher education*, XX-1, 57–73.

Cameron, David (1991), *More Than An Academic Question: Universities, Government, and Public Policy in Canada*, Halifax, Nova Scotia: The Institute for Research on Public Policy.

Canada (1989), *Networks of Centres of Excellence: Report of the International Peer Review Committee and Report of the Minister's Advisory Committee*, Ottawa.

Corporate-Higher Education Forum (1987), *From Patrons to Partners, The Report of the Task Force on Funding Higher Education: Corporate Support for Universities*, Montréal: Corporate-Higher Education Forum.

Davidson, Robert (1988), *University-Industry Interaction in the Social Sciences and Humanities: A Threshold of Opportunity*, Ottawa: Science Council of Canada.

Doutriaux, Jerome and Margaret Barker (1995), "The University-Industry Relationship in Science and Technology," Occasional Paper Number 11, Science and Technology Review, Industry Canada, August.

Expert Panel on Commercialization of University Research (1999), *Public Investments in University*

Research: Reaping the Benefits, Presented to The Prime Minister's Advisory Council on Science and Technology, Ottawa, May 4.

House of Commons, Standing Committee on Industry, Science and Technology, Regional And Northern Development (1993), *Beyond Excellence: The Future of Canada's Networks of Centres of Excellence*, 33rd session, 34th parliament, April 27.

MacAulay, James B., in collaboration with Paul Dufour (1984), *The Machine in the Garden: The Advent of Industrial Research Infrastructure in the Academic Milieu*, A discussion paper for the Science Council of Canada, Ottawa: Minister of Supply and Services.

Maxwell, Judith and Stephanie Currie (1984), *Partnership for Growth: Corporate-University Cooperation in Canada*, Montréal: Corporate-Higher Education Forum.

Networks of Centres of Excellence program (1995), *Policies and Guidelines, Networks of Centres of Excellence Phase II*, NCE, December 15.

NSERC (1985), *Completing the Bridge to the 90's: NSERC's Second Five-Year Plan*, Ottawa: Natural Sciences and Engineering Research Council of Canada, June.

NSERC (1991), *Research Partnerships: University-Industry Cooperative R&D Activities*, Ottawa: Minister of Supply and Services, Canada.

OECD (1984), *Industry and University: New Forms of Cooperation and Communication*, Paris.

Science Council of Canada (1988), *Winning in a World Economy: University-Industry Interaction and Economic Renewal In Canada*, Report 39, Ottawa: Minister of Supply and Services.

Soley, Lawrence (1997), "Phi Beta Capitalism, Universities in Service to Business," *Covert Action Quarterly*, Spring.

Growing the market: Of urinals and university centres—targeting the campus crowd

By Erika Shaker

As the search for ad space continues, more and more of the public space is becoming commercialized—even to the extent that giant ads on the side of buildings are considered a sort of art form. Ads are now present on stickers applied to fruit, on bathroom stall doors and above urinals[1], wrapped around buses and cars, as trailers before movies and on popcorn bags and emblazoned on T-shirts and other articles of clothing. As the disposable income of the audience becomes more appealing, and as competition for ad space increases, more and more surfaces are redefined as innovative ways in which to reach a target market.

And even as corporate logos become a necessary fashion accessory, turning much of the population into walking billboards for Nike, Coke or Pepsi, we are witnessing a new trend: moving from the commercialization of public space to the commercialization of daily existence—of human life itself—of memory, of the defining experiences of our lives.

This was taken to a new level in the spring of 1999 when Tom Anderson, the smitten groom, commercialized his entire wedding to provide his bride (Sabrina Root) with a $34,000 experience "free" of charge. Everything was opened up to sponsorship, from the coffee to the rings to the honeymoon: "Anderson got 24 companies to sponsor the nuptials in exchange for having their names appear six times from the invitations to the thank-you cards... Advertisers had their names appear on the invitations and thank-you cards, on cards at the buffet, on scrolls at the dinner table, in an ad placed in a local independent newspaper, and in a verbal "thank you" that followed the first toast." (Reuters) There was some decorum, however. The bride did draw the line at having banners draped across the church aisle. But the coffee and dress were sponsored, and the happy couple posed, smiling, among their gifts for a photo in the **Philadelphia Inquirer.**

Sabrina's speculation that perhaps Tom might have similar ideas about how to pay for their future kids' college tuition was usurped, however, in the spring of 2000 by two American high school students, Chris and Luke. These clean-cut friends, seniors at Haddonfield Memorial High School in New Jersey, intend to mitigate the soaring costs of post-secondary education by offering their bodies and the term of their university education as living advertisements. "Today's attention relies on the youth of America and where better to reach this audience than directly in the schools themselves," announces the pair's web site, http://www.ChrisandLuke.com.

What can we do for a sponsor? We will wear your clothes; (shirts, shoes, pants) use your equipment (tennis racquets, golf clubs, stereo, computers, DVD, watches) listen to your music, drive your cars, use your tires, drink your soda, eat your chips, fly your airline, and wear your sunglasses...

We are going to be the FIRST corporately sponsored college students. This has never been attempted before. Being the first corporately sponsored college students will allow us and your company to get positive world wide publicity!

Your corporation will get as much publicity as we do. We are not your average students. Unlike student athletes we are not subject to NCAA Sponsorship Rules. We will actively promote your company's name and products around our school, in the press, and throughout the world. Millions of people will associate you with: Chris & Luke: The First Corporately Sponsored College Students! (http://www.ChrisandLuke.com)

The implications of this sort of sponsorship arrangement were alluded to in an article in the **Financial Post**. (Stewart) When asked what sort of products the pair would not sponsor, Karen Ammond, the pair's publicist, explained: "They don't want to do anything that would offend their family.... They're looking for the wholesome product that they can be proud to walk into a school campus and say, 'This cell-phone is great,' or 'You should drink my soda, this is my favourite soda,' and things like that."

However, because advertisers "have long been wary of attaching their sacred brands to people,... Chris and Luke will have to sign a contract with all of their sponsors and promise to abide by a proper code of conduct." In Ms. Ammond's own words, "They will have to sign a morals clause [with sponsors]. The corporation will now become the parent, is really what's going to happen. They'll have to live under the rules of the contract."

Whether or not corporations will be agreeable to their sponsored protegés exercising their freedoms of speech and association is questionable, particularly if that corporation is NIKE. After Phil Knight (CEO of NIKE) heard that his Alma Mater, the University of Oregon, had become a member of the Worker's Rights Consortium (WRC), a student-driven labour rights organization, he announced he would be making no further donations to the university. (Associated Press) According to Knight, "The bonds of trust, which allowed me to give at a high level, have been shredded."

NIKE does belong to another group, the Fair Labour Organization, which enjoys a large business membership and also gives more leeway to manufacturers, allowing them a greater say in how monitoring is carried out and putting limits on the release of inspection results. The association also gives businesses strong representation on its board of directors." The WRC, however, does not allow corporate representation on its board, and "intends to keep corporations at arm's length, conducting surprise inspections with independent monitors and releasing the results of its inspections."[2]

This sort of corporate retaliation could have serious implications for the American universities and colleges increasingly dependant on NIKE's handouts. Currently, the corporation has contracts with almost 200 colleges and many are members of the WRC.

While extreme, the www.ChrisandLuke.com initiative highlights several important issues: the rising costs of tuition (in the United States, Canada and internationally); the increasing willingness on the part of individuals to commercialize the most personal aspects of their lives—even their very person; and the "value" of the coveted student market to corporations. It is ironic that, at a time when the average student debt load in Canada is $26,000, the student market has never been more sought-after by marketers who recognize that "the over 2,000,000 university and college students in Canada represent a very lucrative market. Not only are they significant users of many products and services now, but they are also establishing purchasing patterns and loyalties for the future." (Campus Plus)

This means conducting marketing research, free product distribution on and off campus, corporate campus "reps" organizing spirit- and consciousness-raising events on campuses across the country, as well as team sponsorship, pep rallies, and the much-publicized cola deals.

A recent survey, Campus Scan, provided "a cross-Canada survey of some 500 students in the 18-24 age range. This has given us some interesting insight into these soon-to-be-big-spenders: their motivations, aspirations, fears and insecurities, not to mention their views on media, advertising, brands, and so on." (Saxby)

Campus Scan has a price tag of $9,000, but the company was kind enough to provide me with some cursory information indicating the degree of specificity achieved by careful questioning: "an important part of my life and activities is dressing smartly"; "I consider myself to be health and nutrition conscious"; "I enjoy being extravagant"; "I do not buy unknown brands merely to save money."

And the price tag is well worth it, according to Saxby. "If you like the sound of a profitable relationship with a high-value customer who'll be there for the long haul, then it's time to take a good, hard look at the student market. But first, take some time to learn more about them. Show them that you understand their dreams and aspirations—and offer to help get them there."

Given the products cited in the study, understanding dreams and aspirations has a decidedly materialistic bent: "Alcoholic Beverages (beer, wine, liquor), Automotive, Clothing (men's and women's), Finances, Banking, Health & Beauty (hair products, skin products, birth control, cosmetics etc.), Non-Alcoholic Beverages (soft drinks, bottled water, sport drinks etc.), Packaged Food (chocolate, chips, gum, pasta, noodles, soup, etc.), Sports, Leisure, Movies, Music, Video Games, Telephones, Computers, Email/Internet, Travel." (Sources: PMB

"The bottom line is that college students are open to try products, and often develop long-term relationships with products that are effectively marketed to them."
—Claudio Marcus, executive vice president of Campus Concepts, New York.

Cola wars on campus have become a useful vehicle for discussing corporate intrusion, control and captive student markets. Coca Cola and Pepsi have essentially divided Canadian universities and colleges between them, and have exclusive rights to their student markets.

Spectrum Marketing is a third party company which has benefited from this arrangement. Its business is to get the "best deal" for schools, or the most money "per student." However, the terms of the contracts between schools and cola companies are secret, or fall under the umbrella of "proprietary information." Consequently, members of the public who want to know the terms of the arrangement between the school and the company must submit a freedom of information request. In the case of the University of British Columbia, the request was twice denied, allegedly to preserve the competitive ability of the corporation.

In a CBC radio Ottawa interview, trends reporter Alan Neal discussed with host John LeCharity some of the finer points of these arrangements:

ALAN: Out at UBC (incidentally a Coke university), the students actually filed a freedom of information request, demanding to see the details of the contract...which was overturned.

JOHN: But surely the corporations must realize that students want to know the details of the agreement..?

ALAN: Yes, John, and part of the "communication plan" for these exclusivity agreements actually has a section dedicated to what to say if media and students bring up confidentiality and suppression of information. I was sent in a little brown envelope a leaked copy of one such *communication plan*, and it says that university media people are supposed to say "For competitive reasons, details of this agreement cannot be released." And then are supposed to "*reiterate the positive aspects of the agreement.*. Incidentally, the same plan says that there should be university spokespeople ready to "do follow-up calls to reporters/columnists who wrote negative pieces or did negative reports of the agreement," which all sounds rather ominous to me...(CBC)

The impacts of these arrangements are not just limited to product consumption (although the terms of the contracts often include the promise of the school receiving additional "donations" depending on the amount of product consumed, as a sort of commission, which makes it in the school's best interests to encourage students to consume as much of the product as possible.) The University of Ottawa displayed large banners during finals emblazoned with the statement: "your corporate sponsors wish you well on exams." (CBC) And Chris Bodnar of **The Fulcrum** (U of O student paper) asserted that, after the corporate sponsor came on board, editorial changes to the paper were requested, highlighting the presence of Coke at sports events as key to "raising school spirit." (CBC) And at UBC, students can no longer use the drinking fountains in the education building; all fountains were covered with plastic and turned off as part of the terms of the contract with Coke, which required students who want water to purchase it from the pop machines. (Kuehn)

2000; Canadian Campus Market Research [CCMR]).

Saxby also suggests reasons for gendered niche marketing: according to the study, "Women are more apt than men to see themselves as emotional, energetic and stressed-out. (Marketers might want to be especially nice to these women: They are also more likely than males to describe themselves as compulsive shoppers and impulse buyers.)"

Targeting students by gender, race, school, class year, field of study, or tuition is nothing new to marketers trying to maximize their profit margin—and the lucrative nature of the college market is incentive enough for companies to jump in with both feet. According to www.educationlist.com, college students represent "one of the most lucrative markets currently available to direct marketers. Why? Because they represent your future customers. These young adults will be the affluent purchasers in the years to come. And now is the time when they are forming their purchasing habits. What they buy. Who they buy from. And how they buy it."

Such direct targeting raises privacy issues: if such carefully accumulated information is available, to what purposes can this be used? Certainly, Zapme![3] was found to be providing marketing information on those who used its services to those companies who would benefit from additional access to the student market. We should not assume this is an isolated incident, especially as competition for the college market grows increasingly aggressive.

After all, as Campus Concepts asserts of the American college market:

Why target the college consumer? More than half of the valuable 18-24 year-old consumers attend college. These students spend over $100 billion a year. The average college student spends $6,760 each year. These 14.1 million consumers are the market segment most open to trying new products. They are now developing brand loyalty, giving you the best opportunity to build your brand for today and tomorrow. In addition, these 18-24-year-olds are important centers of influence with their peers and families. They will become tomorrow's leaders, with significant buying power for the rest of their lives.

At Campus Concepts, we understand that college students are not just studying the arts and sciences, they are also developing buying habits and brand loyalties they will keep for the rest of their lives. (http://www.campusconcepts.com/)

On-campus peer-to-peer promos

Marketing to college and university students has become a lucrative employment opportunity for companies like S&MG Promotions. This company (active in both Canada and the U.S.) hires young people to promote products and corporate image at pep-rally-esque events, and campuses are becoming a favourite venue for these sort of fun, product-oriented group activities. S&MG has student reps in many post-secondary institutions across Canada, in order to "partner with [their] clients to deliver a competitive advantage in the areas of sampling/product education, sales/merchandising coverage, retailer training, college marketing and public relations." (http://www.jobs.samg.com/CdnUsWebsite/About.asp).

S&MG's corporate partners include Labatts, Cadbury and Pepsi, who are apparently thrilled to have their products used and promoted in a variety of ways and events on campus (including competitions, beach parties, and pep rallies) and in the presence of the highly desirable college/university market.

And certainly this sort of targeted, feel-good, peer-oriented marketing has been very successful for those corporations involved in the college market, both in Canada and the United States. According to the Varsity Group (http://www.varsity-group.com), a self-declared premier college marketing company:

> College students are a lucrative growth market you can't afford to ignore. They develop strong brand loyalties that can last a lifetime. But the college market can be hard to target. Varsity Group...has developed a powerful platform of strategic marketing services and marketing channels designed to help you connect with the right college students—on campus, online, and on target.
>
> **Reach them where they live. Today's college students have grown up in a media saturated world. It's hard to get their attention. They're skeptical of advertising—if they notice it at all. We've found that college students respond well to peer-to-peer marketing—direct communication on campus with fellow students. (www.varsity-group.com)**

Many of the more effective techniques of marketing to the campus crowd are elaborated in an article by Claudio Marcus, the executive director of Campus Concepts. Marcus discusses the need to use local media outlets such as campus papers, billboards and events. The Internet is also a highly effective way to reach the student market, as students are more likely to be on-line than the majority of the population. But, although the Internet is an effective method of reaching students because it suits their less structured lifestyle, it can't actually put products into the consumer's hands; apparently college students express a strong preference for samples as their favorite way to try products and services. And this is where direct product distribution—the "box o' stuff"—comes in:

> While sampling alone can stimulate product trial, it's most effective when conducted as part of an overall integrated marketing effort. This is particularly true within the college market as college students' insular lifestyles make them less likely to be exposed to mass media vehicles, and sampling in the college market benefits greatly from a marketing program that establishes sufficient on-campus brand awareness. This integrated marketing approach yields its greatest benefits when it's tied to events that are an everyday part of students' lives.
>
> Sampling was a critical component of an integrated effort, according to research done by a major consumer goods company which set up a sampling effort tied to a cam-

pus fitness program that offered a well-known brand and a lesser-known brand. Almost all the students (96%) recalled receiving a sample of the products. Brand perceptions also were significantly enhanced, with 68% of the students indicating that they liked the products "very much" and another 30% indicating that they liked them "somewhat." Actual sales results further supported the company's research findings. (Marcus)

Clearly, both S&MG and Varsity Group have found the same techniques of peer-to-peer on-campus promotions and product sampling to be highly effective, as corporate sales of products will attest after the promotional events have been scheduled.

With cutbacks to higher education in Canada, schools are increasingly vulnerable to the notion that corporate handouts are a necessary part of fund-raising. Such misconceptions serve to defend some of the actions taken by corporations to promote their products on campus, in high-traffic areas, and during school events, to students at a time when tuition fees are rising, virtually across the board, and when the average student debt is $26,000.

The student market is also considered increasingly desirable to corporations because these consumers "are the market segment most open to trying new products. They are now developing brand loyalty, giving you the best opportunity to build your brand for today and tomorrow. In addition, these 18-24-year-olds are important centres of influence with their peers and families. They will become tomorrow's leaders with significant buying power for the rest of their lives. " (http://www.campusconcepts.com/)

The apparent contradiction between the disposable income of students and their desirability as a target market, and their relative impoverishment as more and more students are saddled with debt and food banks on campus are a common occurrence is summarized in one ad campaign launched by Globe interactive. This is the **Globe and Mail**'s attempt to target the campus market with an on-line newspaper: the instant win contest on the web portal announces that students can win one of three $5,000 cash prizes or goods and services from Clearnet Communications, Chapters.ca and Via Rail. The portal and contest is reinforced with bathroom ads (designed by Mosaic Communications, owner of S&MG) which read: "Forget the student loan, this is $5,000 you don't have to pay back." (Johnson) Even crushing student debt is a marketing tool.

(Erika Shaker is the Director of the CCPA Education Project.)

References

Associated Press. OREGON. "Nike Founder Halts Donations." April 24, 2000.

Campus Plus. Corporate marketing information.

CBC. "TRENDS: Exclusivity Contracts On Campuses." Apr.28/99. http://www.ottawa.cbc.ca/cbom/trends/archives/contracts_on_campus.htm.

Chronicle of Higher Learning. "Nike Chief Is Said to Be Rethinking Gift After U. of Oregon Aligns With Anti-Sweatshop Group." Monday, April 24, 2000.

Johnson, Bernadette. "Globe.com seeks campus crowd." **Strategy Magazine**. Sept. 25, 2000. p4.

http://www.strategymag.com/articles/20000925/globecampus.asp

Kuehn, Larry. "Education Roundup." **Our Schools/Our Selves**. #61. Sept. 2000. P9.

Marcus, Claudio. "Break on through to students: Building brand preference in the college market." **Sales and Marketing Magazine.** May 2000. http://salesandmarketingmag.com/promo/0500brea.html.

Reuters. PHILADELPHIA. "Couple Sells Ads to Pay for Wedding." 05/23/99. http://www.design2graphics.com/html/ptp_pages/05_23_99.html.

Saxby, Glenn. "Grads More Valuable than you Know." **Strategy Magazine**. May 8, 2000. Page B15. http://www.strategymag.com/articles/20000508/youth-grads.asp

Stewart, Sinclair. "Squeaky clean, all-American boys seek sponsors for college tuition." **Financial Post**. Oct. 9, 2000. http://www.nationalpost.com.

http://www.campusconcepts.com/

http://www.ChrisandLuke.com

http://www.educationlist.com

http://www.jobs.samg.com/CdnUsWebsite/About.asp

http://www.varsity-group.com

Endnotes

[1] An updated version of the framed advertisement are electronic urinal ads which are activated by urinal usage.

[2] A statement posted on Nike's Web site expressed anger that the university had joined the organization without first notifying the company and without also joining the Fair Labor Association.

"The W.R.C. is a loosely formed organization whose operating tenets include a 'gotcha monitoring' system and an ambiguous living-wage provision," the Nike Web site states. "Neither Nike nor any of our competitors can even join the W.R.C. because they exclude companies from participating in their process — which we believe demonstrates the lack of depth and commitment to serious reform of factory conditions."

"The U. of O., despite its unique relationship with Nike and Phil, is free to align itself with the W.R.C. However, it does not mean that we are required to support those efforts with which we have fundamental disagreements." (Chronicle of Higher Learning)

[3] Zapme! provided computers and limited web access to schools in exchange for the right to target students through on-line advertising.

Public accountability

Con U Inc.: A shopping mall, and so much more...
By David Bernans

The corporate presence on Concordia's campus is most visible and obvious in its corridors, lobbies, cafeterias and washrooms, where slick Zoom Media Inc. advertising panels encourage conspicuous consumption and name-brand identification, where Pepsi machines and Laurentian Bank ATMs are located at regular intervals for students' convenience, and where Sodexho-Marriott Inc. food products are sold. These are just a few of the corporations that have secret exclusivity agreements with the university. Others include Clearnet and Bell Canada.

For some time now, advertising has been spilling out of shopping malls, becoming more and more prominent at sporting and music events, and finding its way onto the formerly public spaces of sidewalks and parks. This is the reality that Naomi Klein (2000, 3-26) calls our "new branded world." Nevertheless, a qualitative leap is made when advertising finds its way into the "ivory tower." Secret exclusivity agreements have helped corporations consolidate their position in public institutions whose mandate is supposedly to promote the free exchange of ideas in the spirit of inquiry.

Although there is no evidence that these agreements have had any direct impact on Concordia's curriculum or research agenda, they create a shopping mall atmosphere that is hardly conducive to the development of critical citizens.

Sodexho-Marriott

The case of the Sodexho-Marriott food monopoly illustrates the extent to which the daily life of students and education workers is shaped by the corporations that surround them. The terms of the Sodexho-Marriott exclusivity deal were so constraining that it was a technical violation of the agreement for students and staff to eat their own lunches on Concordia property. Although these rules were not often applied to individuals, they were applied to groups and associations.

If a club wanted to have a bake sale, if an event was to be held on campus, or if a political meeting was to take place, only high-priced, poor-quality Sodexho-Marriott food would be allowed. In the fall of 1999, students became so fed up that thousands participated in a Concordia Student Union-financed illegal "cheese-in" where students ate non-Sodexho-Marriott cheese, crackers and pizza in opposition to the exclusivity agreement.

After a student referendum and a three-day student strike that combined the Sodexho-Marriott issue with student fee and university governance issues, the university administration and Sodexho-Marriott finally agreed to a special student exemption to the deal (although staff and faculty are still subject to the monopoly provisions in their entirety).

Subsequent to anti-Sodexho-Marriott action, students and other members of the Concordia community organized a food collective that now runs a soup kitchen and a catering service called the *People's Potato*. The *Potato* now serves free high-quality vegan meals on campus on a daily basis, and caters social events at reasonable rates.

Anti-Sodexho-Marriott activism has taken on new life once again as connections between the food services giant and the U.S. private prison industry have come to light. In June of 2000, Concordia student journalist Ariel Troster connected up with the New York-based "Not With Our Money" prison moratorium campaign. The result was a page one article in *The Link* (Concordia's more left-leaning student newspaper). "Incarceration incorporated" (Troster, 2000) is a full-page exposé that explains how the French multinational Sodexho Alliance that controls Sodexho-Marriott is also a major shareholder in Prison Realty Trust/Corrections Corporation of America (CCA).

A forum is also given to the "Not With Our Money" campaign to call for further action from Concordia students on the Sodexho-Marriott front. As protesters were targeting the World Bank and the IMF in Prague, Concordia activists were calling for some local action against the corporate-prison- complex, making "S-26" (September 26) an "International Day Against Capitalism and Sodexho-Marriott".

The price of corporate generosity

Exclusivity agreements visibly change the face of the campus and thus have the capacity to provoke significant, almost visceral, protest action on the part of students. For their mobilizing potential alone, exclusivity agreements can only be ignored at the activist's peril. Nevertheless, both in terms of financial import and in terms of direct influence over research and curriculum, so-called corporate "donation" agreements make exclusivity deals pale to insignificance. Therefore, if protest movements fail to move beyond the necessary stage of knee-jerk reactions to the immediately identifiable service-oriented corporations that target the student as consumer and onto the less obvious R & D-oriented firms that seek to take over the production of both "human resources" (students) and information (research), then the battle to save *public* education will be lost. This conceptual leap, by and large, has yet to be made at Concordia. In this respect, Concordia is typical of education institutions across North America.[1]

Private sector involvement in public education, especially at the post-secondary level, is nothing new. Wealthy individuals and corporate executives have dominated the Boards of Governors (BOGs) of Canadian (and the Boards of Trustees of American) universities throughout the 20th century and continue to do so today. This has meant that the long-term planning, finances and management of public universities, in no small measure, have been and continue to be significantly influenced by corporate interests.

This is, in itself, cause for concern. One need only consider the huge profits banks stand to make from increases to student fees set by the BOGs whose members include many prominent bankers. When student fees go up, as a general rule, so do provincial government guaranteed student loans (once the federal government got out of the business of guaranteeing student loans the banks dropped out of the program). Concordia's own 36 member BOG now has representatives from Royal Bank (Charles Cavell), Laurentian Bank (Ronald Corey), and the Bank of Montreal (Eric Molson).

Although there is no "conflict of interest" here in the legal sense of the term, Concordia students and staff have argued that this constitutes a "social conflict of interest" and have maintained that bankers should resign from the BOG (Bernans, 2000).

What has kept corporate interests in check, however, is a hard-won relative autonomy on "academic" matters that faculty-dominated university Senates have exercised since the 1960s (Tudiver, 1999, 50-54).[2] There has thus evolved a space for critical anti-corporate, and sometimes even anti-capitalist, thinking that is given pride of place in Concordia's 1991 Mission Statement. As modest as this space may be, it constitutes the "ground zero" of *public* education in the model being considered here.

It is the raw material to be transformed in the privatization process.

The breathing space won for critical thought came under attack as soon as political conditions made the enterprise feasible. The corporate offensive came in the form of an "outflanking" maneuver. Rather than overtly trying to force faculty to accept submission to corporate-dominated BOGs on academic matters (an obvious attack on academic freedom), corporations fought for and won changes to intellectual proprietorship policy in publicly-funded institutions, tax laws and research funding that allowed them to gradually increase their influence over research and curriculum through corporate "generosity".

The Business Roundtable in the United States and its Canadian counterpart, the Business Council on National Issues (BCNI), lobbied successfully in the late 1970s and early 1980s for changes to intellectual proprietorship policy that would encourage publicly-funded research institutions to patent and sell their findings and inventions to private industry.[3]

Previously, such research had been non-proprietary. It was promptly published in the public domain for peer review and free public exploitation. The new regime gave public institutions an interest in keeping research results secret in order to garner sales and royalty revenues from private corporations. Combined with generous tax incentives for corporate donations, this gave corporations an interest in funding such profitable ventures.[4]

To reinforce this trend, the federal government has tied much of its research funding to this corporate generosity. The Canadian Foundation for Innovation (CFI), which eats up the lion's share of federal research funding, offers matching funds specifically for research projects with applications that profit private industry.[5] Almost exclusive funding for research that generates corporate interest means that fundamentally non-proprietary research (that can nevertheless produce huge public benefits) has been effectively cut off.

Research on organic farming is no longer being funded, while research into environmentally hazardous biotechnological and chemical solutions to pest problems receives generous government support (Brill-Edwards, 1999). Although the former research can offer benefits to farmers and consumers, it is non-proprietary by nature. It offers no opportunity for private gain. Chemical pesticides research and pest-resistant genetically modified organisms (GMOs) research, on the other hand, may be harmful to the public and the environment, but offer significant revenues to university agricultural research departments and multi-nationals like Dow and Monsanto.

BioChem Pharma

At Concordia University, the most blatant example of corporate generosity's influence over the research agenda has been that of pharmaceutical giant BioChem Pharma Inc. BioChem Pharma's CEO Fransesco Bellini does not exactly sit at an arm's length from the "donation" that he also refers to as an investment. He sits on Concordia's Board of Governors and his company sells the university chemical supplies.

BioChem's donation added more than $1 million to Concordia's $77 million *Campaign for a New Millennium*. Combined with both federal CFI and provincial matching funds of $2 million (Comeau, 1999), this was a hefty shot in the arm for a university hit hard by funding cuts. But the money did not come without strings attached.

Accompanying the donation was a letter from Francesco Bellini to fellow BOG member, Concordia's Rector Frederick Lowy (subsequently obtained by the Concordia Student Union through an access to information request). The letter made clear precisely what kind of research Bellini expected from the new genomic research facility his donation would be funding:

> ...we are excited at the prospect of developing a partnership with the new Biotechnology facility.
>
> If your project is of great interest to us and you are able to get renowned scientists to lead a team with which our scientific team can collaborate and have access to such research, a proposal should be submitted to Dr. Gervais Dionne [BioChem's Chief Scientist] and to Mr. François Legault [Quebec's Minister of Education]. If a positive analysis is given and a relationship is achieved, we could increase our contribution for another million dollars ($1 000 000.00)(Bellini, 1997).

Although the University's own PR publications boasted about the multitude of possible new (and highly profitable) GMOs that could be developed from the gene sequencing to be done on yeast cells

(Comeau, 1999), when student Senators pointed out the undue influence of BioChem Pharma, Vice Rector Research Jack Lightstone claimed that genomic centre work was not to be application-oriented research but rather basic research, and as such, it was not in BioChem Pharma's immediate interest to try to influence the project. Lightstone claimed that no agreement with any corporation had ever compromised the academic independence of the university (Concordia Senate, 1999).

How could the university simultaneously claim that the research was both basic and applied? Because biotechnology research is, by its very nature, both. Concordia's planned genomic research would be done on simple yeast cell "model organisms" to learn about the basic building blocks of life. This "basic" information could also have a variety of profitable applications in the development of new GMOs.[6]

This cross-over between basic and applied research, combined with the legal and institutional changes outlined above, is making it increasingly difficult to maintain the independence of university research from corporate interests. The social magnitude of the loss of this independence has been made manifest in the recent—now infamous—case of the University of Toronto's Dr. Nancy Olivieri and Apotex Inc.

Another Apotex?

The comparison between the cases of these two pharmaceutical giants—Apotex Inc. and BioChem Pharma Inc.— is an obvious one. Both cases involve large donations which put into question the independence of public research institutions. Yet what is missing from the BioChem Pharma case is a Dr. Nancy Olivieri.

Olivieri's well-documented research on treatment for inherited blood diseases led her to the conclusion that Apotex's drug deferiprone may carry serious health risks and required further study before general widespread use. Although publishing these results may have saved many lives, it would have also significantly effected Apotex's bottom line. As one would expect from a private corporation, Apotex did everything it could to protect its profitability, forbidding Olivieri to publish her findings. As one would **not** expect from independent research institutions, Toronto's Hospital for Sick Children (HSC) and the University of Toronto (U of T) sided with Apotex (Canadian Association of University Teachers, 1998).

HSC and U of T fired Dr. Olivieri once she refused to stand by the non-disclosure clause that was part of the Apotex research contract. Thanks to her faculty union and the Canadian Association of University Teachers, Dr. Olivieri has since won back her position, but not before a smear campaign had been launched to soil her reputation (Canadian Association of University Teachers, 1999a).

Could the Concordia-BioChem deal produce a Concordian Dr. Olivieri similar to the U of T-Apotex deal?

In the case of Concordia-BioChem, we are not (yet) dealing with a research contract with non-disclosure arrangements, but rather with a donation agreement with no formal constraints on the independent research to be done. Be that as it may, the most crucial factor in U of T's decision to side with Apotex and against its own faculty member may well have been the $20-30 million *donation* agreement under negotiation between Apotex and the University (Canadian Association of University Teachers, 1999b). The donation, proportional to U of T's $400 million fund-raising drive, is not far from BioChem Pharma's total (promised and actual) donation to Concordia's $77 million campaign once CFI and provincial matching funds are taken into account.

There is no doubt that the prospective donation was the incentive for U of T President Robert Prichard's illegal lobbying to the federal government on behalf of Apotex Inc. with respect to changes in generic drug legislation. His apology to U of T's Governing Council is explicit on this point. The President explained that "the proposed new legislation might make [it] financially impossible for Apotex to fulfill its $20 million donation toward the University's new Centre for Cellular and Bimolecular Research." (quoted in Foss and Luksic, 1999).

It is clear that the financial interests are in place to keep quiet research that would hurt BioChem Pharma's bottom line, just as they were in the case of Apotex at U of T. Yet the likelihood that a martyr similar to Dr. Olivieri will be sacrificed to BioChem Pharma is not very high. This is not because of BioChem or Concordia's superior moral fibre, but for the simple reason that professors with the heroism and integrity of Dr. Olivieri are extremely rare. Why would a researcher risk her career and reputation when all that is required for continued funding and career advancement is silence?

The "chilly climate" for independent thought in Canadian universities is illustrated in a rare confession of corporate influence by University of Western Ontario Journalism Dean Peter Desbarats:

> The moment of truth arrived for me in 1995, when Rogers Communications granted my request for $1 million to endow a chair of information studies, for which I was extremely grateful. When journalists subsequently asked me to comment on the Rogers takeover of Maclean Hunter, all I could do was draw their attention to the donation. They understood right away that I had been, to express it crudely, bought.
>
> This had nothing to do with Rogers. I had begged for the money. It was given with no strings attached. It will serve a useful purpose. But unavoidably I gave up something in return. No one should pretend, least of all university presidents, that this experience, multiplied many times and repeated over the years, doesn't damage universities in the long run (quoted in Tudiver, 1999).

Continuing success of the privatization agenda requires precisely this kind of chilly climate. Once faculty, staff and students are aware of the consequences of rocking the privatization boat and are aware of the rewards of playing along, the complete privatization of public education can proceed with a minimum of disruption. The only way to truly combat the privatization of research and curriculum is for the whole university community to fight these measures with as much vigor as it is fighting the more obvious corporate presence in the corridors, washrooms and cafeterias of our campuses.

(David Bernans is a researcher for the Concordia Student Union. This article is a chapter from an upcoming book.)

Endnotes

1. The exceptional character of the nine month long student strike on the campus of Mexico's National Autonomous University (UNAM) must be noted here. The students' General Strike Council (CGH) joined with faculty, researchers and parents to form the University Front against the Privatization of Education whose general assembly was held in Mexico City's Olympic Stadium. The front has not shied away from the broader issues of (World Bank inspired) privatization of UNAM (Simer 1999, Gilly 2000, Monsivais 2000, Global Exchange 2000).

2. Precisely what matters are considered "academic" can be a matter of considerable debate, as was the case at York University during its 1997 faculty strike. York's administration attempted to start the summer term with scab faculty but the Senate effectively stopped the effort as a threat to the academic integrity of the institution, thus putting pressure on the administration to negotiate a hasty end to the dispute (York University Senate, 1997).

3. The U.S. Bayl-Dole Act, which gives patent ownership to federally-funded research institutions, was passed in 1980 (see Press and Washburn, 2000, 41, Noble, 1997, Noble, 1998). Although commercialization has progressed less quickly in Canada, a committee of the Prime Minister's Advisory Council on Science and Technology has recently suggested a Canadian equivalent to the U.S. Bayl-Dole Act that would add commercialization of federally funded research to universities' core priorities of teaching, research and community service (Tudiver, 1999, 184). In one respect, the Bayl-Dole Act already exists at the institutional level where researchers must accept university ownership of their inventions as a condition of employment (Noble, 1998, 2).

4. Between 1980 and 1998, industry funding of academic research increased at an annual rate of 8.1% in the U.S., standing at $1.9 billion in 1997 (Press and Washburn, 2000, 41). In Canada, non-governmental sources of funding (which includes but is not limited to industry funding of academic research) accounted for 13.1% of total income for universities in 1976-77. By 1996-97, that figure was 23.8% (Canadian Association of University Teachers, 1999c, 128).

5. This trend in federal government funding dates back to the 1980s when the (now defunct) Science Council of Canada adopted the concept of the "service university" whose goal was explicitly and openly conceived as service-provision to private industry. CFI thus follows in the footsteps of Natural Sciences and Engineering Research Council (NSERC) and the Networks of Centres of Excellence (NCE) programs which heavily favoured research projects with applications in private industry (Tudiver, 1999, 145-52).

6. Such applications could include new yeast GMOs in beer-making. Both Bellini and fellow BOG member Eric Molson are on the Board of Directors of Molson Breweries.

Sources

Bellini, Fancesco (1997), Letter to Concordia Rector Dr. Frederick Lowy obtained by the Concordia Student Union through an access to information request, July 30.

Bernans, David (2000), "Top 5 Stories the Concordia administration doesn't want you to know about," *CSU Mid-Term Report*, Spring.

Brill-Edwards, Michelle (1999), "Privatizing Knowledge" paper presented at Canadian Association of University Teachers Conference, *Universities and Colleges in the Public Interest*, Ottawa, October 30.

Canadian Association of University Teachers (1998), "Research Ethics vs. Corporate Interests: Investigator's Disclosure Fuels Ethics Debate" *CAUT Bulletin*, September.

Canadian Association of University Teachers (1999a), "CAUT Brokers Settlement in Olivieri Case," *CAUT Bulletin*, February.

Canadian Association of University Teachers (1999b), "Independent Inquiry Needed in Olivieri Scandal," *CAUT Bulletin*, January.

Canadian Association of University Teachers (1999c), "Government Cuts to Post-Secondary Education," in *Missing Pieces: An Alternative Guide to Canadian Post-Secondary Education*, Ottawa: Canadian Centre for Policy Alternatives.

Comeau, Sylvain (1999), "Genomics Centre is taking shape," *Thursday Report*, April 15.

Concordia Senate (1999), "Minutes of the Meeting of 5 November 1999," Document, US-99-7.

Foss, Krista and Nicola Luksic (1999), "U of T president apologizes for letter," *The Globe and Mail*, September 16.

Gilly, Aldolfo (2000), "The People Will Defend Their Own," from *La Jornada* February 7 reprinted by Global Exchange, URL: www.globalexchange.org, February 9.

Global Exchange (2000), "New York Times and Washington Post Fail to do Homework on UNAM Crisis," URL: www.globalexchange.org, February 9.

Klein, Naomi (2000), *No Logo*, London: Flamingo.

Monivais, Carlos (2000), "The Ultras Par Excelence" from *La Journada* February 7 reprinted by Global Exchange, URL: www.globalexchange.org, February 9.

Noble, David (1997), "Digital Diploma Mills: The Automation of Higher Education," distributed by Canadian Association of University Teachers.

Noble, David (1998), "Digital Diploma Mills, Part II," distributed by Canadian Association of University Teachers.

Press, Eyal and Jennifer Washburn (2000), "Kept University," *Atlantic Monthly*, March.

Simer, Jeremy (1999), "Mexican Student Strike Update," *Joint Publication of The Spark, The Student Activist and the Concordia Student Union*, September.

Troster, Ariel (2000), "Incarceration incorporated: Students decry cafeteria-prison connection," *The Link*, June 6.

Tudiver, Neil (1999), *Universities for Sale: Resisting Corporate Control over Canadian Higher Education*, Toronto: James Lorimer and Company.

York University Senate (1997), Minutes of the April special meeting.

No exclusivity for Coca-Cola at McGill
Or, the silent growth of campus corporatization
By François Tanguay-Renaud

The background

For the past several years, Coca-Cola and Pepsi have been waging battles to stake out Canadian campuses. Beginning with the University of British Columbia in 1995, at least 25 of Canada's 68 campuses have been won over. Montreal's McGill University was therefore not the first university to consider giving Coca-Cola a monopoly when it presented a letter of intent to the company at the end of 1999. This was to be the last step before signing an exclusive cold beverage agreement with the multinational—a deal estimated to be worth around $10 million over 11 years.

The undergraduate Students' Society of McGill University (SSMU) had agreed to sit on the deal as a non-signing "intervener." As a reward for its support, the Society was to get $1.5 million to renovate its students' centre; the remaining cash was to be split down the middle between the students and the university administration. With the Quebec government having shown little interest over the last five years in increasing funding for the education system, the deal appeared, on the university side, to be an appealing alternative to the government's unresponsiveness.

The graduate students' society rejected the deal from the outset. It adopted early on a motion opposing "the participation of McGill University in negotiations to establish exclusivity contracts with any companies or corporations." But for a long time they stood on their own.

For the few who were aware of it, there was little debate offered on the McGill-Coke question. It was framed as a simple matter of consumer choice, with "lack of access to competing brands" often described as a mere "inconvenience." To many it was a compromise, but an acceptable one. As Naomi Klein would put it months later, addressing a crowd of McGill students, "The hardest thing about fighting Coke is not that [its advocates] are telling you it's good, but that they are telling you it doesn't matter...They tell you it is only one of thousands of deals, that it's not in the classroom, that you drink it anyway, that we need the money."

A vocal opposition to the deal nevertheless started to grow on campus at the beginning of 2000. Students began to wonder why Coke had recently sponsored the construction of a "Coca-Cola international student lounge" in the new Student Services Building. They started to question what was motivating the company to fork over millions besides selling sweet, fuzzy, brown beverages. Did the debate go beyond the simple rhetoric of "choice"?

Riding on the momentum created by successful student opposition to deals at the University of Toronto, Simon Fraser University, Université Laval and Université du Québec à Montréal (UQAM), a group of McGill students mobilized against the deal. If 68 student-protesters had been arrested for illegal assembly and mischief over a similar contract at UQAM, McGill was not to stand idle.

The McGill students who were brought together by the issue came from diverse backgrounds. Some had simply grown concerned after reading about the issue. Others were representatives of various faculty associations, Amnesty International organizers, Corpwatch or fair trade activists, journalists for campus newspapers, all with their own set of grievances vis-à-vis the deal. Their course of action was to gather 500 signatures on a petition to force a student referendum on the issue.

With SSMU supporting the deal and already spending part of the projected revenues, the opponents faced an intricate obstacle course. The preamble and the referendum question were rearranged by the "Yes" side to lead students to think that they had to support the deal. The students' society used student funds to buy full-page ads in a campus newspaper to promote the contract. Ultimately, however, those who had initially mobilized against the deal got what they wanted: a student referendum.

But why launch such a campaign?

What People Won't Tell You About Those Exclusivity Deals

The Meaning of "Exclusivity"

As stipulated in article 1.6 of the Memorandum of Understanding that McGill would have imposed on the campus students' associations, the exclusive agreement would have covered:

a. all carbonated and non-carbonated, natural or artificially-flavored non-alcoholic beverages for independent consumption and for use as mixers with any other beverage and otherwise, including, but not limited to: all non-alcoholic beverages with nutritive or non-nutritive sweeteners; natural or artificially flavored non-alcoholic fruit juices; fruit juice containing drinks, fruit-flavored drinks (sweetened or unsweetened); fruit punches and ades, hypertonic and isotonic energy and fluid replacement drinks (sometimes referred to as "sports drinks"); frozen carbonated beverages; bottled/canned carbonated water, ready-to-drink iced teas and coffees; and

b. all drink or beverage bases, whether in form of syrups, powders, concentrates or otherwise, from which such drinks and beverages are made.

This basically excludes tea and coffee, as well as dairy and alcoholic beverages not offered by the cola multinational. But article 3.5 of the Memorandum made it clear that, "Should the Exclusive Supplier acquire similar and acceptable Cold Beverage Products, which were not part of the original Cold Beverage Agreement, the Parties agree to pour the newly acquired products for the remainder of the contract term."

Finally, article 3.3 of the Memorandum of Understanding stipulated that "any cold beverage product advertising, promotion and public relations materials on campus shall be in relation to the Exclusive Supplier's Cold Beverage Products." All advertising and signage to appear in food service outlets and/or on vending machines were also to be "discussed on a case by case basis."

It is therefore not surprising that, following the Pepsi-Concordia deal, a bottled water vending machine from a locally-owned company was promptly removed.

Confidentiality

The exclusive cold beverage agreement, however, would not have only impacted publicity and the selection of beverages available on campus. Students campaigning against the deal were quick to point out other weighty concerns: the McGill-Coke contract threatened to compromise McGill's values.

It was not to be a donation, but a deal with strings attached designed to increase Coke's profits. Nevertheless, it would be difficult for students to become aware of those strings as the deal was to be signed under a confidentiality agreement protecting it from public scrutiny; only two students from the pro-deal students' society would have the right to see it.

After details of their school's 1995 deal were kept confidential, the University of British Columbia's student paper, **The Ubyssey**, filed a freedom of information request. The Privacy Commissioner declined the request, referring in his report to "very persuasive" concealed in-camera statements made by Coke.

Alan Neal, CBC journalist, was once leaked a copy of the "Communication Plan" for one of these exclusivity agreements. It stipulated that university spokespeople should advocate that, "for competitive reasons, details of this agreement cannot be released." They were then supposed to "reiterate the positive aspects of the agreement." Incidentally, the same plan said that university spokespeople should be ready to "do follow-up calls to reporters/columnists who wrote negative pieces or did negative reports of the agreement."

Students were therefore asked to endorse a contract that they would never see.

Sales quotas

However, one of the students who saw the deal at McGill, Kevin McPhee, vice-president of finance of the SSMU, inadvertently shared some of its content with a journalist of the **Montreal Mirror**. He admitted that the deal would last at least 11 years and that it would be the first time McGill signed a deal with sales quotas. McGill students would have to consume a certain amount of Coke products or the university would incur a penalty, probably an extension of the contract at no cost to Coke.

Likewise, at UQAM, in exchange for a $5.4 million offering, Coca-Cola demanded that the university oversee an increase in consumption of 130% over 10 years. If the quota was not met by the end of the term, the contract would be extended for two more years at no additional cost to Coca-Cola. The University of Saskatchewan similarly had to pay Coca-Cola last year for failing to meet sales quotas in its exclusive pop deal.

At UBC, the exclusivity agreement included a quota per unit (not per volume). Coke then introduced a bottle version (higher volume, higher price), causing sales to decrease. The multinational used this tactic to demand a sales increase. Students started lobbying for can-vending machines, but Coke had full control over placement and location of vending machines. The company went even further and imposed a minimum price for clubs buying Coke products from the UBC students' society. Thus, it is now more expensive to buy on campus than off.

Via this quota system, the financial well-being of McGill would have been directly linked to Coke sales on campus. As McGill student Nick Vickander commented to the **Globe and Mail**, "Being so strapped for cash, it is questionable whether McGill's independence as a public institution could be preserved under these circumstances."

Freedom of expression

At another level, previous corporate-university deals in the United States—like Reebok's deal with the University of Wisconsin—included anti-disparagement clauses that prohibited the university from criticizing the corporation. Whether this was part of the McGill contract was of course unknown, as the university refused to make the deal public.

But students pointed out that a Georgia high school had suspended a student for wearing a Pepsi shirt on Coke Day and refusing to remove it for a photo. At Kent State University, the Amnesty International group was denied funding from the university because the speaker from the Free Nigeria Movement they wished to bring in for a talk might have spoken "negatively about Coca-Cola."

Closer to us, two York University students who displayed anti-Pepsi banners at a school football game were asked to leave and were threatened with letters of reprimand. Some campus editors have also been approached to "make an effort to mention in their sports articles that the Coke Fun Team was at the game to help 'raise spirit'."

In order to fulfill sales quotas, it could not be in the university's interest to allow vocal criticism of the multinational's public/professional behaviour.

The bigger picture

Commercialization of public space

For Naomi Klein, speaking at McGill during the referendum campaign, cola companies, like most major companies, sell their brand image, not their product: Coke is peace and diversity, Pepsi is cool and young. Coke is selling itself as an idea, and it needs people who are forming brand loyalties in order to do that. Thus, "You here at McGill, if you sign that deal, you become part of the production process, not the marketing process," Klein argued. "Their image becomes real by sponsoring your school."

Robert Baldwin, a professor of plant biology at the University of Saskatchewan, commented on how Coca-Cola makes itself noticed: "When I walk from campus to my office, I must see the Coke logo 50 times." He also expressed outrage at a pixelboard sign erected on campus: "The university built this big flashy sign to promote events on campus, and Coke can flash their logo whenever they want."

Exclusive beverage contracts are only the tip of the iceberg. As McGill Physics Professor Shaun Lovejoy commented during the referendum campaign, "Commercialization has been visible for some time, from the advertising in university bathrooms to the growing corporate presence" on campus. "But it also shows itself at the research level and the hiring of faculty level where commercial interests hold enormous growing influence."

Likewise, in a letter aimed at encouraging McGill's Principal, Bernard Shapiro, to respect the referendum results, Bill Graham, president of the Canadian Association of University Teachers (CAUT), wrote : "I believe that universities must be accountable to the public and that the recent commercialization drive poses a serious threat to public confidence in the independence, integrity and autonomy of our universities. We need to resist that."

Some argue that the trend has been occurring so incrementally that we have hardly noticed. "It began innocently enough in the early 1990s when, in the depths of the recession, companies earned PR laurels as 'good corporate citizens' by giving financial help, directly or indirectly, to cash-starved institutions," wrote Henry Aubin of the **Montreal Gazette**, commenting on the McGill situation. Since then, it has become easy to rationalize each new increment on grounds of precedents. "Thus, when the Youth News Network sought to come to Montreal-area schools, interspersing ads in its televised newscasts, supporters could point out that, in exchange for labels from students, Kellogg's and Campbell's had already lavished educational materials on Quebec schools."

At McGill, in a like manner, supporters of the exclusivity agreement with Coke pointed out that McGill had been closely involved with corporations like Molson, Sony, or Nortel for decades, and that Chapters Inc. already had an exclusivity contract on books.

Checkered ethical history

Coca-Cola's history is marred with accusations of union- busting, systematic racism, and human rights abuses. "If we are willing to overlook such a past and sign a long-term agreement with an abusive corporation, how will we be able to criticize their future decisions?" asked some students.

Those students mentioned, for instance, that Coca-Cola, through its Nigerian-owned franchise holder, sponsored and supported events and demonstrations organized by General Sani Abacha's military dictatorship. In order to invest and conduct business in Nigeria, Coca-Cola interacted and had to favour the interests of the military regime. By dealing with Abacha and his subordinates in any fashion, Coca-Cola, the world's most recognized business enterprise, gave legitimacy to his dictatorship.

The students noted that the leaders and shareholders of Coca-Cola have profited through Abacha in the sale of a valueless and nutritionless soft-drink at the cost of an average day's pay to the people of the highly populated region, where nutritional and financial resources are quickly disappearing from their grasp.

Disturbing letters were also circulating on campus during the referendum campaign. **Harper's** Magazine, for example, has reprinted a letter from Colorado School Board official John Bushey, in which he urges principals to help sell at least one Coke product every other day to students and staff, in return for cheques ranging from (US)$3,000 for elementary schools, to (US)$25,000 for high schools. The contract quota stipulates that the board must sell 70,000 cases of "the product," at least once every three years. "If 35,439 staff and students buy one Coke product every other day for a school year, we will double the required quota."

The students pointed out that Coca-Cola is the very corporation that was sued for discrimination by some of its black employees in April, 1999. Those employees indeed claimed that blacks were paid less and had fewer opportunities to advance than white employees. And what about all those stories, printed in several newspapers and books from around the world, of union-busting in Coca-Cola plants and corporate sponsored death-squads in Latin America. What about Coca Cola's attempt to convert rainforests in Belize into orange groves, or its history of misleading the public about its record on plastics recycling? How easy is it to forget that Coca-Cola was a proud sponsor of the Berlin Olympic Games during the Nazi era?

Along the same line, those students asked how a public and independent university like McGill could associate itself with a company solely accountable to its shareholders. They cited, as an example, the comments of Coke's former CEO, Douglas Ivester, that the typical person drinks *only* four ounces of soft drink out of an average of 64 ounces of liquids per day, and that "[this] still leaves our industry with 60 ounces to go after. Put another way, we're only tapping four- 64ths of the opportunity."

Did Coca-Cola have anything to say?

For its part, Coca-Cola Bottling refused to discuss the details of the deal during and after the referendum campaign. It even refused to say how many campuses in Canada it had made exclusively its own.

"We see our role as making our beverages available where people are thirsty. It's a pretty simple objective," said Sandra Banks, a spokesperson of the company, to Kate Swoger of the **Montreal Gazette**. She added that there was a great need for such drinks at McGill. "In the end, it's definitely a proposal that we will make to help satisfy those needs and, ultimately, help grow our business as well."

The fnal outcome

The campaign proved to be arduous. Information sessions, debates after debates, class presentations, hours of leafleting and tabling. For a complete month, Coke was everywhere at McGill. At least two to three stories per issue of each campus newspaper focused on the Coke debate. Personalities like Naomi Klein came to address students. The Canadian Association of University Teachers and the Canadian Federation of Students lent their support to the cause.

There was so much noise that the mainstream media had no choice but to listen. A new breath was indeed given to the campaign as the main Montreal and Canadian newspapers published dozens of articles, features and editorials on the issue. Anti-Coke activists also appeared several times on the main television channels.

Nobody could avoid the issue any more. Not even Coke, which felt compelled to send representatives to the McGill campus to take the pulse of the situation. Some would even undertake to convince McGill students. "This is my university, this is my job," said Coke representative Samuel Houde to a group of students who had assembled around him. "You would be foolish to say no to free money!"

The results of the vote came down on March 10, 2000. To the question "Do you authorize the Students' Society of McGill University to enter into a campus-wide, exclusive cold beverage agreement?", a record 5,000 voters cast ballots, and 56.4% voted NO.

McGill waited a month before responding to the results of the student referendum. "There's no interest on the part of students, and unless students invite us, we are not interested in taking this thing any further," announced Vice-Principal (Academic) Luc Vinet. In an interview given to **Maclean's** Magazine, Vice-Principal (Administration and Finance) Morty Yalovsky also stated that, "We take the outcome of the vote very seriously. At this point, we are not going to pursue the agreement."

❖ ❖ ❖

Facing $80 million less in government funding than the national average, McGill has been in dire straits over the past decade. McGill's libraries rank among the worst in the country, according to **Maclean's**, and buildings are unsafe and inaccessible. Because of this lack of funds, the university is thus looking for alternative sources of funding.

Private sources? Some have said that, the more dependent a university becomes on private funding, the more this university becomes privately accountable. Some have said that, for every penny a university gets from elsewhere, the louder it is telling governments that cuts are acceptable. One thing is sure, though: If governments do not massively reinvest in post-secondary education, we are bound to see many other attempts at establishing partnerships with the private sector.

As far as Coca-Cola is concerned, however, McGill students have said NO. In order to "connect" with them at McGill post-referendum, Coca-Cola will thus have to convince the administration to defy the wishes of its student body and renege on its decision.

Would this be possible? Vice-Principal Yalovsky recently declared that the deal was simply an arms-length business contract that is currently in a "holding position." The results of the student referendum, he added, have never been binding on the university.

(Francois Tanguay-Renaud is a student at the McGill University School of Law.)

The advantages and disadvantages of corporate/university links: What's wrong with this question?

By Claire Polster

Several years ago, a friend gave me a wonderful mini-book called *Women's Wit and Wisdom*. There are several marvellous quotation in this book, my favourite of which is "the only interesting answer is that which destroys the question". I'd like to use my time today not to answer the question of the advantages and disadvantages of corporate links for the public university, but to make the case that we should not engage with this question. Among other reasons, this is because it diverts our attention from quite a different question which ultimately sheds more light on the implications of corporate links and also leads to more effective strategies to respond to them. This question is "what do corporate links do to the public university, i.e., how do they transform what it does and what it is?".

While I will spend some of my time answering the alternative question I propose, I am going to devote the bulk of my talk to critiquing the question of the pros and cons of corporate links, focusing on the motivation, assumptions, and ultimately the conception of the university underlying it. I have chosen to do this for two reasons. First, although I have spent most of my academic career looking at the larger social forces and dynamics that are advancing the corporatization of the university, I am becoming increasingly concerned about the ways in which people's thinking (particularly academics' thinking, but that of others as well) also draws us into, and makes us complicit in, advancing this process. In critiquing the question of the advantages and disadvantages of university/industry (U/I) links, I want to reveal how many of us get caught up in advancing the corporate agenda, even as we wish to resist it. My second reason for focusing on the limitations in our thinking is that these are relatively easy things for us to change. And although changing how we think is not a sufficient condition to defeat the corporate agenda, I am increasingly convinced that it is a necessary one.

So to begin explaining why I think it is a mistake to consider the advantages and disadvantages of corporate/university links, let me first address the motivation that lies behind this question. There are at least two reasons why many people in the university community and elsewhere are interested in assessing the advantages and disadvantages of corporate/university links. Perhaps the main reason is that many people believe that these links are inevitable. As such, they want to understand both their benefits and harms so that they can find ways to maximize the former and minimize the latter and thereby preserve if not enhance the public university. There is arguably a way in which this motivation is somewhat contradictory, as one cannot manage or negotiate with the inevitable. Nonetheless, this motivation is quite widespread.

The second reason why people, and particularly academics, engage in discussing the advantages and disadvantages of corporate links-which may be more significant than one might be inclined to concede at first-is their desire to be, or to appear to be, reasonable, fair minded, and/or progressive as is befitting members of the academic community. It is bad form in the liberal university to completely reject things out of hand. Rather, we are encouraged to examine issues from all possible sides, which usually serves to complicate the picture. In this context, to uncompromisingly reject university/industry links is to risk being branded as a dogmatic and unsophisticated thinker. Indeed, after hearing my university President imply this in an interview on a local television station, I had my own moment of radical self doubt in which I feared I was losing my critical edge, given that I am no longer willing to entertain arguments about the virtues of these links.

I will come back to the flaws in these motivations, but I would now like to turn to four of the assumptions that many people make when they attempt to answer the question of the pros and cons of corporate links. These are:

1 that the advantages and disadvantages of these links are clearly distinguishable
2 that the magnitude of each advantage is generally proportional to that of its corresponding disadvantage
3 that each advantage and disadvantage has a limited number of clearly identifiable-and hence manageable-impacts
4 that these advantages and disadvantages can be explored and assessed without considering the larger context within which the university exists

It will not surprise you when I say that each of these assumptions is seriously flawed. Let me briefly address the flaws of each of these assumptions and of the general conception of the university that underlies them.

The first assumption, namely that the pros and cons of corporate links are clearly distinguishable, is highly problematic. Even seemingly obvious advantages of corporate links can, at the same time, be highly disadvantageous for the university. For example, corporate funded chairs seem to be unquestionable beneficial for the university as they amount to additional, free money and resources. Notwithstanding their benefits to certain members of the university community, however, such chairs may produce substantial and often unanticipated costs for universities, which force them to divert funds from already undersourced areas. Thus, rather than enhancing the university - or at the very same time that they do this - these chairs also lead to its internal underdevelopment. Similarly, spin of companies, which may increase a university's prestige and revenue stream, may simultaneously harm the very institutions that they help. In addition to consuming substantial financial resources of the university, they also often use up great amounts of the time and energy of professors and staff which can no longer be used in the service of students of other communities that are important to the university.

The second common assumption made when assessing the pros and cons of corporate links is that the size an advantage is proportional to the size of its corresponding disadvantage. So, for example, it is commonly assumed that the more money and individual citizen or corporation donates to the university, the more the potential leverage they may acquire in the institution, or that the more money an academic stands to make from some research initiative, the more likely they are to become embroiled in some conflict of interest. This assumption is currently reflected in university policies such as those that mandate that senior administrators vet research contracts that exceed $100,000 or that more attention be paid to the terms and conditions of larger rather than smaller donations to the university. The mistake here is the failure to recognize that the potential impact of corporate links is by no means proportional to their magnitude. For instance, very small donations can have substantial effects on a university - in both the short and the long term - such as when the mere loan of a piece of "state of the art" equipment to the McGill University got the donor a seat on the music faculty's curriculum committee.

The third assumption behind the question of the advantages and disadvantages of university/industry links is that their effects are clearly identifiable and discrete. This is perhaps the most problematic of the assumptions. It overlooks less visible and intangible impacts of these links. It also overlooks the ways in which the impacts of links interact over both the short and long term. For example, while the professional and/or financial benefits of research partnerships for academics, universities, and businesses can be clearly identified and measured, less tangible impacts of these arrangements, such as the erosion of academic autonomy, the weakening of institutional democracy, and the displacement of a collegial research culture by a competitive one are less easily measured and accounted for, though no less significant. Also less visible are the cumulative impacts of these links, such as the erosion, in the short term, of the university's willingness to serve the needs of groups who cannot afford to sponsor research, and the potential foreclosure, in the long term, of the university's ability to serve those needs.

Finally, the assumption or practice of looking at the pros and cons of university/industry links without taking the broader social context into account is problematic. That which appears to be advantageous from within a local perspective is often revealed to be disadvantageous when a broader perspective is adopted. For example, when the current social context is taken into account, the large sums of money that universities may generate from private activities can arguable be seen to be harmful in that they both facilitate and legitimate further government withdrawals from university funding. Also, given that the increasingly popular matched-funding programs of government to serve to concentrate public funds in the hands of the richest and most research intensive Canadian universities, smaller universities, and many larger ones, actually undermine their long term interests when they participate in these programs, regardless of how successful they might be.

The problems with all four of these assumptions stem from a common source, namely a flawed conception of the nature of the university and of the impact of corporate links upon it. Implicit in the discussion of the pros and cons of corporate links is a conception of the university as a machine, comprised of various parts, which each have discrete effects on the operations of the whole. Corporate links are viewed as an additional, new part of the machine, whose various effects need to be adjusted so that they do not harm and may actually enhance the workings of the whole. These are simplistic and misleading conceptions of the university and corporate links. It is far more accurate and illuminating to conceive of the university as a living organism. As for corporate links, they are not an **add-on** to the university, such that after their establishment one has the old university plus these links. Corporate links are an **add-into** the university, which produce the qualitative changes that pervade its multiple and interacting aspects and dimensions including its culture, operating practices, funding systems, reward structures, etc. To effectively grasp and respond to the implications of corporate links for the university, one cannot engage in a cost/benefit analysis of their discrete impacts. Rather, one must reorient to the question of these links, focusing on what they make the university fundamentally become or on how they qualitatively transform what the university is.

I don't have time either to fully illustrate what I mean by this different orientation to corporate links or to fully elaborate on what these links make the university become. To give you a sense of both, however, I'd like to briefly address a paper I've written on the implications of the university's involvement in intellectual property (IP), which may be the ultimate expression of corporate links.[1]

There is much debate in the literature about the advantages and disadvantages of university involvement in IP. Some benefits that supporters point to include its increasing university revenues, facilitating more exciting and synergistic research, and enhancing the university's contribution to both science and economic competitiveness. Some disadvantages its opponents point to include its promoting secrecy, competition, conflict of interest, and inattention to less commercially valuable avenues of research.

Although all these points are valid, to focus on them is to miss the more significant implications for the university of its involvement in IP, to overlook what it does to the university and compels it to become. In the paper, I argue that its involvement in IP limits the liberal university's ability to reproduce itself, in two ways. It leads to the destruction of the commons of knowledge on which the university relies, and it inhibits the university's ability to serve the public interest, which is also crucial to its long term survival.

I further argue that a university's involvement in IP both pushes and pulls academics onto a track of private knowledge production, resulting in the university producing a more limited range of knowledge, to which access is increasingly restricted, and which serves the needs and interests of an increasingly limited sector of society, namely those who can afford to sponsor research. Ultimately, the university's involvement in IP has the potential to destroy any difference between it and any other private knowledge institution. There will remain no university dedicated to a robust conception of public service. And there will thus remain no university that is worthy of—and likely to receive—public support.

This is what corporate links ultimately mean for the university. They transform it from a public serving institution, i.e., a public resource for social development, into a knowledge business, i.e, a private resource for economic enrichment. No amount of debating the pros and cons of corporate links will lead to this conclusion. Indeed, becoming engaged in this debate actually prevents one from ever arriving at this conclusion.

More importantly, debating the pros and cons of university links will keep us in a place from which this transformation of the university cannot be stopped. What is particularly tragic about the efforts of some academics and others to discern and to mitigate the disadvantages of corporate links— through various policies, regulations, etc.— is that, although they believe their actions are protecting and preserving the public university, they are actually facilitating and advancing its transformation.

For example, one measure being advocated to redress the growing secrecy in the university that is a product of corporate links is to impose limits on the period of time academics may withhold information from the public domain. While this measure may remedy some problems, such as increased duplication and waste in knowledge production, it does nothing to reverse the displacement in the university of a public research culture by a private one. On the contrary, it serves to both facilitate and legitimize this qualitative transformation.

In the present context, the only way to keep the public university from becoming a knowledge business is to stop corporate links before they start, or to rid the university of those that currently exist. Their "harmful effects" cannot be mitigated once these links are established because the effect of these links are not additive in nature but are fundamentally transformative.

This brings me back to the flaws in the motivation of those who seek to answer the question of the advantages of university/ industry links. Earlier I suggested that the main reason people wish to answer this question is their assumption that these links cannot be stopped, but that their harmful effects which threaten the public university can be neutralized. I have suggested that things are actually the other way around. Corporate links are not inevitable: they are human products and they can be stopped. Moreover, **unless** they are stopped, their harmful effects which fundamentally threaten the public university **cannot** be neutralized. Indeed, despite any good intentions we may have, our efforts to manage and contain these effects will only facilitate and advance the public university's transformation.

As for concerns about being—or being branded as— simplistic, I have tried to show that refusing to engage in debates about the advantages and disadvantages of corporate links is not simplistic in the least. What **is** simplistic is the view of the university as a machine that produces this debate, as well as debates about how to mitigate the harmful effects of corporate links, which needlessly tie us up in complex intellectual knots about acceptable degrees of secrecy, disclosure, corporate control of research results, etc., and ultimately get us nowhere in terms of preserving the public university.

Indeed, when one abandons a mechanistic conception of the university and orients to the transformative impact of corporate links upon it, these debates do not only seem simplistic and sterile, but also quite insidious. Either by default or by design, they keep us from engaging in the far more significant and urgent debate we must have in our country, namely the debate about the kind of university Canadians want and Canadians need. And they keep us from acting clearly and decisively in defense of our vision.

To summarize, corporate links are transforming our universities from public serving institutions into knowledge businesses. This is not an advantage or a disadvantage for a public university. This is a conversion of the public university from one thing to another. Whether this conversion is a good or a bad thing is the debate that Canadians—both inside and outside the university—must have. Discussing the pros and cons of corporate/university links only stifles this debate and promotes university policy by stealth whereby the choice is being made for us rather than by us.

Difficult as it is, then, I want to urge all of you to urge everyone you know to refuse to participate in the advantages/disadvantages debate and to ensure that the larger issues at stake be put firmly and squarely on the table. "Public serving institutions or knowledge businesses?"—that is the question.

(Claire Polster teaches in the Department of Sociology at the University of Regina. She can be reached by e-mail at claire.polster@uregina.ca)

Endnotes

[1] This article is called "The Future of the Liberal University in the Era of the Global Knowledge Grab." It is published in *Higher Education*, vol. 39, pp. 19-41.

Globalization and the restructuring of Canadian community colleges: Critical perspectives

By Diane Meaghan

Restructuring is perhaps the most significant issue affecting higher education today. With an increasing interest in controlling public expenditures, the metaphor of the market is central to a number of discourses that call for institutions of higher education to become more efficient, adaptable and accountable by utilizing a corporate template as a panacea for post-secondary educational ills.

It is important to provide some perspective on the ideological concepts that are shifting colleges and universities from a public to a private good that are transforming these institutions, academic work and learning.

Of particular interest is the way that policies and practices that favour economic rationalism and the market are being implemented, together with the manner in which colleges are organizing activities through procedures adopted from the world of business and becoming businesses through marketing initiatives, student recruitment and enhanced fiscal autonomy.

These policies and practices arise in a distinctive political, economic and social context of globalization as part of an economic discourse of free trade and market primacy at the international level (Meaghan and Casas: 1995).

Beginning in the 1970s, economic, political and social relations were transformed by a growing acceptance of the dominant discourse of the globalization agenda that valorized economic rationality, neo-classical economics, and the minimalist politics of neo-liberalism. In the new globalization model linking global social relations with local practice, the message of international financiers characterized the state as inefficient, suggesting that market forces will make governments more competitive through restructuring and downsizing.

Regional trade organizations proclaimed the need for deregulation, particularly of capital and labour markets, a reduction in the level of taxation and public spending, privatization or abatement of the welfare state, and a reduction of state functions that have resonated with Western governments.

In what Michel Foucault's (1991) terms a "regime of truth," the Canadian government shifted public resources from the welfare state to economic development as a single-focus solution to current problems, and developed policies and practices that favoured efficiency, productivity, profitability, labour market flexibility, and neo-Fordist managerialist models of administration. This approach stressed the need for Canada to become more competitive, resulting in policy initiatives to enhance training the labour force, to reduce unemployment insurance, and to respond to the deficit and inflation with greater competitiveness.

In the 1995-96 federal budget, cost-sharing was replaced by block grants that removed $3.7 billion dollars by 1996-97 as transfer payments to the provinces. This resulted in substantive reductions of financial transfers to the provinces under the Canadian Health and Social Transfer [CHST] for income assistance, health and post-secondary education (Fisher and Rebenson, 1998:80-1).

Between 1983-1995, the decline in federal contributions to post-secondary education totalled $13.5 billion, according to Neil Tudiver (1999:65). Since constitutional responsibility for education has remained within the provinces and provincial grants represent the single largest source of revenue, the problem of the federal government was compounded when provinces such as Alberta and Ontario instituted their own debt reduction initiatives (Tudiver, 1999:65).

The globalization theory has structured the transformation of higher education by increasingly making these institutions central to national strategies to secure global markets (Lyotard, 1984). According to Janice Newson (1998:71), education policy is a particular favoured form of micro-economic revision because of the perceived role that it plays in restructuring the economy along the lines of macroeconomic choices with an emphasize on efficiency, productivity and global competitiveness.

This demand-side approach places a high valuation on education in order to supply particular skilled workers for the existing division of labour in business and industry. Increasingly, linkages between universities and colleges as sources of knowledge and with corporations are being undertaken to produce value-added processes and products for the marketplace.

Western countries have been indirectly influenced by proposals for reform by the World Bank, such as its 1994 report "Higher Education: The Lessons of Experience" recommending that countries move from a single state source of funding to multiple sourcing (including student fees, donations, commercialization and partnerships), and further suggesting that government funding should become more closely tied to performance (Slaughter and Leslie:1997).

The Organization for Economic Cooperation and Development (1994:37) has had a more pronounced effect on higher education in Canada, the United States and the United Kingdom, particularly as a result of the 1989 document "Education and Economy in a Changing Society" that urged ministries of education to improve management and accountability in higher education. The OECD has become a major source of ideas, knowledge and policies that legitimate educational reform, making higher education ancillary to the requirements of international competition and product innovation.

Howard Buchbinder and Pinayur Rajagopal (1998), in describing another source of regulations in the NAFTA agreement, suggest that globalizing influences concerning the imposition of standards are being encouraged to bring practices within Canadian universities in line with government policies.

In "The Canadian Opportunities Strategy" (1999), the federal government articulated the way in which post-secondary education was to contribute to a "knowledge society." A climate of "learnfare" encouraged education and training to merge, as knowledge came to be viewed as instrumental, flexible, related to short-term goals, and a value-added commodity.

Corporations have demanded that higher education apply successful business principles to reduce costs, become more efficient, find new markets, and increase income (Greider:1997). The government has responded by exhorting universities and colleges to incorporate business-like practices associated with accountability, privatization and managerialism.

In reconstructing education to be less a part of social policy and more a sub-sector of economic policy, Neave (1988) points out that governments have demanded that universities develop more efficient managerial techniques, science and technology have been singled out to highlight commercial endeavours, and university-industry partnerships have been established to generate wealth.

"The Report on the Commission of Inquiry on Canadian University Education" (1991) identified practices adopted by administrators in Canadian universities to re-engineer work processes and reduce costs in a manner favoured by the Corporate Forum on Higher Education, the Business Council on National Issues, the Institute for Research on Public Policy, and the Public Policy Forum. Recent government initiatives such as the establishment of the Expert Panel on the Commercialization of University Research (1999) have encouraged teaching and research in Canadian universities that is market-based through the use of performance-based funding.

A key document for colleges in the Canadian restructuring initiative was the paper "Agenda: Jobs and Growth: Improving Social Security in Canada" produced by the Human Resources Development Canada (1994). It made the point that the wealth of individuals—and indeed, the nation—turned on the issue of skills acquisition. Whereas public funds had formerly been designated to the colleges through federal-provincial agreements, they now became available to private sources through indirect federal training purchases.

The result was a reduction in the amount of federal training funds going to colleges, and a rapid growth in the private training sector, despite the entrepreneurial approach undertaken by many colleges. Ontario's response to this form of economic pressure was revealed in the "Ontario Council on University Affairs" (1995) that called for professional programs to be rationalized and funding for the approval of new programs to be tightened.

The release of two Premiers' Council reports entitled "Competing in the New Global Economy" (1988) and "People and Skills in the New Global Economy" (1990) called for training to shift from the provincial government to private partnerships.

The "Ontario Premier's Council on Economic Renewal" (1995) went further in making the connection between learning and earning. In the new economic model, both education and work were to become key issues of "revitalization."

Over the past decade and a half, Canadian colleges have been confronted by pressures from a severe decline in funding. Various institutions have responded by substantially raising and deregulating tuition, reducing programs and staff positions, and encouraging marketing and fund-raising activities. These institutions also face an unprecedented expansion in enrolment over the next five years, due to the entrance of the grandchildren of baby boomers.

Similar to the universities, economic constraint is not the only, or even the major impetus for restructuring, although financial pressure is critical to effect structural and programmatic changes (Tjeldvoll:1998). It is assumed that efficiency, productivity and skills brought to the marketplace will contribute to the economic well-being of the province, and that colleges as institutions should become more commercial and entrepreneurial, and more bureaucratic and corporate in nature.

Colleges have served the economic, technological, social and cultural objectives of society. These institutions have fulfilled their mandate by providing quality post-secondary education and by extending access to higher education (Terenzini, 1996:9). They have met the needs for a skilled and educated labour force; they turn out graduates who prosper in the economy, and they preserve and transmit culture to ensure productive citizens for society. Charged with the responsibility to dispense both vocational and avocational education, colleges provide technical skills training in career-specific programs. These institutions assist students to acquire generic skills, critical thinking, problem-solving capabilities, liberalized social attitudes, and the ability to communicate. Responding to the needs of students and the requests of employers for a literate and educated workforce, a college education was designed to be easily accessible and practical rather than theoretical in nature.

Colleges also fulfill a commitment to social equity in responding to the needs of local communities, and in an era of rapid change they have made some strides in human resource development in attempting to shift to a post-industrial knowledge-based society.

Despite these achievements, colleges are being directed to increasingly become corporate, not communal, and certainly not collegiate (Downery, 1996:81).

Unlike universities, colleges were not founded on a collegial model that encourages academic freedom, peer evaluation, and shared decision-making. Nor have colleges had a bicameral system of governance, with a Board of Governors accountable for financial matters and a Senate responsible for academic issues.

Managerialism, the recognition of the right of senior administrators to oversee in an unfettered manner, is not a new idea, as pointed out in the Skolnik report (1986),"Survival or Excellence?: A Study of Instructional Assignment in Ontario's Colleges of Applied Arts and Technology", and in the Pitman Report (1986), "The Report of the Advisor to the Minister of Colleges And Universities on the Governance of Colleges of Applied Arts and Technology" (1986).

Corporate managerialism is part of the retrenchment of existing practices that supports a hierarchical management structure, strengthens a corporate bureaucratic model of governance, and encourages teaching and learning processes directed to the interests of business and industry. What is presently innovative is a strong marketing approach based on managerial principles favoured by both the federal and provincial governments, designed to transform these public institutions into organizations that will serve a more competitive state. Colleges are busy developing a corporate image to sell professional services and provide training programs, both at home and abroad.

While colleges have employed a managerial and corporatist approach since their inception, teaching was always at the forefront of activity. During the past 10 to 15 years, however, colleges have rapidly been restructured by bureaucratic and financial accountability practices such that the values, structures and processes of these institutions have increasingly been subsumed under the directives of marketing initiatives.

The increased use of the language of business that redefines students as "clients" and corporations as "partners" is an example of concepts borrowed from the world of business. Talk about efficiency and rationalization shifts the thinking within colleges from an educational enterprise to a discourse of economic conservatism (Slaughter, 1998b:236). The new relationships between colleges and their "customers" place the latter in a far stronger position than the arms-length relationships of the past, by dictating to colleges the kind of service that is required through contracts and donations.

Such initiatives represent a shift in program design away from faculty and students to employers and business enterprises (Trigwell and Reid, 1998:145). The result has altered the relationship among government, college and society, reforming governance, management and academic productivity (Neave, 2000:10).

As governments imposed deep cuts in public funding of colleges, provincial operating grants did not keep pace with expanding enrolment, costs and inflation. Colleges were transformed from operations based on social demand to institutions that utilized a user-pay principle, shifting the burden of a college education to the individual.

Tuition policies prescribed that students should pay for a substantial portion of their education through high tuition fees, or incur significant debt loads (Hack, 1998:14). As a result, average tuition rose by 58% between 1989 and 1997 across Canada; a federal task force estimates that educational debts for students reached $25,000 by 1998 (Tudiver, 1999:68).

The concept of "student as client" draws academics into an education as commodity discourse, changing the pedagogical relationship of teacher and student to one of provider and purchaser of a service (Meaghan, 1996;1999a:3). Given that colleges cater more to working-class students than universities, and that they have a higher portion of part-time students who are penalized through loans applications, many first-generation college students, women, visible minorities and immigrants have suffered as a result (Slaughter, 1999b:215).

Services that were once provided through central operating budgets have been offloaded to be purchased within departments at cost recovery. Campus-wide services such as parking, sports facilities and food services operate at full-cost recovery and in some cases generate a profit. Fund-raising drives that appeal to corporations, alumni and staff designed to establish modest endowment programs have been undertaken with great institutional fanfare.

In an attempt to slow the rate of public spending, support staff have suffered the most through loss of jobs, a significant increase in workload and stress, and through proposals to outsource custodial, printing and technical services that fail to take into account value added to service by long-time, loyal employees.

College structures concerning governance are currently being bypassed, or in some instances eliminated, providing little or no input into decision-making for faculty, staff, departmental administrators, and students. Administration which historically supported teaching has garnered control that is utilized to pursue activities quite apart from academics, such as fund-raising, marketing, and forging connections with the private sector (Tudiver, 1999:2). Industry-government-college partnerships, either led by industry as in the case of selling training programs, or in the form of amalgamated programs to develop technology-enhanced learning, have been undertaken to market college services, institute flexibility in resource allocation, and achieve economies of scale. Many colleges have endorsed product advertising, established computer and clothing boutiques, and made campus bookstores a profit venture.

On an ad hoc basis, a number of colleges are being privatized "through the back door." Although these institutions remain legally public and utilize public funds, they set up alternative "public/private" corporate entities within which to fund-raise, market services, and engage in producing training packages for industry and courseware for students, particularly in Asia and the Pacific Rim.

Such enterprises have resulted in the development, delivery and evaluation of college curricular materials by contract personnel or by commercial firms with college credit awarded for such programs. This form of institutional segmentation has led to the commodification of knowledge and a growing concern that standards of quality education have been compromised, with little regard for entrance and exit standards in some cases.

The encouragement of greater specialization among divisions has become another flash point. Some faculty, departments and institutions are viewed as "winners" in the brave new world of colleges that allocates resources to "economically-valuable" disciplines. Such stratified initiatives mask the privileging of men who predominate in teaching, learning and administrative functions in these areas (Slaughter, 1998a:237). All colleges have moved to more cost-effective instructional delivery systems through computer-mediated learning (Meaghan:1995b).

Although these methods were initially introduced to facilitate distant education, the introduction of computer-enhanced learning may be attributed to wanting to replace the "sage on the stage" with the new pedagogical model of the "guide on the side" where faculty are incidental to the design, delivery and evaluation of learning (Barrett and Meaghan, 1995:22).

The use of electronic media expands the market of students while decreasing costs for buildings and course development, the later being handled by payment of an honorarium with copyright held by the college. While it is suggested that the "anywhere" and "anytime" flexible delivery of instruction through the use of a CD-ROMs or the Internet extends access to students, David Noble (1998) explains how electronic technologies have caused faculty to lose control of curriculum, have removed faculty from the teaching process, and converted classroom teaching into products.

Peer tutors, technicians and non-academic staff have eliminated the need for some faculty to prepare and deliver courses (Noble, 1999), while the reality of the virtual college is fast approaching (Pascarella and Terenzini, 1998:160; Coaldrake:1999; Meaghan:2000).

Efforts have intensified in the 1990s to apply accountability measures (to assess both colleges as institutions and employees) through the introduction of total quality management (TQM) schemes, outcomes-based education, and performance indicators. Externally-applied, quantified measures remove conceptualization and control, and reorganize the social relations of academic work. Performance indicators, in particular, dilute the influence of academics, shifting control over academic work processes from faculty to management through the development of common standards and the means of regulating academic work.

In linking academic assessment with issues of funding, these procedures reconstruct the relationship between the way academic work is performed, on the one hand, and how, on the other hand, it is interpreted and evaluated. Margarite Cassin and Graham Morgan (1992:2 53) suggest that in the process of rendering academic work accountable in universities, such devices make visible aspects of professorate work which is the most and the least efficient and cost-effective.

These techniques are similarly employed in the colleges to decrease expenditures, monitor faculty, and attempt to raise the standard of pedagogical practice.

In adopting procedures from the world of business that favour greater flexibility, faculty are divided into a core of full-time career academics who are relatively well remunerated and receive benefits of supplementary health and disability insurance, pensions, and a dental plan, offset by a large and growing group of part-time, contract and casualized faculty (many of whom are women), who receive low pay, few benefits, and lack job security.

Although slower to impact on the colleges than universities, a two-tiered faculty complement has resulted in redundancies and full-time faculty positions not being filled upon vacancy. This has led to the growth in numbers of part-time faculty who in most instances have a very different view of what is needed and required from full-time faculty with respect to salary and benefits, job security, working conditions and the restructuring taking place within the colleges.

The changing social relations of academic work have intensified long-standing problems between faculty and administration in a number of colleges. Faculty observe that college education has shifted from a culture of learning and credit acquisition to one of self-directed and, at times, off-campus training.

Decredentializing and deinstitutionalizing college education recently led one college president to remark that "grades don't matter any more" (De Sousa et.al.:1997:16). For the faculty who have retained jobs, work intensification has produced concessions in the form of modularized courses, shortened semesters, larger classes, year-round programs, and very little time for course preparation, curriculum review, and professional development (Meaghan, 1997:16).

A recent survey by Jerry White (1999) of the Centre for Research on Work and Society at York University found a high degree of dissatisfaction and plummeting morale among Ontario college faculty, due to deteriorating working conditions, depreciation of salaries, and the perception that academic decisions are being exclusively made by a few senior managers. At the same time, cutbacks have also occurred in the infrastructure that supports teaching and learning, resulting in reductions in library acquisitions and maintenance of the physical plant.

The best-case scenario views the preservation of the current generation of academics and the core function of teaching in a mixed economy together with corporate service; a worse-case scenario perceives of this as the last generation of career college teachers, as these institutions rapidly adopt a market approach to education.

College programs are likely to continue in future to be differentiated through partial and full-cost recovery fees, providing market-driven services that will continue to be privatized. The status of colleges in future may nonetheless be enhanced with an increase in transfer courses, greater college-university linkages, and the introduction of seamless systems. Added to these phenomena is the perceived value of a college education pragmatically leading to a job with placement rates between 87% and 92%, although only about half those numbers find jobs in their area of training (Roseman, 2000:C1).

Lines between academically-centred education and vocationally-oriented training, and the distinction between applied and basic research are liable to be blurred. The rising tide of vocationalism may conversely push skills training into the university curriculum. Marketing of college services, particularly international marketing to generate profit, will likely increase as public sphere funding declines.

At the same time, colleges are liable to be more closely monitored through government policy and made more accountable in future. Most likely there will be a strengthening of the current trend to highlight bureaucratic and corporate procedures in the name of efficiency and cost containment. Such arrangements will intensify work practices with less participation, however, in decision-making processes for the majority who work and learn in these institutions.

As labour market segmentation expands, so will barriers of access, particularly for women, racial minorities, immigrants, and lower-income students. Reducing the selection of courses in Humanities and English and Communications subjects is cause for concern that students will not develop social analyses, critical thinking, and literary abilities. Affordable, accessible and pluralistic programs which offer courses in aboriginal studies, labour and women's studies, as well as French-language programs, are vulnerable to reduction under a market orientation.

(Diane Meaghan is a professor of General Education at Seneca College.)

References

Barrett, Ralph and Meaghan, Diane. (1990). Unionism and Academic Collegiality: The Politics of Teaching in an Ontario Community College. In Jake Muller (Ed.), **Canada's Changing Community Colleges: Education as Work/Education for Work** (pp.76-89). Toronto: Garamond Press.(1995, June 15).

"Technoeducation and Teacherless Learning: Learning-Centered Education in Ontario's Colleges." Paper presented to the Canadian Anthropology and Sociology Society, Learned Societies of Canada annual conference, Brock University. (1998, February 17-21).

"Proletarianization, Professional Autonomy and Professional Discourse: Restructuring Educational Work in Ontario's Community Colleges." Paper presented to the International Conference on the 150th Anniversary of "The Communist Manifesto", Havana, Cuba.

Buchbinder, Howard and Rajogopal, Pinayur. (1998). Canadian Universities: The Impact of Free Trade and Globalization. **Higher Education**, 31 (2) pp. 283-99.

Cassin, Margarite & Morgan, Graham. (1992). The Professorate and the Market-Driven University: Transforming the Control of Work in the Academy. In W. Carroll & L. Christiansen, Ruffman & R.

Coaldrake, Peter. (1999, March). The Changing Climate of Australian Higher Education: An International Perspective. **Higher Educational Management**, 11, (1), 117-35.

De Sousa, Luis. & Boland, Brady. & Ferrone, Darlene. (1997, May). Grades Don't Matter. "Impact", Toronto: Seneca College Student Association p. 16.

Foucault, Michel. (1980). "Truth and Power." In Carl. Gordon (Ed.), **Power/Knowledge** (pp. 34-76). New York: Pantheon.

Fisher, Donald & Rubenson, Kjell. (1998). "The Changing Political Economy: The Private and Public Lives of Canadian Universities." In Jan Currie & Janice Newson (Eds.), **Universities and Globalization: Critical Perspectives** (pp.67-89). Thousand
Oaks, CA: Sage.

Greider, William. (1997). **One World Ready or Not: The Manic Logic of Global Capitalism**. New York: Touchstone.

Human Resources Development Canada. (1994). **Agenda: Jobs and Growth: Improving Social Security in Canada**, Ottawa, Queen's Printer.

Lyotard, Jean. (1984). **The Postmodern Condition: A Report on Knowledge**. Manchester: University of Manchester.

Meaghan, Diane. (1995a, October 21). "The Corporate Agenda: An Intrusion in Education." Paper presented at the Corporate Agenda in Education Workshop, Diversity in Education Conference, Toronto Waldorf School, Toronto, Ontario. (1995b, November 23).

"An Academic Response to the Council of Presidents' 'Learning-Centered' Model of Education." Paper presented to the Seneca College Board of Governor's. Toronto: Seneca College.(1996).

"Transformational Trends in Higher Education: Restructuring the Academic Labour Process Through the Introduction of a Corporate Agenda" (1996). **Socialist Studies Bulletin**, 4, (1), 45-57.(1997).

Clear and Present Danger: Restructuring Ontario's Community Colleges. "Education Monitor, 1," (4), 16-18. (1999).

"Dangerous Liaisons: Restructuring Ontario's Community Colleges to Meet Market Needs." In Denise Doherty-Delorme and Erika Shaker (Eds.), **Missing Pieces: An Alternative Guide to Canadian Post-secondary Education**. (139-142). Ottawa: Canadian Center for Policy Alternatives, Ottawa, Ontario.(1999, November).

"Restructuring Community Colleges: Retrenchment of the Factory Model." **The Local**, OPSEU, Local 560, Seneca College.

Meaghan, Diane and Casas, Francois (1995, September). Educational Restructuring for the New Global Economy: Corporations and Curriculum Control. **Our Schools/Ourselves**, pp. 34-43.

Neave, Gary. (1988). "Education and Social Policy: Demise of an Ethic or Change of Values?". **Oxford Review of Education**, 14, (3), pp. 273-83. (2000).

"Diversity, Differentiation and the Market: The Debate We Never Had But Which We Ought to Have Done." **Higher Education Policy**, 13, pp. 7-21.

Newson, Jan. (1998). "Transnational and Supranational Institutions and Mechanisms." In Jan Currie & Janice Newson (Eds.), **Universities and Globalization: Critical Perspectives** (pp. 78-94).Thousand Oaks, CA: Sage.

Noble, David. (1998, March). "Digital Diploma Mills: The Coming Battle Over Online Instruction." (Part 11). Toronto, OCUFA. (1999). Digital Diploma Mills (Part IV). http://communication.ucsa.edu/da/ddm4.html.

Ontario Council on Universities Affairs, "21st Annual Report", Toronto: Minster of Education and Training.

Ontario Premier's Council on Economic Renewal (1995). "Lifelong Learning and the New Economy". Toronto: Ministry of Finance.

Organization for Economic Cooperation and Development. (1994). **Education at a Glance: OECD Indicators**. Paris: OECD.

Pascarella, Ernest & Terenzini, Patrick. (1998). "Studying College Students in the 21st Century: Meeting New Challenges." **The Review of Higher Education**, 21, (2), 151-65.

Pitman, Walter (1986). The Report of the Advisor to the Minister of Colleges and Universities on the Governance of the Colleges of Applied Arts and Technology. Toronto: Minster of Colleges and Universities.

Rosman, Carol. (2000, March 13). "College Funding Under Review." **The Toronto Star**, p.C1.

Skolnik, Michael. (1985). **Survival or Excellence: A Study of Instructional Assignments in Ontario's Colleges of Applied Arts and Technology**, Toronto: The Ontario Institute for Studies in Education.

Slaughter, Sheila. (1998a). "Supply-Side Economics, National." Higher Educational Policy and Institutional Resource Allocation: ASHE Presidential Address. **The Review of Higher Education**, 21, (3) pp. 209-44.(1998b).

Federal Policy and Supply-Side Institutional Resource Allocation at Public Research Universities. **The Review of Higher Education**, 21,(3), pp. 209-44.

Slaughter, Sheila & Leslie, Larry. (1997). **Academic Capitalism: Politics, Policies and the Entrepreneurial University**. Baltimore, MD: Johns Hopkins University Press.

Terenzini, Patrick. (1996). "Rediscovering Roots: Public Policy and Higher Education Research." **The Review of Higher Education**, 20, (1), pp. 5-13.

Tjeldvoll, Arild. (1998). "The Service University in Service Societies: The Norwegian Experience." In Jan Currie & Janice Newson (Eds.), **Universities and Globalization: Critical Perspectives** (pp. 134-56). Thousand Oaks, CA: Sage.

Trigwell, Keith & Reid, Anna. (1998). "Introduction: Work-Based Learning and the Students' Perspective." **Higher Education Research and Development**, 17, (2), pp. 141-53.

Tudiver, Neil. (1999). **Universities for Sale: Resisting Corporate Control over Canadian Higher Education**. Toronto: James Lorimer and Company.

White, Jerry. (1999). "Voices From the Classroom: The Ontario Colleges and the Question of Quality." Toronto: Center for
Research on Work and Society, York University.

Private universities, public menace
By James Clancy

Every year or so, it seems the right wing in Canada sets its sights on another aspect of Canadian public life which it wishes to see turned over to the private sector. Through sympathetic governments, they've already met with tremendous success in their drive to privatize Crown corporations; Air Canada, Petro-Canada, and the soon-to-be U.S.-owned Canadian National are just a few examples.

We've also seen their push for a two-tier "for-profit" health care system meet with support from more than one provincial government in this country.

So now they've set their sights on the education of Canada's young people and the very future of our country. In a recent announcement, the government of Ontario—Canada's most populated province—lays out the right wing's most recent battle cry, which is to introduce private, for-profit universities to Canada.

While the government of Ontario can generally be relied upon to defy reality in support of its radical conservative agenda, the Premier's announcement was especially surprising in its shallowness and its misrepresentation of the facts.

To build an argument, one must first lay down a series of facts, and this is where the government of Ontario failed most miserably. At the outset of his announcement, Premier Harris states: "There is not enough education choice in Canada when it comes to universities"—a statement so far removed from reality as to be laughable.

For the student seeking to enter a post-secondary institution, Canada offers as wide a range of choices as any country in the developed world: from the university-level courses offered at local community colleges across the country to regional universities such as the University of Northern British Columbia or Lakehead University, to major metropolitan learning centres like McGill University or the University of Toronto.

In fact, each year Maclean's—Canada's national political magazine—makes a great deal of its rating of Canadian universities, demonstrating that there's a vast array of choices for Canadian students. A system as diverse and accessible as Canada's is, by its very nature, competitive and fair; that's the whole point of universality. World-renowned centres of excellence have developed at universities across the country, a *real* fact which defies every aspect of the government of Ontario's argument.

But the Harris government's folly doesn't end there. The Premier then proceeds to build the main points of the government's argument on this shaky ground.

With reassuring words, we are told that private universities "will be open to the general public" and will "almost certainly have loans and scholarships available for students who can't afford normal tuition." How very kind of them.

What Harris is saying, between the lines, is that these schools will be open for anyone who can afford them. The offer of greater student debt to accommodate the occasional poor student is a sugar-coating for a bitter pill. Through the U.S. experience, we've learned that in only the rarest circumstances—or through the accumulation of massive debt— do the poor or even the middle class enter that country's élite private universities.

Harris also tells us that he's concerned about the number of Canadian students willing to move to the U.S. and pay high tuition fees at large private American universities. What the Premier doesn't recognize is that the creation of a few private universities and colleges in Ontario will do nothing to dissuade the wealthiest and brightest Canadians from attending élite private American institutions like Harvard and Yale. Instead, what will happen is that the new private universities and colleges in Ontario will seek to recruit middle-class students whose parents can either afford to fork over $45,000 a year in tuition or who are willing to incur huge debt loads.

The final point the government attempts to make should be called "the big lie." The Premier states that the private institutions will exist only to complement the public education system. This, of course, is nonsense. Once private universities are competing for funds, faculty and other resources with the public universities, there can only be a thinning of available resources.

The government's argument to the contrary must be based on some kind of voodoo economic theory that new money will suddenly appear from nowhere: the same money, perhaps, that the Ontario government has been diverting *from* post-secondary education.

Proponents of private universities and colleges like to cite, as an example of a success story, the case of Bond University in Australia. Bond University, attended by fewer than 2,000 students, is a vanity campus, named after the Bond Corporation which sponsors it. If this is the Ontario government's vision of our education future, then the Canadian equivalent would be a chain of universities sponsored and named after Dow or TSE 300 companies.

In that case, I don't look forward to the day when our children are taught by graduates of the Coca-Cola College, our surgeries are performed by alumni of Monsanto University, and our resources are administered by graduates of Wal-Mart U.

The reason this vision of the future of education is so frightening is that the private universities that the Ontario government proposes will not be accountable to the public. The "for profit" education system they propose would be accountable only to shareholders, alumni, and the special interests which have laid out sponsorship dollars.

The point the Ontario government wishes to ignore is that the public system which educated most Canadians is in large part responsible for the wealth that we enjoy as a country. From the UN recognition of our desirability as a place to live to the TSE's banner year, credit for the creation of wealth in this country should be given to its working people and the public system which helped them gain the skills to create that wealth.

That system is the very public education system that the Ontario government is now setting out to undermine.

If Premier Harris and his cabinet colleagues are genuinely concerned about ensuring the future quality of post-secondary education in Canada, they should be joining us in calling for the enhancement of the public education system which has brought us this far.

They should be joining us when we demand that federal and provincial governments quit starving our colleges and universities—instead of leading the call for even more cutting.

They should be joining us when we urge greater access to our colleges and universities so that more Canadians can have the skills they need to build a strong future for this country—instead of working to build a system which provides access only to the wealthy.

They should be joining us in a meaningful discussion about how we can improve the public education system, to make it more flexible, more progressive, and better equipped for this new millennium—instead of espousing half-truths about its "beautiful ivory towers."

Our nation and our economy were built on the skills and knowledge gained through an education system based on accessibility, affordability and quality. The way to build our future as a nation is to strengthen and enhance that system and to provide even greater numbers of Canadians with the skills to succeed.

To argue for anything less, as the Ontario government does, is to betray this country's future.

(James Clancy is National President of the National Union of Provincial and General Employees—www.nupge.ca)

Neoliberalism, corporate hegemony and the university

By William K. Carroll and James Beaton

> "I believe that our economic future depends on our ability to create, use and manage knowledge as effectively— more effectively—than the rest of the world...To do this, we need to unbundle our funding and allow universities to compete for research grants; we need to allow variation in tuition fees to promote institutional excellence; and we need to permit private institutions to play a role our university system. Let the market, not the government, determine which universities succeed and where our centres of excellence are."
> —Peter Godsoe, Chancellor of the University of Western Ontario and Chair and Chief Executive Officer, Scotiabank. Speech presented to the Canadian Club of Toronto, March 4, 1996.

As the statement above suggests, the modern university is facing a "survival of the fittest" mentality that favours intense competition for private investment, deregulation of fees, and public investment that is conditional upon industry partnerships. This thinking arises from a larger neoliberal ideology emphasizing minimal government intervention in private enterprise, an emphasis on the rights of the individual to acquire and exchange property, and individual responsibility for success or failure on the market.

As the market moves into the university and the university moves into the market, the distance between intellectual labour and business priorities narrows. Increasingly, faculty are required to meet performance standards showing their research can be used by industry or is of some economic utility. Research funding granting agencies look favourably upon industry partnerships. Students are increasingly viewed as "customers" who are purchasing an educational "product."

In this paper, we discuss the changing political-economic context in which universities operate and the involvement of corporations in universities.

The Invisible Hand and the Ivory Tower

In a globalized economy where competitiveness is key, all universities are equally considered sites for producing economically advantageous research or a skilled labour force for capital. The university is viewed by both industry and government as a key economic institution where precompetitive products are developed and transferred to industry, innovations and new technologies are patented and licensed, and industry relevant skill-sets are taught so graduates can be "job-ready" upon graduation.

Universities that have suffered from public funding decreases in the 1980s and 1990s are attempting to recoup their losses and grow financially through privatization and commercialization. This may involve increasing tuition, partnering with industry, forming spin-off companies, patenting and licensing inventions, and investing assets in the financial market.

Neoliberal regimes are moving away from the redistributive demand-side Keynesian/welfare role to promote economic development through supply-side strategies that emphasize corporate competitiveness and conditions for investment. A dynamic higher education sector is considered by business and government as important to attracting international investment and expanding into international markets. Research can render old ideas, technology and productive processes obsolete, thus allowing for a destruction of the old productive forces and the development of more competitive productive strategies.

Teaching is essential to ensuring that the labour is skilled. Given the importance of the universities to the productive capacities and profitability of capital, industry officials may feel as though they have to be involved in the management, culture and direction of the university.

Neoliberal policies define knowledge and research as exploitable commodities for private wealth rather than for the public good. Neoliberal discourse recasts the private interest as being the public good. Disciplines that are not overtly market-driven are justified on the basis of their benefits to the economy. The Liberal Arts are faced with market pressures and are increasingly justifying themselves on the basis of why criticism is good for business. The inability to justify a discipline in terms of the market or the needs of industry may mean a stagnant or reduced budget.

Corporate participation in the university

Governments at all levels are encouraging business partnerships in university teaching and research. Current federal and provincial policies are increasingly making significant portions of funding contingent upon the formation of corporate partnerships or achievement on industry-relevant performance indicators.

One important example at the federal level is the Canadian Foundation for Innovation (CFI). The specified mandate of this multi-million-dollar granting agency (its initial budget was $800 million) is to increase the "capability" of Canadian universities, colleges, hospitals, and other not-for-profit institutions in partnership with the private sector to conduct scientific and technological research and development (Martin 1997). Significantly, the receipt of the public funds is contingent upon private sector partnership.

There are numerous other examples at the federal and provincial levels where research and operational funding is increasingly conditional upon certain industry-relevant performance indicators and corporate partnerships.

While current state policy is facilitating corporate partnerships, it is also likely that the state retrenchment initiated in the 1980s has facilitated the university's turn to business and market forces as both a guiding force for decision-making and source of revenue. Universities have begun massive fund-raising campaigns, probably facilitated by corporate representation on governing boards. For instance, the "Great Minds for a Great Future Campaign" at the University of Toronto aims to raise a minimum of $575 million by 2002. As of 1999, the campaign team had raised over $481 million (University of Toronto Annual Report, 1999). The campaign executive represents such business luminaries as Tony Comper (CEO of the Bank of Monreal), Charles Baillie (CEO of Toronto-Dominion Bank), Al Flood (Chair of the Executive Committee of the Canadian Imperial Bank of Commerce), Peter Munk (Chair of Barrick Gold), and former Ontario Premiers William Davis and David Peterson.

Campaign teams can be thought of as points of connection between universities and corporations. However, university boards of governors are also important and influential in that they control the financial resources of the university. For this reason, representation on the board of governors becomes a matter of concern. The changing social composition of governing boards is indicative of a changing balance of power between intellectuals, administrators, and economic and political élites as shifts in class power create spaces for business to transform the process of teaching and research (Barrow 1994: 250).

The transformation ultimately involves an ideological control that becomes embedded within the normative values of the corporate ideal (ibid: 250-251). When corporate officials sit on university boards, they not only have a forum to represent business concerns to the university, but they can also import a particular way of thinking into the decisions of where to allocate resources and raise revenue. Many decisions that were once made by faculty are now centralized to management. This major transformation in the university is referred to as a "budget-based rationality" (Newson 1994).

In our research on corporate participation on university boards, data were gathered for the top 250 corporations, corporate directors and university board members for 1976 and 1996. Between those years, the *dominant stratum* of the corporate elite—individuals who direct two or more Top 250 firms—shrank by 12%, from 485 people to 425. But, despite this decrease in the total number of corporate linkers, the number of corporate linkers active on university boards—whom we call *university linkers*—remained constant, at 52; thus as a proportion of all corporate linkers, those engaged in university governance increased modestly, from 11% to 12%.

The three academics serving on university and corporate boards in 1996 are presidents of their respective institutions, signalling a trend in which university administrators are reaching out to dominant corporations. Whereas in 1976 university presidents did not serve on multiple boards of dominant corporations, by 1996 this internally-generated relation had become an established practice for university chief administrators.

In both years, as Table 1 shows, a majority of the university linkers were *function-*

ing capitalists, that is, insiders (executives or board chairs) of corporations. But there is also a shift to a greater representation of outside directors (31%) in 1996. Moreover, whereas in 1976 nearly all of the outside directors were corporate lawyers, by 1996 the outside corporate directors take in a greater range of occupations, including academic advisors, consultants and *eminence grise*. Such *organic intellectuals*—not themselves capitalists but implicated both in the accumulation process (through their multiple corporate directorships) as well as in the governance of universities—may be said to mediate the relation between capital and universities.

Another angle from which to view this changing network is to consider which economic sectors of corporate capital are represented by their executives on university boards. Here, our cases include all the corporate-university linkers who held an executive position in a corporation, regardless of whether the firm was big enough for the Top 250. Table 2 shows a definite shift from heavy representation of industry on university boards to greater presence of capitalists primarily engaged in investment companies. In particular, by 1996 there are fewer university linkers from the primary and secondary industrial sectors, and more from utilities/communication companies and especially investment companies.

Executives in major investment companies, who control productive capital through ownership of financial paper (typically as strategic blocs of share capital), might well be considered prime candidates for university governance, as these beleaguered public institutions turn to private funding sources. In effect, we find evidence here of transition from an era in which the top layer of the capitalist class was represented predominantly by leading lights of industrial capital to one in which "post-industrial" paper entrepreneurship finds a stronger presence in university governance.

In addressing the question of the differences in corporate representation among the universities, Table 3 displays in its first two columns the number of university linkers who participate in the governance of each university in our sample. There is, in accordance with previous research, enor-

Table 1: University linkers by principal occupation

Principal occupation	1976	1996
Top 250 executive	50	44
Other executive	35	25
Legal advisor	10	12
Academic advisor	2	6
Consultant	0	6
Eminence grise (retired officials)	0	6
State official	0	0
Other outsider	4	2

Table 2: University linkers grouped by economic sector of their home corporation

Economic Sector	1976	1996
Primary industry	12	3
Manufacturing	34	20
Utilities/communication	10	14
Commerce	7	9
Financial intermediation	24	23
Investment companies	10	31
Property Development	2	0
Other	0	0

Table 3: Corporate linkers and corporate contacts for university governing boards

University	Number of linkers 1976	Number of linkers 1996	Numbers of corporations 1976	Numbers of corporations 1996
York	8	9	31	25
Montreal	1	9	3	19
McGill	5	5	19	20
Toronto	4	3	9	11
New Brunswick	0	3	0	8
British Columbia	0	3	0	7
Alberta	0	3	0	11
Dalhousie	6	3	17	6
Queens	9	2	33	10
Concordia	2	2	4	4
Calgary	2	2	4	10
Simon Fraser	0	2	0	5
McMaster	8	1	23	2
Western Ontario	3	1	12	2
Guelph	1	1	3	2
Waterloo	1	1	4	2
Ryerson	1	1	3	10
Laval	0	1	0	9
Manitoba	0	1	0	2
Carleton	1	0	3	2
Bipartite Density			0.04	0.03

mous variation between institutions: four universities have no corporate linkers on their boards in either year, (Memorial University of Newfoundland, University of Ottawa, University of Saskatchewan and University of Victoria); York and McGill have five or more in each year. Dalhousie and Toronto also have several corporate linkers on their boards in both years. Hence, three long-established schools, including the two major upper-class anglophone universities in the metropoli of Montreal and Toronto, have maintained a range of corporate connections via their governing boards.

York's strong ties to corporate capital date from its inception as a project behind which Toronto-based capital mobilized in the late 1950s (Axelrod, 1982). Yet there is also an interesting redistribution of linkers—from the concentration of linkers on the boards of a few key universities in the heartland of post-war corporate capital and at the heart of the Canadian bourgeoisie as a social class (the two major Toronto universities, anglophone Montreal, Queens, McMaster, Dalhousie)—to a more dispersed network that takes in a *greater range* of schools, and of regions.

In 1976, only 14 of the 24 universities had corporate interlockers on their boards and five boards claimed 36 of the 52 linkers. By 1996, 19 universities had recruited corporate linkers to their boards, and the leading five claimed 29.

The redistribution of university linkers points up several changes: 1) a decline in corporate representation on some university boards—most stunningly Queens and McMaster, but also Dalhousie; 2) increased presence of corporate linkers on the boards of universities in western Canada, as corporate head offices have moved westward; 3) increased representation on the UNB board; and 4) increased representation on two major francophone universities, which were quite marginal to the corporate-university network in 1976—particularly Université de Montréal.

UNB presents a good example of the shift from isolation to corporate integration. The list of university governors from the

1976-77 UNB Calendar makes it clear that at that time board members were local municipal leaders and the like; there was no apparent strategy of seeking or maintaining corporate representation. Yet by 1996 there are three corporate linkers on the board, including the university president, as well as the scion of Toronto's Eaton family, Fredrik Eaton. For UNB, this means a major shift in corporate contacts, as each linker serving on the board generates multiple ties to the largest Canadian corporations. In this way, the UNB board moves from having no ties to corporate capital to having direct contact with eight major corporations **(see the last two columns of Table 3)**.

Comparing across the decades, then, we find that: 1) the network becomes *more inclusive* of universities in Western Canada (Calgary, UBC), eastern Canada (UNB) and French Canada (Montréal, also Laval); and 2) except for York, McGill and Toronto, there is considerable shifting in the extent to which members of the dominant stratum participate on university boards.

Table 4 shows the differences in the degree to which sectors of corporate capital participate in university governance. Considering the mean number of universities with which corporations have board-level ties, the declining prominence of financial institutions is striking. In 1976, the 50 leading financial institutions were on average tied to 1.34 of the 24 universities—far more than other corporations; but by 1996 their average is indistinguishable from several other sectors, including investment companies. This pattern fits with the argument that since the 1970s there has been a recomposition of corporate capital in Canada, with the chartered banks and widely-held life insurers now playing less central roles as mediators of particular in-

Table 4: Mean number of university contacts for top 250 corporations grouped by economic sector, 1976 and 1996

	1976	1996
Resources	.52	.85
Manufacturing	.49	.54
Utilities-communication	.83	.84
Financial intermediation	1.34	.82
Investment companies	.72	.87
Trade	.27	.30
Real estate	.00	.00
Other	1.00	.38
All companies	.65	.64
Eta	.128	.035

Table 5: Mean number of university contacts for top 250 corporations grouped by nationality of control, 1976 and 1996

	1976	1996
Canada	.93	.79
USA	.34	.22
Other American	.00	1.00
Britain	.50	.80
France	.25	.33
Germany	.00	.00
Netherlands	.25	.00
Other European	.00	1.00
New Zealand	.00	1.00
Japan	.00	.25
Hong Kong	.00	.50
Other Asia	.00	.00
South Asia	.00	.50
Eta squared	.086	.066

terests, as certain family-based empires such as that of the Desmaraises take up more central positions through their investment companies and financial conglomerates (Carroll and Lewis, 1991).

In a similar vein, Table 5 compares the mean number of ties to universities for Canadian-controlled and foreign-controlled companies. In 1976, Canadian-controlled firms had substantially more directorate ties to universities, but by 1996 this difference had attenuated somewhat. Interestingly, U.S.-controlled firms also show a drop in their already sparse ties to universities, suggesting that economic continentalization is not propelling American-controlled corporations toward increased contacts with Canadian universities. Instead, it is other foreign-controlled companies—whose controlling interests are in Britain or the Pacific Rim—that show a small increase in board-level ties to universities. This development seems consistent with *an incipient globalization of capital relations*—especially as regards the increased (though still quite modest) involvement of Asian-Pacific capital in the corporate-university network.

By way of conclusion, and in the spirit of the largely empirical character of this study, we shall restrict ourselves to recapitulating the main findings and their immediate substantive implications. Three points stand out in particular. Firstly, although we find no increase in the dominant stratum's overall presence on university boards, there is evidence of increased ties emanating from inside universities as major university presidents become members of the corporate élite's dominant stratum. By 1996 it had become an established practice for university presidents to serve on multiple corporate boards.

Such ties may indicate a deepening of corporate-university relations, as chief executive officers of universities and corporations rub shoulders in corporate boardrooms and participate in a common managerial culture.

Secondly, although the overall incidence of corporate-university interlocking remained stable during the two decades, there are several senses in which these relations became more *inclusive*. This is evident in the spatial distribution of university linkers, which by 1996 spanned most of the country. It is evident in the number of universities whose boards include one or more members of the dominant stratum. It is evident in the increased number of organic intellectuals who knit together universities and corporations through their participation in governing both— whether they be retired politicians, active university presidents, or other advisors to corporate capital. All this points to a broader class hegemony, as the persuasive force of corporate-capitalist priorities is registered more widely, rather than being largely ensconced within the boards of a few élite institutions.

The new liberalism is indeed a move away from old-style élitist conservatism. In the neoliberal world, all universities are equally considered sites for producing factors of production in the quest for international competitiveness, and most university boards now include one or more member of corporate capital's dominant stratum.

A more inclusive hegemony might well be more persuasive in some quarters, but those committed to alternative visions of higher education can also point to broadened corporate involvement as an anti-democratic tendency as the corporate ideal displaces other possibilities of the university.

Thirdly, this research illustrates how corporate-university relations have evolved with the changing character of the Canadian political economy. State retrenchment beginning in the 1980s has led to major changes, which include a turn by universities to massive fundraising campaigns. In addition to retrenchment, many governments have made funding conditional upon forming business partnerships and satisfying performance requirements in terms of market and industry relevance. Deregulation of the financial sector has weakened the preeminence of chartered banks as central nodes in corporate finance and in directorate interlocking (Carroll and Lewis 1991), while corporate takeovers issued in a new wave of investment companies, some of whose executives have been recruited to university boards, possibly in appreciation of their prowess in raising and multiplying funds.

The rise of high-tech companies since the 1970s adds a further nuance to the picture, as it is directors of domestically-controlled high-tech companies who show an elective affinity for university governance. However, among dominant companies as a whole, the tendency for domestically-controlled corporations to be linked to universities at the board level has attenuated slightly as the growing number of large firms controlled in the Pacific Rim (and in Britain) have modestly increased their representation on university boards, suggesting that incipient circuits of global accumulation may be laying the basis for closer international integration of corporate elites on issues of higher education.

(William Carroll is a professor of sociology at the University of Victoria. James Beaton is a doctoral student in sociology at York University.)

References

Axelrod, Paul. 1982. *Scholars and Dollars: Politics, Economics, and the Universities of Ontario 1945-1980*. University of Toronto Press. Toronto.

Barrow, Clyde W. 1990. *Universities and the Capitalist State: Corporate Liberalism and the Reconstruction of American Higher Education, 1894-1928*. Toronto. The University of Wisconsin Press.

Carroll, William K. 1986. *Corporate Power and Canadian Capitalism*. University of British Columbia Press. Vancouver.

Carroll, William K. 1993. "Canada in the crisis: Transformations in capital structure and political strategy," in Henk Overbeek (ed.), *Restructuring Hegemony in the Global Political Economy*. London: Routledge, pp. 216-45.

Carroll, William K. 1996. "Globalization and the recomposition of corporate capital: A cross-national study." Research Proposal to Social Sciences and Humanities Research Council of Canada, with Malcolm Alexander and Meindert Fennema as international collaborators.

Carroll, William K., and James Beaton. 2000. "Globalization, Neo-liberalism and the Changing face of Corporate Hegemony in Canada," *Studies in Political Economy* 62, Summer 2000, 71-98.

Carroll, William K., and Scott Lewis. 1991. "Restructuring finance capital: Changes in the Canadian corporate network 1976-1986," *Sociology* 25 (3), 491-510.

Godsoe, Peter. 1996. "Canadian Universities: Competing to Win". Address to the Canadian Club March 4. Scotiabank.

Gramsci, Antonio. 1971. *Selections from the Prison Notebooks*. New York: International Publishers.

Hatzichronoglou, Thomas. 1997. "Revision of the high-technology sector and product classification." STI Working Paper 1997/2, Organization for Economic Co-operation and Development, Paris.

Martin, Paul. 1997. *Budget Speech 1997*. Ministry of Finance. Government of Canada.

Newson, Janice A. 1994. "Subordinating democracy: The effects of fiscal retrenchment and university-business partnerships on knowledge creation and knowledge dissemination in universities." *Higher Education* 27: 141-161.

Niosi, Jorge. 1978. *The Economy of Canada*. Montreal: Black Rose Books.

Niosi, Jorge. 1981. *Canadian Capitalism*. Toronto: James Lorimer.

Ornstein, Michael. 1976. "The boards and directors of the largest Canadian corporations: Size, composition, and interlocks." *Canadian Journal of Sociology* 1, pp. 411-37.

Ornstein, Michael. 1988. "Corporate Involvement in Canadian hospital and university boards, 1946-1977", *Canadian Review of Sociology and Anthropology* 25(3).pp 365-388.

Ornstein, Michael. 1989. "The social organization of the capitalist class in comparative perspective." *Canadian Review of Sociology and Anthropology* 26: 151-77.

University of Toronto. 1999. *University of Toronto Annual Report, 1999*, University of Toronto, Ontario, (http://www.utoronto.ca).

Whither education for citizenship in a globalized, free market world?

By Bernie Froese-Germain

Shifting education goals

A fundamental shift is occurring with respect to the goals of public education—a shift taking place at all levels of education. In short, the trend is one of education for, and through, the market (and consequently, away from education for democratic citizenship). This is education tailored to serve the needs of the market for consumers and workers, and increasingly delivered through competition-inducing market mechanisms such as charter schools and vouchers.

The signs of this shift in reconceptualizing the major goals of education are prevalent and going largely unquestioned:

- In his address to the *Congress on Educating Active Citizens* held in Victoria last year, Ken Osborne (1999a) remarked that the policy statements and other education pronouncements coming out of the ministries of education of all political parties are heavily laced with terms such as "skilled and adaptable workers", "entrepreneurship and innovation", "economic growth", and "competitive global environment."

- The report of a federal advisory panel on skills (entitled *Stepping Up: Skills and Opportunities in the Knowledge Economy*) found that a major challenge facing Canadians is that our "attitudes toward entrepreneurship, risk taking and success are not changing fast enough." To address this 'concern', it recommends that Canadian schools teach 'the basic concepts of risk management, innovation and entrepreneurship,' and that "all levels of the education system—from elementary to post-secondary—have a contribution to make toward the development of a more competitive, entrepreneurial culture." (Galt, 2000)

Perhaps the most absurd expression of this entrepreneurial mindset in recent memory was the proposal, rejected by the Alberta government in 1998, to start a charter school of commerce for young children. It promised anxious parents a number of features to give their kids a leg up in the highly competitive global economy, including a curriculum in which commerce is the central theme throughout all subject areas.

- In 1999, another federal advisory panel—the Expert Panel on the Commercialization of University Research—issued a report whose recommendations, according to the Canadian Association of University Teachers (1999), "encourage the steering of research toward the commercial interests of private corporations, undermine the tradition of open communication between scholars, and provide for the expropriation of the results of university research to the corporate sector." The CAUT also notes that the panel "blithely presents the interests of Canada and those of private corporations as one and the same."

- Education is increasingly being viewed as a business like any other. Indeed, education as a profitable, exportable commodity is an explicit goal of the federal government's education strategy. In a presentation to the second annual Canadian Education Industry Summit, a conference convened in October 1998 to promote privatization and investment in the education-for-profit industry, Sergio Marchi, federal Minister for International Trade, told participants that, not so long ago, the term "education industry" would have been unthinkable. But now we do see education as an industry, and today you have examined the incredible array of opportunities it offers. And because education is an industry, we need to bring the same discipline and approaches to it that we have to more traditional industries. (Proceedings of the Second Annual Canadian Education Industry Summit)

The federal government's presence at a conference promoting education privatization did not go unnoticed. It was strongly criticized by a coalition of public interest groups and public education supporters.

- On the international scene, organizations such as Asian Pacific Economic Cooperation (APEC) and the Organization for Economic Cooperation and Development (OECD) have a powerful influence on the education systems of member as well as non-member countries. As Kuehn (1999) observes, the OECD's system of education indicators (on which the CMEC's Pan-Canadian Education Indicators Program is modelled) is "largely focused on elements of education that are seen as developing 'human capital' and thus making a contribution to economic growth" (p.118), to the detriment of socio-cultural education objectives.

Kuehn also notes that the Program for International Student Assessment (PISA), recently established by the OECD to measure and report on student achievement in reading, math and science—subject areas considered essential for career preparation and which parallel the CMEC's School Achievement Indicators Program (SAIP) assessments—dovetails nicely with this human capital-based approach to education.

- On more than one occasion, Ontario Premier Mike Harris has made public statements devaluing a liberal arts education in favour of a focus on math, science and technology programs to better prepare students for jobs. The premier's comments reveal a profound misunderstanding of the fundamental difference between education and training, and illustrate that the line between them is becoming blurred in people's minds—certainly in the minds of politicians. At a recent CAUT conference on the commercialization of higher education, Noble (2000) offered this conceptual distinction between education and training:

In essence, training involves the honing of a person's mind so that that mind can be used for the purposes of someone other than that person. Training thus typically entails a radical divorce between knowledge and the self. Here knowledge is usually defined as a set of skills or a body of information designed to be put to use, to become operational, only in a context determined by someone other than the trained person; in this context the assertion of self is not only counter-productive, it is subversive to the enterprise. Education is the exact opposite of training in that it entails not the disassociation but the utter integration of knowledge and the self: in a word, self-knowledge. Here knowledge is defined by and, in turn, helps to define, the self. Knowledge and the knowledgeable person are basically inseparable. (p. 101)

In keeping with the thrust of Harris's message, the Ontario government, in the name of 'accountability', is considering tying a portion of post-secondary education funding to the labour market success of university graduates: how many and how quickly graduates find jobs in each discipline, average starting salaries, etc. Alberta is already using such 'performance indicators' to determine some percentage of higher education funding.

In such an environment, one might ask: what are the prospects for a broader, more balanced education for citizenship?

Education for citizenship and democracy

It is significant that, up until the past decade or so, educating students for citizenship was still very much at the core of what public education was all about in Canada (Osborne, 1998/99). We seem to have lost sight of this ideal as the education focus rapidly shifts from creating citizens to producing workers.

So what exactly do we mean when we talk about citizenship education? Or, perhaps more to the point, what do we mean by citizenship?

Citizenship is a complex and continually evolving concept. Any attempt to conceptualize it (and hence to conceptualize citizenship education) must be informed by numerous contextual factors. Contemporary Canadian society is rapidly changing, pluralistic in every sense of the word—religious, racial, ethnic, linguistic, cultural. Our post-modern, post-industrial 21st century world is consumed by transformative economic, social and political change. Powerful forces are tearing at the nation state, resulting in a 'borderless' world thrust upon us by globalization on the one hand, and by increasing fragmentation caused by tribalism on the other: what Benjamin Barber has described as "Jihad vs. McWorld". Kingwell (2000) believes we need to rethink our ideas about citizenship in the context of the injustice of global markets and the banality of global culture, and work towards defining a "global politics to balance and give meaning to these troubling universal realities." (p. 23)

Over the last century, approaches to citizenship education in Canada have evolved in tandem with changes to the concept of citizenship. According to Osborne (1998/99), as assimilation gave way to multiculturalism; unilingualism to bilingualism; uniformity to diversity .... [B]y the 1970s, Canadian citizenship had come to consist of six principal elements. It aimed to give students, first, a sense of identity as Canadians but also as citizens of the world; second, an awareness of and respect for human rights; third, an acceptance of the responsibilities and obligations of citizenship; fourth, a reflective commitment to broad social values; fifth, the capacity to participate in public life; and sixth, the ability to think about and act intelligently on the implications of all five of these elements. (p.17)

Sears and Hughes (1996) acknowledge that no consensus exists about the meaning of citizenship education because citizenship itself is a "contested concept" (p.124). In their typology, they describe a spectrum ranging from élitist and passive conceptions of citizenship education (i.e., the workings of our parliamentary democracy and electoral system, the right to vote) to more activist conceptions. In the latter vein, some observers advocate the need for a participatory, intentional citizenship which combines critical thinking with "critical doing."

Clark and Case (1999) further refine the analysis. Taking as their starting point that citizenship is and should be the primary focus of social studies, they describe a citizenship education matrix consisting of four 'camps' located along two intersecting axes. The camps are:

- citizenship education as social initiation: passing on the understandings, abilities and values that students require if they are to fit into and be productive members of society;

- citizenship education as social reformation: empowering students with the understandings, abilities and values necessary to critique and ultimately improve their society;

- citizenship education as personal development: fostering students' personal competencies and interests so that they develop fully as individuals and as social beings;

- citizenship education as academic understanding: promoting mastery of the bodies of knowledge and forms of inquiry represented in the social science disciplines so that students have at their disposal the most sophisticated means to make sense of the complex world they face.

The authors explain that the *social initiation* and *social reformation* camps represent a range of positions along a social acceptance/social change axis such that, "at one extreme, the point of citizenship education is to promote complete conformity with mainstream social norms and practices; at the other extreme, it is to promote total transformation of the social fabric."

Similarly, the *personal development* and *academic understanding* camps represent a range of positions along a subject-centred/student-centred axis such that, "at one extreme is a view that the best form of citizenship preparation is achieved by nurturing the whole child by focusing exclusively on students' interests, concerns, problems, values and so on; at the other extreme, the best form of citizenship preparation is thought to be achieved by disciplining the mind exclusively through exposure to the bodies of knowledge and forms of reasoning found in the social sciences." (Clark & Case, pp. 19-20) This conceptual framework attempts to capture the diversity of perspectives on citizenship education.

The multi-faceted nature of citizenship education makes it a malleable concept which can be conveniently interpreted to suit particular needs. Wall (2000) found, for example, that among the motivations for the resurgent interest in citizenship education is to "promote citizenship supportive of a free market economy" (p.8). On this point Sears and Hughes (1996) remark that,

In the current round of educational reform...the emphasis is on 'perceived economic priorities' and 'little has been said about citizenship" (Osborne, 1992, p.375) except, perhaps, that good citizens pay their own way, contribute to the nation's economic well-being, and ensure success in the international marketplace. This is hardly citizenship 'in the widest sense of the term,' as Conley calls for: it is citizenship downgraded and down-sized, if not totally dismissed. (p. 123)

This is a serious distortion of the concept as it is generally understood.

Whose story makes history? The debate over history teaching

The teaching of history has become a political and ideological flashpoint in all of this, given its role as the traditional instructional 'home' for citizenship education.

Much of the history debate revolves around fundamental questions such as what history should we be teaching (conventional political, constitutional, military history vs. social history), how should it be taught (chronological ordering of facts and events assessed by standardized tests vs. the nurturance of critical and creative thinking), and why should it be taught and studied?

Osborne (2000) provides a good synopsis of some of the key issues in the debate. He attributes Jack Granatstein's controversial 1998 book *Who Killed Canadian History?* with launching a renewed debate about the teaching of history in Canadian classrooms.

It provided the impetus for corporate-sponsored initiatives such as the Dominion Institute and more recently, the Historica Foundation (which has an endowment of $10 million and counting). The brain-child of Lynton (Red) Wilson, chairman of Bell Canada Enterprises Inc., Historica was set up to promote the teaching of history through popular media (television, the Internet) in order to fill a perceived gap in students' history knowledge.

This perception is fueled in part by the Dominion Institute's simplistic history surveys, results of which have been widely reported in the media (critics of this exercise describe it as "a dangerous game of trivial pursuit of civics knowledge" (McKay, 1998)). Commenting on Historica, the following quote from a Quebec journalist (cited in Pitts, 1999) illustrates the difficult and divisive path that lies ahead for those anxious to document the 'official' version of our national story. The message is, 'don't go there':

> 'This temple of official history would certainly give birth to the mother of all quarrels—with aboriginals, unions, immigrants, ethnic groups, classes, political parties...BCE and the Bronfman Foundation are putting their finger in a wasp's nest if their goal is to establish an official, genuine History of Canada.'

While Granatstein and Osborne may start from the same place —that history teaching in the schools is of critical importance— they differ markedly on what and why history should be taught. Osborne (2000) notes, not without some irony, that the "most striking aspect of the debate [about history teaching] is its total lack of historical context." He describes five distinct Canadian "history crises" dating back to the 1890s (Granatstein's book being a catalyst for the current crisis), which he says "identified the same problems—boring, divisive or unknown history—and came up with the same solutions: national curricula or national standards," solutions which he notes "are unlikely to be effective." Indeed, Osborne (2000) states that the "[nation-building] vision of history teaching that held sway for much of the 20th century …...had little noticeable effect on national unity."

Although denied by Historica Executive Director, Tom Axworthy, the national unity agenda appears to be a strong factor motivating the renewed interest by the business community, among others, in history and citizenship education. In its operational plan, Historica is explicit about its intention to "support efforts that foster a national Canadian history curriculum" and to "work with the Council of Ministers of Education in developing a pan-Canadian civics curriculum"—in other words, promoting a 'shared narrative' focused on nation-building as part of a national curriculum (given the political sensitivities involved, the CMEC is no longer moving ahead on this front) (Wall, 2000). Webster (2000) captures the corporate sector's reaction to the 1995 Quebec referendum results in this vivid description:

> Quite a few powerful businessmen must have woken up on the morning after the referendum thinking Canadian history looked less like a big

snowy map sprinkled with obscure dates and places and much more like a blood-stained spreadsheet. (p.30)

Witness also Prime Minister Chrétien's not-so-subtle remark that, "If history were better taught, the country would be healthier. No doubt about it." (Osborne, 2000). Not only are schools viewed as the key to our global economic competitiveness, it seems they are also perceived by some as the cause of—and solution to—our national unity woes. Osborne (1999b) believes that using history to bolster national unity is ultimately misguided, noting that,

The teacher's task is to help students understand the kind of country they live in, not to preach national unanimity... Appeals to national unity can be used to steamroller local traditions and cultures and to stifle dissent...The Canadian history teacher must be able to show students how Canada seeks to reconcile unity with diversity.

Rather than impose external controls in the guise of national standards and a national curriculum, Osborne (2000) proposes a two-pronged approach to ameliorate history teaching: improve the quality of history curricula, beginning with a "sustained public debate," and improve the quality of teaching through enhanced working conditions which allow teachers "time to read and reflect and strengthen their understanding of history as a discipline."

Re-connecting the dots

While connections among concepts such as public education, democracy, the public good, equity and citizenship may have been self-evident in the past, this no longer appears to hold true. These relationships bear restating given their significance: in essence, strong democratic societies require informed, committed, active citizens and, as Booi reminds us, "democracy emphasizes the importance of *all* citizens and of rule by *all* the people." (p.41)

A strong system of public education, rooted in the principles of equity, universality and accountability, is essential to the preservation and promotion of democracy because citizenship is fostered in large part through our public schools. Educators have a responsibility to re-establish these fundamental relationships in the public mind.

A little knowledge of Canadian history sheds some light on these connections. In discussing the origins of public education, Saul (2000) notes that, lest we forget, "a fully funded, universal public school system [was and continues to be] the key to our functioning democracy." (p.A14) Osborne (1999a) reminds us that "public education in Canada, as in other countries, began as preparation for citizenship." (p.3)

Unfortunately, the goal of educating for citizenship is being severely compromised by education reforms which are eating away at the fundamental principles of democracy embedded in the public education system. These reforms include:

- an over-reliance on private sector funding fuelled by cutbacks to the public funding base (Shaker (2000) describes private sector initiatives such as the Youth News Network as "strategic corporate philanthropy");
- a drastic reduction in the number and power of school boards—in favour of

unelected parent councils—thereby undermining the long-standing system of local governance of schools by individuals who are democratically elected and publicly accountable;

- measurement-driven, outcomes-based accountability which is woefully inadequate to effectively assess the objectives of citizenship education; and

- increasing commercialism and privatization, and the trend toward market-based reforms which remove education from the public domain.

As Osborne (1998/99) describes it,

> We no longer see students as citizens but as workers. We value not citizenship and the society that sustains it, but economic success in the global economy. The week before I wrote these words, my local newspaper featured statements from 39 candidates in elections for surrounding school boards. It is perhaps not surprising that, of the 39, the great majority spoke of computers, high-tech, the global economy, excellence, and the other educational buzz-words of the moment, and only two even mentioned the word citizenship. It is in this climate that schools are urged to form partnerships with business, that literature is downgraded to literacy, that history disappears from the curriculum, that knowledge and appreciation are abandoned for skills, that understanding is reduced to performance standards, attainment targets, and intended learning outcomes. (pp.16-17)

The citizenship education debate is one which goes to the very heart of the goals of education. According to Labaree (1997), analyses of the causes of problems with U.S. schools range from the pedagogical and organizational to the social and cultural. While these are important, he believes that the

> central problems with American education are fundamentally *political*. That is, the problem is not that we do not know how to make schools better, but that we are fighting among ourselves about what goals schools should pursue. Goal-setting is a political, and not a technical, problem. (p.40)

Toward this end, he goes on to describe several competing visions of the goals of education in the U.S. Briefly, these goals are:

- education for democratic equality: schools should focus on preparing citizens to serve the needs of democracy and the common good; this goal "expresses the politics of citizenship" and views education as a "purely public good";

- education for social efficiency: schools should focus on training workers for a competitive marketplace; this goal "expresses the politics of human capital" and views education as a "public good in service to the private sector," providing economic benefits to society;

- education for social mobility: schools should prepare individuals to compete for social advantage; this goal "expresses the politics of individual opportunity" and views education as a purely "private good for personal consumption." (pp.42-43)

Labaree argues convincingly that the latter two market-oriented goals have combined to seriously erode the goal of education for democratic equality. He is particularly critical of the social mobility goal which has come to dominate the others, with some negative consequences for the shaping of American education. As he notes, "if education is indeed a private good, then the next step (according to the influential right wing in today's educational politics) is to withdraw public control entirely and move toward a fully privatized system of education." (p.73)

As highlighted in the introduction, Canadians are also struggling with educational goals. Osborne (1999a) describes what he sees as a growing imbalance in the social, cultural and economic goals of education.

Educators' voice in the debate

If restoring a sense of balance—even recapturing citizenship as an all-encompassing goal of education—is to become a priority, it cannot occur without the involvement of teachers.

The teaching profession faces several critical issues in this regard. To start, teachers must add their collective voice to the current discussion. The profession needs to articulate its understandings of, and approaches to, both citizenship and citizenship education. A useful starting point for this discussion (for both teachers and the public) might be a series of questions posed in a discussion paper by Caplan for the CMEC Third National Forum on Education held in May 1998:

- What can schools realistically do to help prepare children for life and responsible citizenship?
- Are there commonly shared Canadian values that schools should be trying to transmit to students?
- What impact are business values and priorities having in shaping the outlook of today's students?

Citizenship education must receive priority in the curriculum (including, but certainly not limited to, history and social studies courses and programs), and more broadly within the goals of education. Equally important, any meaningful approach to citizenship education cannot be compromised by the means of assessment— i.e., standardized tests of the multiple choice/fill-in-the-blanks variety.

As they say in the vernacular, schools need to "walk the talk." In addition to looking at curriculum and instructional approaches, other important aspects of education must come under scrutiny, including the organization and governance of schools, and broader school-community relations (Cogan & Dericott, 1998).

The notion of a passive versus active orientation to citizenship, alluded to earlier, must also be addressed. The latter approach strives to create "intentional citizens" capable of both critical thinking and its corollary, "critical doing."

How the profession resolves these and other issues will clearly have important implications for the teaching of citizenship education in our schools. At present, the dominant players in the debate are the academic and research communities (including the Citizenship Education Research Network and the McGill Institute for the Study of Canada) and the corporate sector (Historica, Dominion Institute, C.R. Bronfman Foundation).

Teachers and their organizations are beginning to enter the fray. One recent initiative is a project by the Canadian Teachers' Federation called *Living Democracy: Renewing Our Vision of Citizenship Education*, a major objective of which is to engage the profession, as well as the broader community, in this important dialogue.

Canadian educators are committed to a broader and more balanced vision of the role of public education in our society. They want to ensure that the goal of education for democracy doesn't get drowned out in the din over the other competing goals of education. Their involvement in this debate is critical, particularly at a time when the utilitarian, instrumental version of education predominates.

Missing Pieces, the title of this volume, may be more apropos for this article than I originally thought. Education for democracy, arguably more necessary than ever, may end up becoming a critical piece of what is pushed aside in our schools as we restructure education to satisfy the corporate rather than the broad public interest. It's a little unsettling to note that, in a slick popular ad campaign with the slogan "I am Canadian", one beer corporation seems to be equating Canadian identity with consuming its product. We mustn't allow the goal of educating for citizenship to be reduced to a form of "education for citizenshop."

(Bernie Froese-Germain is an Ottawa-based education researcher and writer.)

References

Booi, L. (2000, Summer). "Public Education, Democracy and Equity." *ATA Magazine*, 80(3), p. 41.

Canadian Association of University Teachers. (1999, Sept. 30). *CAUT Commentary on The Final Report of the Expert Panel on the Commercialization of University Research*. Ottawa. Available online at: http://www.caut.ca/English/CAUTframe.html

Caplan, G. (1998, March 30). *Good Schools, Good Citizens: A Discussion*. Reference document coordinated by the Canadian Teachers' Federation for the sub-theme on "Transitions Into and Through the School Systems", CMEC Third National Forum on Education, St. John's, Newfoundland, May 28-30, 1998. Available online at: http://www.cmec.ca/nafored/english/ctf.stm

Clark, P., & Case, R. (1999). "Four Purposes of Citizenship Education." In R. Case & P. Clark (Eds.), *The Canadian Anthology of Social Studies: Issues and Strategies for Teachers* (pp. 17-27). Vancouver, BC: Pacific Press.

Cogan, J. J., & Dericott, R. (Eds.). (1998). *Citizenship for the 21st Century: An International Perspective on Education*. Sterling, VA: Stylus Publishing.

Galt, V. (2000, Jan. 26). "Panel Advises Teaching Kids Business Basics." *Globe and Mail*.

Historica (undated). "Operational Plan Executive Summary." Available online at: http://www.histori.ca/historica/eng_site/about/plan.html

Kingwell, M. (2000, Sept./Oct.). "The Accidental Citizen: Rethinking Civic Membership in the Age of Globalization." *This Magazine*, p. 23.

Kuehn, L. (1999, June). "Globalization and the Control of Teachers' Work: The Role of the OECD Indicators." *Our Schools/Our Selves*, 9(6), #60, pp. 117-129.

Labaree, D. F. (1997, Spring). "Public Goods, Private Goods: The American Struggle Over Educational Goals." *American Educational Research Journal*, 34(1), pp. 39-81.

McKay, R. (1998, Summer). "The Trivial Pursuit of Civics Knowledge: A Dangerous Game." *Canadian Social Studies*, 32(4), p. 113.

Noble, D. F. (2000). "Digital Diploma Mills: Rehearsal for the Revolution." In J. L. Turk, *The Corporate Campus: Commercialization and the Dangers to Canada's Colleges and Universities*. A CAUT Series Title. Toronto: Lorimer & Co.

Osborne, K. (2000, May 27). "Who Killed Granatstein's Sense of History? Misguided Criticisms." *National Post*, pp. B1, B3.

Osborne, K. (1999a). "Fostering Educated and Active Citizens." Plenary Presentation to the CSBA/CEA/BCSTA Congress on Educating Active Citizens, Victoria, BC, July 1999.

Osborne, K. (1999b, Mar.). "Who Killed Canadian History? – Book Review." *Canadian Historical Review*, 80(1), pp. 114-118.

Osborne, K. (1998/99, Winter). "Education for Citizenship." *Education Canada*, 38(4), pp. 16-19.

Pitts, G. (1999). "Red Wilson's History Crusade Gathers Steam." *Globe and Mail*.

Proceedings of the Second Annual Canadian Education Industry Summit: Investment in the Education-for-Profit Industry. "Session 6 – International Opportunities: Taking Canadian Education Products and Services to Market." The Hon. Sergio Marchi, Minister for International Trade, Department of Foreign Affairs & International Trade, Toronto, Oct. 7, 1998.

Saul, J. R. (2000, Mar. 24). "How We Will Make Canada Ours Again. The Lafontaine-Baldwin Lecture." *Globe and Mail*, pp. A14-15.

Sears, A. M., & Hughes, A. S. (1996). "Citizenship Education and Current Educational Reform." *Canadian Journal of Education*, 21(2), pp. 123-142.

Shaker, E. (Ed.). (2000, July). *In the Corporate Interest: The YNN Experience in Canadian Schools*. Ottawa: Canadian Centre for Policy Alternatives.

Wall, D. (2000, May). *Contemporary Approaches to "Citizenship Education"*. Draft report prepared for the Canadian Teachers' Federation.

Webster, P. (2000, March/April). "Who Stole Canadian History?" *This Magazine*, pp. 29-31.

International context

Private higher education at McGill and beyond: A fact sheet
By Pauline Hwang

Introduction

Since taking office in 1993, the federal Liberals have cut more than $7-billion in provincial transfer payments from health, post-secondary education and training.

Canadian universities today face chronic government underfunding, an increasing dependence on private funds, and the prospect of competition from foreign corporations through free trade agreements. With these challenges, one of the options McGill has considered is a privatization of some or all of its programs. This fact sheet surveys the situation of public vs. private universities across Canada, and examines the impact of these options on the autonomy and accessibility of higher education at McGill and across Canada.

Between 1992 and 1998...

Government operating grants to universities: DOWN 24 %
Operating income from student fees: UP 67 %
Operating income from non-government gifts and donations: UP 29 %

Across Canada

B.C.

Private universities and colleges number 1,100. 64 of them are accredited, meaning they have access to provincial student aid and private partner dollars. A loophole in B.C. legislation allows universities with degree-granting authority in other jurisdictions to establish easily in B.C. As a result, many private U.S. universities have set up operations in this province.

> "Many students fear that this move will lead to a two-tier education system for the rich and the poor...they claim that education is only a right, not a business for people to reap magnificent profits... Frankly, it is difficult to see what all the fuss is about." – Michael Taube, Fraser Institute analyst

The University of Phoenix, for example, offers degrees from the state of Arizona, though they have an office in Vancouver. U of Phoenix is an American private, for-profit institution that has 67,000 students enrolled on campuses across 15 states and another 10,000 on-line. The cost of a 4-year undergraduate degree at Phoenix is $40,800. The U.S. Department of Education recently ordered the school to pay $650,000 in fines after an audit exposed "system-wide problems" in student aid programs. Opponents also charged it failed to meet the state's required levels of library resources and qualified, full-time faculty.

University of British Columbia's former president, David Strangway, has been working since April 1998 to "offer better schooling to those who can afford it" through a "private, non-profit liberal arts university for affluent students" in Squamish, B.C. It would service 800 – 1,200 students, 50% of whom would be international.

Alberta

Alberta is set to become the first province in Canada to offer fully private college degree programs. A major step toward allowing fully private degree programs is the introduction of independent organizational evaluations for private post-secondary institutions. This replaces a requirement, in place since 1984, that such schools had to be affiliated with an Alberta university. Though final details remain to be worked out, the private institutions will likely continue to receive money from the provincial government.

Ontario

Private degree (student-pay-all) programs at the University of Toronto now include a $25,000 Masters in mathematical finance and a $30,000 Masters in telecommunications. Telecommunications giant Nortel sponsored the program and the "Nortel Institute," and receives non-exclusive rights to market any inventions supported by their funding. Donald Cormack, a Graduate Studies associate dean, says "That's what we're here for: to produce students who are going to be productive. If we don't, industry will come back and criticize us."

On April 28, 2000, the Ontario government announced it would consider permitting the establishment of private, degree-granting institutions, "including for-profit and not-for-profit institutions". They say the move will make available educational 'alternatives', at "no government expense," and that it responds to public demand for market-specific training. Private institutions would have access to the Ontario Student Assistance Program (OSAP), and the maximum amount a student can claim will be $4,500.

The government is considering over two dozen proposals for private universities, including proposals from the Apollo Group (which owns the private University of Phoenix already in B.C). In 1990, Bette Stephenson, former Conservative Minister of Colleges and Universities, proposed a private, not-for-profit university in Queensville, called "Wolfe University." It would specialize in engineering, information technology, and science. Earlier in 2000, she commented that recent meetings with the ministry have yielded a response that is "totally positive, there's been no negative involved."

Quebec

In April 1999, administrators and faculty at McGill University proposed the creation of an affiliated private liberal arts college.

Tentatively named "McGill College International," projected tuition would be $28,000 per year for an undergraduate degree. (See details in the "MCI proposal" section.)

At Concordia University, Rector Frederick Lowy also refuses to reject the idea of a private college as an ultimate solution. He says, "[The MCI] proposal reflects the frustration of all the universities as they do not have enough funds. If we can't get the money from the government, then we'll have to find another way to do it, which is what they [McGill] are proposing."

New Brunswick

New Brunswick is the only province that has no legislation restricting the use of the term "university" or degree-granting status (although that may soon change). In September 1999, Unexus University became the first Canadian degree-granting university residing solely on the Internet. Owned by Learnsoft Corporation (which is based in Kanata, Ont.), Unexus is a for-profit, private university that charges its students (primarily middle-aged executives) as much as $28,000 for a degree.

Newfoundland

An aviation school owned by the Career Academy closed down unexpectedly. The 19-year-old private Academy has 14 campuses in Newfoundland, Nova Scotia and Ontario. Its 1,400 students were displaced by the school's sudden collapse Aug. 14, 1999, due to financial problems. About 120 former Career Academy students spent two weeks camped out on the front lawn of the provincial legislature, demanding to complete their studies somehow. Among this and other incidents, Newfoundland's government has decided to temporarily stop granting licences for new private colleges and launch a public review of their private post-secondary industry.

Debunking the private university arguments

"No cost to taxpayers."

Proponents of private universities argue that, although the program benefits only a selected group of students, taxpayers will bear none of the education costs. However, private institutions receive public funding in several ways: interest-free government student loans, tax breaks for students, tax breaks for private funders, faculty research grants, "free-riding" on public resources like libraries, zoning changes and municipal services for private universities and related real estate developments, etc. Students from laxly-regulated private institutions also have a much higher loan default rate than public university students.

In the U.S., private universities receive about 30% of operating revenue from direct and indirect government subsidies. The institutions state that they are "publicly-assisted." In reality, taxpayers will end up supporting private universities at little benefit to the general public.

"Brain drain."

The "brain drain" (of young, talented intellectuals fleeing Canada for better opportunities elsewhere, usually the U.S.) is a reason often cited by corporate lobbyists for

Defining some terms and acronyms

PSE: post-secondary education

Privatization: retreat of public funding, ownership, control and regulation in PSE, replaced by private funding, ownership, control and deregulation of such things as tuition fees. (often accompanying by its cousin, 'corporatization' – see below)

Corporatization: influence of business interests in shaping aspects of PSE, including tuition levels, allocating of funding to various programs, course material suppliers, corporate partnerships, intellectual property arrangements, research agenda, PSE management, etc.

Public vs. private universities: Since the 1960s, this distinction has been understood to depend on sources of funding. A publicly-funded institution receives direct capital or operating grants from provincial and federal taxes. Private universities can be either not-for-profit or for-profit.

(In McGill's case, it is technically a private institution founded in 1821, and owned by the Royal Institute for Advancement of Learning. However, when public funding became a major source of revenue for McGill in the 1960s, we have since been considered "public." McGill's 2000-01 budget projects that 56.6% of our operating revenues will come from public sources.)

> "...there is, in fact, no such thing as an entirely private, or for that matter, an entirely public university in Canada." – Association of Universities and Colleges of Canada[6]

Secular vs. Non-secular universities: In Canada, most established private universities have been in some sense religiously-based. The new and proposed private institutions generating public attention, however, are secular.

Not-for-profit vs. for-profit universities: Not-for-profit universities (and organizations in general) reinvest excess revenue from activities back into their operations. For-profit institutions, in contrast, "seek to maximize their profits and, in the event that such institutions offer shares, seek to provide the highest possible return to shareholders."[7] All public universities are not-for-profit, whereas private ones may be either.

(The University of Phoenix in BC and Unexus University in New Brunswick are the two for-profit universities in Canada.)

On-line/Physical location universities: "On-line universities may become an increasingly important player in the debate over public and private institutions in Canada. On-line institutions can be accredited in one jurisdiction, yet still operate via the Internet in another jurisdiction, thereby possibly circumventing the latter jurisdiction's policy on private institutions." – AUCC[8]

GATS: General Agreement on Trade in Services. A multilateral agreement concluded in 1994 designed to govern international trade in services. Now among the WTO agreements, which include GATT (General Agreement on Tariffs and Trade), TRIPS (Trade-Related Aspects of Intellectual Property Rights), TRIMS (Trade-Related Investment Measures), etc.

WTO: World Trade Organization. A Geneva-based organization comprising 135 member countries with agreements on international exchange in goods, services, investment, intellectual property, etc. (see "GATS".) Target of major protest in Seattle in late 1999.

FTA: Free Trade Agreement. Signed between Canada and the U.S.A. in 1989.

NAFTA: North American Free Trade Agreement. Signed between Canada, the U.S.A. and Mexico in 1993.

FTAA: Free Trade Area of the Americas. Proposed extension of NAFTA to apply to all of the Americas, creating a hemisphere of liberalized trade.

National treatment: Requires governments (for example, the Canadian government) in a free trade agreement to treat all companies equally, regardless of where the company is based. In NAFTA, foreign firms are not even required to have a "local presence" in Canada to operate here and be given the same "rights" and economic consideration.

tax cuts and other policies that benefit the wealthy. McGill and other universities hope that experiences in new, élite private institutions will also entice these students and professors to stay.

First, the brain drain is often criticized as a political construct that values the talents leaving the country but not the talents entering (i.e., through immigration). For example, this is one (particularly offensive) way of framing the "brain drain," stated by a public policy consultant in Ottawa, and former senior official in the Privy Council: "We should not take comfort in the fact that we continue to be a magnet for qualified immigrants if our own sons and daughters see no future in the country in which they were born."[9]

Second, assuming the brain drain does in fact exist (itself quite debatable), those who do leave cite numerous reasons—such as wage levels, opportunities for promotion, tenure, job stability, and innovative research—at least as often as high taxes. We can keep these professors in Canadian institutions without creating private universities, and without choosing tax cuts over post-secondary funding.

"Private universities provide educational choice."

With tuition of $21,555 per year,[10] for whom would private universities offer choice? It is difficult to avoid reality that the quality of education students could access (i.e., smaller classes, better equipment, more qualified professors, etc.) would depend on their (or their family's) disposable income. In this way, it is hard to imagine that higher education will be able to equalize class disparities to a significant extent.

In response to the recent decision by the Ontario government, the Canadian Federation of Students "believes that if the ministry were sincerely interested in expanding choice for students, it would reduce tuition fees, re-regulate tuition fees for all post-diploma, professional and graduate students, and restore the $400 million cut to operating grants in 1996. It would build publicly-funded institutions in rural and northern communities."[11]

"Elementary and secondary school education is already two-tiered, so what's the big deal?"

This is an important argument to be addressed by both sides in the debate. As Chris Ragan, McGill Associate Professor of Economics, argues, "There are some very hypocritical double standards in this country. If anything, confronting disparity in elementary and high school is *more* fundamental—yet we're completely happy with a two-tier educational system at those levels."

The public/private system in earlier education has not gone unnoticed, however. As Erika Shaker of the Canadian Centre for Policy Alternatives puts it, "we should be working toward more equity, not less, in all levels of education." Even within the public school system, "fund-raising and user-fees also move us toward an education system where schools can enhance programs based on the wealth of families or communities."

In 1996, for example, the final report of the "Commission des états généraux sur l'éducation du Québec" recommended abolishing private high schools (with average tuition of $1,000) and strengthening the public system. The recommendation was struck down by the Quebec government.

Privatizing higher education has generated more attention, perhaps for reasons such as these:

1. Its urgency as a current consideration, while private (often historically religious) elementary and secondary schools have evolved in Canada over at least two centuries.

2. Privatization of some levels of education should not be used as a precedent for further privatization, creating a unidirectional spiral effect

3. Two possibilities that could lead to lower "value" for a Canadian degree: if élite universities grant degrees that are more prestigious in comparison, or if the quality of private institutions is not adequately regulated.

4. Allowing Canadian companies to operate in the university sectors means these education markets must be permanently opened to foreign companies on an equal footing (thanks to free trade deals – see section below).

"We must compete with American universities for the top students."

This argument deflects attention from the reality that, for the vast majority of Canadian post-secondary candidates, Canadian universities are the only option. By spending time, resources and tax dollars to create 'competitive,' elite private universities for top students, we avoid our obligation to provide a quality education to every able and motivated student in Canada.

Furthermore, most new and proposed private universities in Canada are far from the model of famous private not-for-profit corporations like the U.S. Ivy League schools. Because they are more targeted, often geared toward career training, and have little or no endowment, it is difficult to imagine these private universities competing with the prestigious American ones. Even so, many Canadian students who decide to attend American universities are also making a personal choice about lifestyle, environment, or career location, meaning they may choose to go to the U.S. nonetheless.

"No alternative. Our university system is just not up to par anymore."

Government underfunding of Canadian universities has led to a $3.6 billion accumulated deferred maintenance bill[12], stagnated faculty salaries, and increased student fees and debts. The government has chosen tax cuts over social programs, despite public opinion which consistently ranks health and education as top spending priorities.

The Ontario government, for example, is giving an across-the-board $200 tax rebate in the fall—a move that costs the total ($1 billion) of university tuition province-wide. The best alternative to meet current future demand for higher education is government reinvestment in university operating grants. Universities such as McGill have stated they are only considering privatization schemes (student-pay-all professional programs, international programs, and the MCI) because of the dire situation imposed by government policy. Staff, faculty and administration should join in loudly and creatively demanding public reinvestment in higher education.

The McGill College International Proposal (MCI)

The McGill College International (MCI) Proposal was created by an ad hoc committee of professors working since April 1999. The initial idea was to create something that would revitalize McGill, attracting more money and top international students to McGill. The plan became known as the MCI (though the name will change because "MCI" is also apparently a phone company).

> "MCI would be of considerable financial benefit to McGill, particularly to the library. More importantly, it would revitalize us academically, at a time when budgetary cuts and a declining Maclean's ranking raise questions about our future." – MCI Committee Q & A document

In a nutshell, this 3000-student, private, liberal arts college at McGill would be funded entirely by tuition, roughly projected to $28,000 per year plus $8,000 food and residence, for a three-year undergraduate degree. Students would enjoy small classes, a broad non-specialized curriculum in "global studies," an international internship, and would live in residence for the first two years to facilitate evening discussions and classes. Ten percent of revenue would be set aside for scholarships for deserving students. The emphasis for these affluent students (most of them international) would be on education rather than training.

McGill would benefit by this private college paying departments for instructor services, the library for use of its material, and classroom rental. The idea would be that cost-sharing between the MCI and McGill would bring badly-needed improvements to library facilities, as well as attracting talented professors—including young, visiting, international, etc. For example, if MCI paid the proposed $225,000 per 100- student cohort to the McGill library, that would bring in $6,750,000 at 3,000 students; McGill's total library budget for 1999-2000 is $14,724,000. The proposed classroom rental fee for 3,000 students would give McGill an additional $3,000,000. In this way, rather than free-riding off McGill infrastructure, the flow of resources will be from MCI to the rest of McGill:

> "The whole point of this from the get-go was in a sense for profit which would be funneled back into McGill...It would now be a for-profit program, in that it would be completely funded by students or private donations, not by taxpayers. The students wouldn't see themselves as subsidizing anything, they would be paying the market price for their product or service."[13]

MCI instructors would include McGill instructors, hired per course, "folding chairs" or tutorial positions for non-tenure-track recent post-doctoral graduates, and visiting professors, lecturing on their specialities (could also give pro bono lectures to McGill at large). The college would take advantage of McGill's international reputation, with the McGill name lending weight to an MCI degree even if Quebec would not accredit the program.

The Faculty of Science rejected the proposal in December of 1999, but the Faculty of Arts in January 2000 approved a formal committee to explore the idea. However, in May 2000, the Faculty of Arts rejected that committee's request to pursue foundation funding to do a thorough feasibility study, effectively killing the MCI plan—at least for a little while. Concerns at McGill included philosophical approval of a two-tiered system, the danger of resources flowing from McGill itself to the MCI, the possible devaluing of the standard McGill degree, tension on campus between McGill students and MCI students...

> "One thing that was key was that the dean, after we had defeated the motion, reiterated that we were not rejecting innovative degree programs. What we were rejecting was the idea of a private college at McGill." – Andrew Kovacs, then President of the Science Undergraduate Society, January 2000.

In a sense, the Faculty of Management is an example at McGill where this privatization has already occurred. They offer an expensive international MBA program and at least one other joint program between engineering and management. That the MCI concept will resurface in the faculties of arts or science after a year or two would not be surprising.

Phenomena related to privatization

Private universities are not sprouting out of the blue. The context includes attempts to privatize and commercialize many services that, in Canada, have traditionally been public. Examples include water monitoring, health care, electricity, and many more. The context also includes extensive corporate influence, and international trade and investment frameworks.

The links between corporatization and privatization stem from a market-driven approach that is increasingly applied to public services, reinforced and accelerated by trade liberalization.

Free trade agreements (FTA, NAFTA, FTAA, GATS) consider education and other previously public services on an economic basis only. Cultural differences, social policy, and democratic and local governance of education are non-issues in the drive toward economic integration.

Integration and "harmonization" of services and standards, with the U.S. in particular, means largely adopting their traditions of two-tiered systems and market ideologies, while Canada's systems (rapidly becoming extinct) gave us a unique reputation for quality of life.[14]

Possible "barriers to trade" in post-secondary education include:
- educational standards,

- regulations favouring public institutions,
- price-setting,
- monopoly granting of degrees,
- qualification standards for professionals,
- governance regulations, and
- government subsidies to public institutions.[15]

Under NAFTA, new services will automatically be included in the agreement. Existing services that were initially under "governmental authority" will be eventually harmonized into the agreement, unless specifically designated otherwise. Most disturbingly, once public and private service providers are allowed, a) national and provincial governments must treat them equally—putting into question the subsidies uniquely given to public education services, and b) the decision to commercialize the sector is legally irreversible. Furthermore, "they don't look at it in terms of local jurisdiction, they look at it nationally. If Ontario offers private universities, Canada is offering private universities."[16]

Under GATS, there is a weak exemption for services under "governmental authority," but it is possible that higher education no longer falls under this authority. The Canadian government has not requested an "unbound exemption" from GATS terms for educational services.[17]

The weak GATS exemption is eliminated in the proposed FTAA agreement:

"The consensus among negotiators is that "The FTAA services agreement should have, in principle, universal coverage of all service sectors," with no mention of an exemption for services delivered in the exercise of governmental authority. There is only reference to governments maintaining "the right to regulate services." As well, again in contrast with the GATS, negotiators are saying national treatment "should apply to all service sectors and to all service suppliers." With this framework, services as diverse as health, education, library, museum, cultural, and sewer and water services and other public services would have to be opened up to foreign, for-profit suppliers."
– Patty Barrera, Common Frontiers-Canada, commenting on FTAA negotiations document leaked by American officials.

It has become clear to most players in the higher education sector that free trade may represent a significant challenge to the Canadian public post-secondary education sector.

What we can do:

- Voice concerns to McGill administration, and the federal and provincial governments, calling on them to make accessible, quality higher education a priority.

- Collaborate with other student groups across Canada in lobbying and campaign efforts.

- Promote accessible, autonomous education through such initiatives as the "Free University of Toronto," a cooperative effort of U of T students, faculty and community members to provide completely free and independent education. Volunteer professors and community leaders offer courses primarily in the evenings, in three terms throughout the year.

- Expose sources of anti-public-education material, including: the Fraser Institute, Business Council on National Issues, Business-Higher Education Forum, the C.D. Howe Institute, and other notoriously right-wing think tanks.

- Examine the effects of the Free Trade Area of the Americas agreement on higher education, especially leading up to next negotiation summit, the "Summit of the Americas" to be held in Quebec City in April 2001.

(Pauling Hwang is a youth orgnizer and activist)

Other sources of info

Association of Universities and Colleges of Canada, "Private Universities in Canada: A Background Paper."

Calvert, John and Larry Kuehn. *Pandora's Box: Corporate Power, Free Trade and Canadian Education.* Toronto: Our Schools / Our Selves. July/August, 1993.

Canadian Association of University Teachers: www.caut.ca
Excellent source of discussion papers, information on corporate-university governance linkages, public policy bulletins, etc.

Canadian Centre for Policy Alternatives. *Education Monitor*, and other useful material. www.policyalternatives.ca

Canadian Federation of Students: excellent information available from the national and provincial offices, well-researched, from a student perspective, nationally-coordinated.
www.cfs-fcee.ca

Clift, Robert. "Background Paper on the General Agreement on Trade in Services (GATS) and Post-Secondary Education in Canada." Confederation of University Faculty Associations of British Columbia. November 29, 1999. http://www.cufa.bc.ca/briefs/GATS.html

"Decoys instead of Dollars for Post-secondary Education", OCUFA report, 2000. http://www.ocufa.on.ca/Research/v1n2.htm

Handelman, Steven. "A Tale of Two Universities: The Shapiros of McGill and Princeton warn of a crisis in education." *Time*, March 29, 1999.

Harden, Joel. "Trade Liberalization and Post-Secondary Education." A presentation for the Canadian Federation of Students – Ontario. E-mail chair@istar.ca for a copy.

McGill College International: Report of the Arts and Science MCI Committee on a proposed new BA degree program. http://blizzard.cc.mcgill.ca/PGSS/mci.html

Newson, Janice and Howard Buchbinder. *The University Means Business: Universities, Corporations and Academic Work.* Toronto: Garamond Press, 1988.

Report of the Task Force: Towards a new McGill (1996): http://blizzard.cc.mcgill.ca/uro/Read/ch2.htm#C

(1) Post-Graduate Student Society's letter to the administration on the MCI:
http://www.mcgill.ca/PGSS/pgssmci.html; and
(2) Principal Shapiro's response to that letter: http://www.mcgill.ca/PGSS/shapirolet.html

"Private Universities: Privileged Education." Canadian Federation of Students Fact Sheet. May 2000, Vol. 7, No. 1.

Travers, Jim. "Schools plan could cause scandal." *The Toronto Star.* May 9, 2000

Vinet, Luc. "Tradition and Innovation: An International University in a City of Knowledge." McGill discussion paper on plans and policies, 1999 http://blizzard.cc.mcgill.ca//documents/innovation/

Press, Eyal and Jennifer Washburn. "The Kept University." *Atlantic Monthly*, March 2000.

Endnotes

1. From a letter to the McGill Reporter in 1996. http://blizzard.cc.mcgill.ca/uro/Rep/r2817/shapiro.htm
2. OCUFA report, "Decoys instead of Dollars for Postsecondary Education", 2000. http://www.ocufa.on.ca/Research/v1n2.htm
3. Schmidt, Sarah. "Private programs make their way to U of T." *Varsity News*. September 23, 1997.
4. *Ibid*.
5. Stewart, Walter. "Don't Sell the School" *The Third Degree*. Vol. 3 No. 1, Spring 1991, p. 19
6. "Private Universities in Canada: A Background Paper." Association of Universities and Colleges of Canada, p.2
7. *Ibid*.
8. *Ibid*.
9. Mitchell, James R. "What Really Matters: Higher Education in an Era of Globalization." A Paper Prepared for the Association of Universities and Colleges of Canada. Ottawa: Sussex Circle, March 2000.
10. average tuition per year for American private universities (approx U.S.$14,500)
11. Canadian Federation of Students-Ontario, May 2000
12. "A Point of No Return: The Urgent Need for Infrastructure Renewal at Canadian Universities." A Study prepared for the Canadian Association of University Business Officers (CAUBO), April 2000
13. Chris Ragan, McGill Associate Professor of Economics, interviewed on July 21, 2000
14. Calvert, John and Larry Kuehn. "Pandora's Box: Corporate Power, Free Trade and Canadian Education."
15. Harden, Joel. "Trade Liberalisation and Postsecondary education"
16. *Ibid*. Also see Travers, Jim. "Schools plan could cause scandal." *The Toronto Star*. May 9, 2000
17. See http://www.cufa.bc.ca/briefs/GATS.html

Public Education:
Citizen's rights for sale—cheap!
By Sarah Dopp and Karl Flecker

The public interest is surreptitiously being handed over to corporate interests. Public education, itself, is speeding along the road of trade liberalization. While many of us are trying to slam on the brakes, the rulers at the World Trade Organization (WTO) and transnational corporations are seemingly, oblivious to the dangers as their corporate cruiser speeds along a profit highway.

One would think that public education and trade liberalization are incompatible. After all, public education is a basic right. Under the United Nations' Universal Declaration of Human Rights, Article 26[1], everyone has the right to education. Education shall be free, at least in the elementary and fundamental stages. Education is clearly a public service that could not possibly be commodified by any progressive society—right? Meanwhile, trade is generally understood to refer to goods and commodified services movement across borders.

Two seemingly disconnected concepts—but let there be no doubt: the two have become increasingly intertwined. There are fundamental questions to be asked.

Worldwide public education expenditures now exceeds $2 trillion. In corporate-speak, this means 50 million teachers, 1 billion students, and hundreds of thousands of educational establishments and institutions, each with a bundle of service contracts, all of which adds up to a lucrative market.[2]

Under the ideology of the World Trade Organization, rights are now being granted to corporations, as though they were citizens: rights that allow them to establish a commercial presence to deliver education and demand that their operations be established in other jurisdictions. Extending such entitlements to corporate entities comes at the expense of real people's human rights.

How did this get started?

The re-packaging of public services in general began with the North American Free Trade Agreement (NAFTA), which enabled our unique and valued services to be privatized.

Trade liberalization of "educational services" specifically fell prey to the General Agreement on Trade in Services (GATS), which began under the General Agreement on Tariffs and Trade (GATT). The GATS is a comprehensive framework of rules and disciplines for trade in services—all economic activity that is not directly related to the production of goods, tangible commodities with price tags attached. The GATS classifies educational services as primary education, secondary education, higher education, adult education, and other educational services. (Services not covered by the previous four categories.)

The WTO drivers on the road to excess profit view our national and provincial regulatory framework which protects public education (through various funding supports, regulated tuition's, and qualification standards for professionals) as 'barriers to trade.' Using obfuscating principles called Most Favoured Nation (MFN) and National Treatment, the WTO's corporate drivers are prepared to demand that member countries extend the same treatment provided to domestic providers of educational services to out-of-country corporate providers.

Under these principles, the Canadian government would be obligated to provide the same subsidies and funding support to private educational institutions as it does for public institutions. The effect would be to undermine the public system and redirect public funds to for-profit, private establishments.

In a background paper on the topic of education, prepared by the WTO Secretariat, we see that education is categorized into two lanes. One is termed 'public consumption," referring to education that receives government funding and thereby reduces the cost of tuition. The second lane is termed 'private consumption,' which refers to tuition determined by the institution, also known as deregulated tuition.[3]

The WTO document acknowledges the importance of education to the prosperity of an economy, but simply sees it as a commodity and therefore subject to international trade rules. As a result, government commitments to preserving public education could be considered an obstacle to investment.

There can be no doubt that the corporate purchase of public services usurps our rights as individuals, as well as the rights granted for the common good. In public education this means that democracy, accessibility and affordabil-ity now come with a price tag.

The WTO's designs on public education include a clear plan by which education can be provided as an international service. Products, such as instructional materials, books and even documentation sent via the Internet which are produced in one country and 'consumed' in another, are considered to be supplied across borders and thus subject to WTO rules. Services utilized in another country are considered consumption abroad and also subject to WTO rules. Even individuals—e.g., instructors teaching abroad and students studying abroad—are covered by rules governing the movement of natural people.

Any one of these applications leaves the public system, which already suffers from decades of underfunding and increased commercialization, to yet further erosion.

Following the map of corporate interests that seek to invest in education will result in accountability of the system being judged by corporate shareholders using a bottom-line assessment tool. The interests of the public—the 'common good'—will be superseded quite simply by private gain interests.

The reality of this attack on public education is occurring in jurisdictions across Canada. The University of Phoenix—the largest for-profit university in North America—established a campus in Vancouver in January 1999 to grant American degrees. Under the GATS, it can demand the same subsidies as publicly-funded universities in B.C. and could demand to establish additional campuses in other provincial jurisdictions seeking access to other provinces' educational markets.

Most provincial governments have so far resisted corporate pressure to establish private universities, but the line in the sand is shifting quickly.

Examples include the establishment of private, accredited, degree-granting universities in British Columbia. David Strangeway's private university plan for Squamish, B.C. tops the list. The Ontario government recently announced it will pursue private universities as part of its strategy to address the increased demographic demand for a higher education. New Brunswick has established legislation allowing corporate ventures to use the title of "university" and grant degrees without provincial accreditation.

The opening of these legislative windows enable corporate entities to seek their WTO and NAFTA sanctioned entitlements which can enable them to provide services in any jurisdiction they choose; to access public funds to finance their private ventures, and to effectively dismantle the public education system.

So who are the marketeers putting a price tag on public education and driving this agenda forward? Private 'education industry' corporations serve to benefit profitably from liberalized trade. The WTO contracted the Global Alliance for Transnational Education (GATE) to take an inventory of all 'barriers to trade' in education.

Prior to the Millennium Round of the WTO in December 1999, Pierre Pettigrew, Minister of International Trade, publicly tried to reassure Canadians that health care and education would not be on the table. In a press release from the Department of Foreign Affairs and International Trade, he states: "Canada's position is both forward-looking and balanced. Our economy is based on exports, and we must continue to press for increased access for goods and services. At the same time, we will continue to safeguard Canada's vital social interests."[4]

The stated position of commitments to expand the Canadian export market opens the Canadian market to importing, and, while the Canadian government has not committed educational services, the U.S. and European Union have both expressed intent to include education and health care. The Canadian government will find itself under increasing pressure, as negotiations proceed, to follow suit.

The "Team Canada" approach of export promotion, selling our services and bringing business home permeates virtually all aspects of society, Canadians hold little faith in our government's commitment to public services.

Given our government's eagerness to operate among the movers and shakers of the WTO and the private sector, the preservation of a public education system and the protection of our basic rights will only come from our commitments and abilities to affect social change.

It is imperative that we work together: faculty with students, public sector workers with the broader community. No single constituency can fight in isolation. We all have vital stakes in an education system that is public and accessible. Our communities and economy depend on the knowledge and jobs universities and colleges generate. We must remain vigilant in our protest against these attacks. We have a great deal of work still ahead of us. The Canadian government will continue to talk from both sides of its mouth, offering meaningless assurances that we have nothing to fear. The right will continue to label us "protectionists" and fear-mongers. We are already seeing the transformation of education, but, more importantly, we are exposing and resisting it.

(Sarah Dopp is the Coordinator for Operation 2000, a project of the Polaris Institute. Karl Flecker is a policy analyst in the equity field at Queen's University.)

Endnotes:

[1] Universal Declaration on Human Rights, United Nations, 1948.
[2] Educational International-Public Services International, "The WTO and the Millennium Round: What's at Stake for Public Education?"
[3] "Education Services Background Note by the Secretariat," Council for Trade in Services, September 1998.
[4] Department of Foreign Affairs and International Trade, "Pettigrew announces Canada's Position on the WTO Negotiations," November 15, 1999.

The fire this time? Understanding the movement against trade liberalization
By Joel Harden

"Let us embrace the spirit of adventure. Let us sail the uncertain seas. And let us resolve to complete that voyage and do so, together."

What you just read may sound like a heartfelt speech to graduating students, but the actual audience, and the intended message, was far less inspiring. These remarks were made on Dec. 9, 1998 by Sergio Marchi—then Canadian Minister for International Trade—at the 22nd Annual Miami Conference on the Caribbean and Latin America.

Marchi was not spurring on his audience of international trade bureaucrats and policy-makers to a grand sailing adventure around the world. His address was intended to bolster the confidence of those interested in liberalizing any and all barriers to international trade—be it through new free trade deals or the dismantling of any governmental measures that inhibit potential markets for corporate profits. Marchi urged his audience to support the current negotiations for a Free Trade Area of the Americas, a hemispheric agreement touted by trade experts as being the most comprehensive plan to date in prying open domestic markets to foreign direct investment.

The ideological justification behind the push for greater liberalization in world trade is known among trade experts as the 'Washington Consensus.' In a provocative article for **The New Yorker**, William Finnegan offers a fitting description of the idea:

> "Global free trade supports global economic growth. It creates jobs, makes companies more competitive, and lowers prices for consumers. It also provides poor countries, through infusions of foreign capital and technology, with the chance to develop economically and, by spreading prosperity, creates the conditions in which democracy and respect for human rights may flourish."

Like Marchi, the vast majority of politicians and journalists have swallowed the Washington Consensus holus bolus. But, while apologists for capitalism and trade liberalization have emphasized their like-mindedness, successive protests have burst onto the political scene like numerous leaks in a gigantic dam. Defenders of public education have figured prominently in this outburst of activity. Students, in particular, have played an important role.

This is, of course, hardly surprising. International organizations promoting trade liberalization have applauded when Canadian policy-makers have slashed funding for public education, deregulated aspects of post-secondary education, or introduced privatization in various ways. In present-day capitalism, where the ebb and flow of markets (and the weighty players behind them) determine the future efficacy of social programs, public education activists are recognizing the significance of the current fight against trade liberalization.

Cutbacks are setting the stage for the onset of freer trade in services, where new tiers of élite (or sub-standard) education will be introduced at the expense of public education, and the right of every citizen to expand their human capacities through learning.

In this short article, I draw attention to the agenda of trade liberalization, but not to talk about its unhindered progress, limitless possibilities, or inevitable march forward. Here I argue that the current revolt against trade liberalization is an important new movement with an enormous amount of potential. The success of this movement will depend on the work of activists to broaden their efforts, and tear down artificial divisions between those opposed to freer trade.

The concerns many people have about trade liberalization must be translated into wider, broader-based actions. To this end, I cite the example of the 'fire last time'—the explosive mobilizations of protest in 1968—as an important example for those fighting trade liberalization today. The 'fire last time' is an illustration of the power everyday people can have when they act in unison against a common adversary. If today's fight against free trade is to become the 'fire **this** time,' it must follow in these historical footsteps.

Confidence rising:
This movement is for real

Even the most die-hard defenders of free trade would have difficulty disputing the obvious confidence their critics have gained in recent years. Demonstrations against the global institutions promoting trade liberalization fetched crowds of hundreds five years ago. Today it is common to expect many thousands at protests that call the record of free trade and corporate excess into question.

The Summer of 2000 alone saw a cavalcade of activity—militant anti-McDonald's groups of farmers in France, thousands of people picketing the Democratic and Republican Party conventions in the United States, and thousands again in Windsor to protest the FTAA being negotiated by the Organization of American States (OAS). In September, 10,000 activists blockaded the World Economic Forum in Melbourne (Australia), preventing 200 of 700 delegates from entering. This demonstration marks the second time the WEF has been disrupted in as many meetings. In Prague, thousands of activists swarmed the streets of Prague (Czech Republic), defying ordinances against their protests timed with a joint meeting of the International Monetary Fund and World Bank.

Few would dispute that these large mobilizations of protest are indicative of a contagious new mood. Even the **Globe and Mail**'s Peter Cook is willing to concede the existence of a 'protest plague.' Still, many might argue against the claim that these events represent an actual movement forming against trade liberalization. The recent course of events, like the upheavals of the late 1960s, is doubtless viewed by some as fits of wandering rage, a rudderless string of dissent that will soon run its course. These arguments may be convincing for those who have not analyzed the current period closely, or others who are anxious to see this outburst of activity subside. But, despite these misgivings, too many factors suggest we are witnessing a movement indeed, and one that is gaining confidence with each explosion of protest.

The first indication that a movement is forming is evident in the way each demonstration feeds off the last. Soon after activists disrupted the WTO Ministerial in Seattle, the call was out to organize for the April 16 2000 Mobilization for Global Justice in Washington D.C. The same was true in Ontario, when activists used report-back meetings from Washington D.C. to build momentum for protests at the June 4-6 2000 meeting of the OAS in Windsor.

The Internet has certainly played a key role in coordinating this activity with minimal levels of bureaucracy and cost. Events in Seattle, Washington D.C., Windsor and Melbourne were covered instantly by independent media sources, and sent to all corners of the globe via the Internet. Sound and video clips of police violence, enormous crowds, and provocative speeches were broadcast around the world. These clips were not just transmitting information but motivation to activists elsewhere planning the next round. The movement has quickly become international in scope, thanks in large part to the use of new information technologies.

But the role of information technologies alone does not explain why trade liberalization has become a lightning rod for a new movement of protest. This movement has grown exponentially because the issues impacted by trade liberalization are so broad, and the profit-oriented motives of its adherents so obvious. Just as big business has attempted to rally its troops behind new trade pacts, activists have harnessed a contagious mood of unity in this struggle as well, where environmentalists, trade unionists, activists from Southern nations, and students march side by each with little or no awkwardness.

'Teamsters and turtles—together at last' was the slogan many associate with the 'Battle of Seattle' in late 1999, highlighting how, for the first time in recent memory, trade unionists and environmentalists found common cause in their struggles. Before the June 4-6 2000 protests in Windsor against the OAS, trade union activists worked closely with organizers from the Canadian Federation of Students and other activist collectives.

The solidarity on display in this movement has been much different from the last wave of militancy witnessed in Canada during the 1995-98 'Days of Action' in Ontario. There, leaders held hands during 11 city-wide strikes voicing common cause in speeches, and mobilized large sections of their membership. Still, the 'Days of Action' movement—while politicizing and mobilizing new layers of people to take on the Mike Harris government—had its working basis of unity among leaders; demonstrators went home after protests with no meaningful opportunity to decide what the next step was. These decisions took place in the boardrooms of trade union leaders. When controversies among the union leadership proved divisive, the 'Days of Action' movement collapsed after a single meeting that decided against escalating to province-wide action. An earlier opportunity to support an illegal province-wide strike by Ontario teachers in 1997 was similarly squandered by this climate of divisiveness at the top.

The current movement against trade liberalization is different because it has been based on solidarity from below, from new working relationships between activists in different social movements. Activists in the United Students Against Sweatshops—some of whom were first politicized through the American Federation of Labour/Congress of Industrial Organizations' Union Summer program—have signed solidarity pacts with Steelworkers for fair labour practices, and supported union struggles on campuses across North America.

The militant environmental organization Earth First! has also signed pacts with the Steelworkers regarding sustainable production, and its activists have worked closely with unions elsewhere. In Ontario, the Canadian Federation of Students recently joined a boycott of Molson Canada products to support members of the Canadian Autoworkers' Union occupying a plant in Barrie slated to close. Though the boycott did not prevent the plant from closing, it did force Molson to provide job transfers, a lowered pension ceiling, and severance packages far richer than what was previously offered. Not long after, the CAW provided funding for two buses for students to attend the April 16 2000 Mobilization for Global Justice in Washington D.C. This is the mood of solidarity that sets the fight against trade liberalization apart.

Ample evidence exists to argue that we are witnessing the birth of a new broad-based social movement. "This is what democracy looks like," "Ain't no power like the power of the people 'cause the power of the people don't stop," "Human need, not corporate greed"—these are the commonly-heard slogans that illustrate what many have called the 'Spirit of Seattle' at the heart of the fight against trade liberalization. There is a pervasive belief—backed up with convincing evidence—that the world financial system is not what its functionaries claim it to be, that it must be refused and replaced with better alternatives.

With each teach-in, rally, march or direct action that takes aim at trade liberalization and capitalism itself, people are becoming aware of the hypocrisy at the heart of the system. After three decades of trade liberalization, the assets of the world's 200 wealthiest people has increased to $1 trillion, more than doubling the $440 billion in 1996. 850 million people at the same time go hungry each day in impoverished Southern nations, and 160 million suffer from malnutrition. In Canada, the nation that ranks first in the United Nations Development Index, 3% of the population controls 80% of the wealth, and the bottom 20% of families now live on an average annual income of $17,058.

These are the conditions in which the movement against trade liberalization is emerging. A growing minority of the public is justifiably outraged about international trade bodies far beyond democratic reach, and the apologetic governments that defend them. Margaret Thatcher's once-celebrated declaration of the 'TINA' ('there is no alternative' to freer trade) syndrome has been rejected and replaced with what Susan George describes as the 'TATA' ("there are thousands of alternatives") approach to corporate globalization.

Citizens who have been told to have faith in political élites and business experts are now taking matters into their own hands, asserting alternatives to trade liberalization as they rally, blockade, and speak out against the injustices of the world in which they live. The revolt against trade liberalization may be new, its future uncertain, and its potential a matter of debate. But there can be no doubt, given its resonance, persistence, and international appeal to a committed (and growing) minority, of its considerable importance.

Students join the movement

Students have certainly been a catalyst in the new movement against trade liberalization. One of the hottest issues on campus today is the concern activists have about the fight against free trade and the power of multinational corporations. The most recognized grouping in North America has been the United Students Against Sweatshops (USAS), a network that formed in the past four years as more students learned that university/college apparel was being produced in deplorable working conditions. The USAS has seen explosive growth, and currently boasts a network of 160 campus chapters.

This strength in numbers has been channelled at campus administrators to win codes of conduct for the production of items bearing the insignia of colleges and universities. These codes of conduct have been won in the United States and Canada through a series of efforts—from the lobbying of administrators to the occupation of campus offices. Most recently, students at the University of Toronto occupied their President's office for several days to force the hand of local officials who had delayed the implementation of a code of conduct. In the end, the students won: the U of T—renowned for its dogged resolve in promoting poor labour relations—implemented a code of conduct for the production of apparel bearing the university's name.

Students in Canada have been key agitators in the movement against trade liberalization. Most Canadians will remember images of student protesters being pepper-sprayed by police during the 1998 APEC Summit held at the University of British Columbia, and the callous words Prime Minister Jean Chrétien uttered—"Pepper? I put it on my plate"—that haunt him to this day. Students in British Columbia were front and centre during the "Battle of Seattle" in late November 1999. Student activists from Manitoba, Ontario, Quebec, Nova Scotia and throughout the United States were in Washington, D.C. to demonstrate against the IMF and World Bank from the 16-18 of April 2000.

The Canadian Federation of Students has figured prominently in the movement, particularly in the June 4 2000 protest against the Organization of American States in Windsor. The concern about corporate rule has often carried over into disputes at the local level on campus. Students at McGill University in Spring 2000, for example, defeated an attempt to introduce a beverage exclusivity deal with Coca Cola. Campus activists elsewhere have protested the domination of corporate representatives on local university/college governing bodies, and the mutation of these structures into craven machines of corporate fundraising.

The anti-corporate inclination of student activism today is also a response to the way in which campuses have become festivals of market advertising. It is common to see university or college halls swarmed with salespeople hocking credit cards, cellphones, and countless other items. Washrooms are plastered with ads facing a captive audience, and the audience often becomes amateur graffiti artists in retaliation.

Today, students are viewed by many as a niche market, as "customers" of "education factories" run by administrators who act like executive officers of large corporations. Add to this the impact of soaring tuition fees, burgeoning class sizes, deteriorating campus services, and significant hours of work in the part-time jobs most students pursue to make ends meet. These are fertile conditions for alienation, and undoubtedly the reason students have played a leading role in the fight against trade liberalization.

Touching a nerve

Two predominant responses have met most attempts to provoke an honest debate about the implications of trade liberalization: insatiable curiosity from concerned citizens, and a mixture of dismissals and paranoid delusion from those charged with defending the free trade fort. Illustrative of the first trend, a mass teach-in held at the University of Toronto in November 1997 drew thousands as Susan George of the European Transnational Institute, Tony Clarke of the Polaris Institute, Elizabeth May of the Sierra Club and others surveyed the ruins left in the wake of corporate globalization. Successive teach-ins around the world have widened the debate about capitalism and trade liberalization, arming more citizens with evidence that contradicts the supposed virtues of untrammeled free trade.

Such efforts have led to serious questioning in many quarters that has, for the most part, been quickly dismissed. When citizens have taken to the streets in protest, they have faced outright dismissals by media pundits and political leaders. When demonstrators marched on Washington, D.C. to protest (among other things) the debt crisis of impoverished nations created by the brutal structural adjustment programs of the IMF and World Bank, Thomas Friedman of **The New York Times** called them "flat earth advocates."

In a letter written to Michael Conlon, National Chairperson of the Canadian Federation of Students, Canadian Trade Minister

Pierre Pettigrew rejected Conlon's concerns about the WTO's General Agreement on Trade in Services for higher education. Paul Jackson, Associate Editor of the **Calgary Sun,** speculated that protests against trade liberalization were well organized because they were receiving outside help. Jackson suggested that Libya's Moammar Ghadhafi, Iraq's Saddam Hussein, or Afghanistan's Osama bin Laden was financing this latest round of insurgency.

More distressing than such alarmist responses is the degree of state surveillance and police violence that has met protests against trade liberalization. During the demonstrations in Seattle, Washington, D.C., and Windsor, organizing centres housing activists were raided, demonstrators were assaulted by police, jailed shortly before demonstrations, or held in jail for inordinate lengths of time. Millions of dollars in public funds have been spent to finance large policing operations or purchase "crowd control" materials. Civil rights to free expression have been suspended inside entire city blocks surrounding trade meetings. The right for citizens to wear gas-masks was declared illegal in Detroit during the June 4-6 2000 protests against the OAS in Windsor.

The Canadian Security Intelligence Service (Canada's own version of the CIA) recently stunned the activist community when it released a document entitled: "Anti-Globalization—A Spreading Phenomenon." In CSIS's opinion, the 'anti-globalization' movement was remarkably effective, and posed serious problems for holding future trade meetings in Canada. Activists were credited with showing remarkable skill in utilizing the Internet to assign tasks and carry out mobilizing activities. In a curiously insightful passage, CSIS argued that the disparate groups in the movement registered an impact "out of all proportion with their individual strengths", a point emphasized by those sympathetic to the movement as well.

But the surveillance and violence activists have endured stems from the real concern demonstrations against trade liberalization have caused. Far away from the noise in the streets, the protests against freer trade have touched a nerve in some of the world's most influential boardrooms. A report conducted by Burson-Marseller (a prominent Washington, D.C. publicity firm) for an unknown client was leaked to the press, and its content detailing corporate concern with recent events was instructive. The report—entitled "Guide to the Seattle Meltdown: A Compendium of Activists at the WTO Ministerial"—analyzed the different actors behind the 'Battle of Seattle.' The authors cautioned that the effectiveness of the protest meant "significant short-term ramifications for the business community," and warned of "the potential ability of the emerging coalition of these groups to seriously impact broader, longer-term corporate interests."

Mainstream media reports have frequently discredited the movement against trade liberalization, but the reaction that has been elicited in the halls of power is proof enough that a nerve has been touched. The question on most people's minds is where the movement is headed, and its prospects for success or failure. Will this movement collapse under the weight of its own expectations? Will it be contained by the powers that be? Or will current mobilizations grow stronger? These are the questions I turn to now.

The fire this time?

A common criticism directed at the new movement against trade liberalization is that it lacks a coherent, focused program for change. In an effort to defend the movement from its critics, Naomi Klein has argued that the decentralized nature of the movement is, on the contrary, a source of strength. Klein envisages a future for the movement that builds on the same decentralized decision-making model of affinity groups that have built demonstrations to date. For her, the absence of an overarching revolutionary philosophy in the movement is not its most pressing problem. Of greater concern is the inability of activists in the movement to determine what the next tactical step in the anti-capitalist struggle will be. It is worth citing Klein at length here, for she grapples with the key debates taking place in the movement right now:

> "An odd sort of anxiety has begun to set in after each demonstration: Was that it? When's the next one? Will it be as good, as big? To keep up the momentum, a culture of serial protesting is rapidly taking hold. My in-box is cluttered with entreaties to come that promise to be 'the next Seattle.' [S]omeone posted a message on the organizing e-mail list for the Washington, D.C. demos: 'Wherever we go, we shall be there! After this, see you in Prague!' But is this really what we want—a movement of meeting stalkers, following the trade bureaucrats as if they were the Grateful Dead?

> "The prospect is dangerous for several reasons. Far too much expectation is being placed on these protests: The organizers of the D.C. demo, for instance, announced that they would literally 'shut down' two $30 billion transnational institutions, at the same time as they attempted to convey sophisticated ideas about the fallacies of neo-liberal economics to the stock-happy public. They simply couldn't do it; no single demo could, and it's only going to get harder. Seattle's direct-action tactics worked because they took the police by surprise. That won't happen again. Police have now subscribed to all the e-mail lists. L.A. has put in a request for $4 million in new security gear and staffing costs to protect the city from the activist swarm."

Klein's concerns about where the movement is headed raise important questions that must be put to healthy debate. Nevertheless, her pessimistic position about the movement's resonance with the wider public represents a retreat, and gives undue credit to right-wing critics who allege that the fight against freer trade is without broad-based support.

Klein's cynical claim that the movement faces a 'stock-happy public' is a flawed assessment of the economic realities most people face as they try to understand what the fight against free trade means for them. The biggest barrier activists face is not the devotion people have to their mutual funds and RRSPs. As Jim Stanford has explained, with personal savings, consumer debt, and real income at record low levels, most people can ill-afford the portfolios needed to reap the benefits of today's volatile stock markets (if indeed they can afford them at all).

The real challenge the movement faces today is not a public uncritical of free markets and free trade. Most people will remember the Asian economy crisis only three years ago, and are terrified of losing whatever savings they may have when international capitalism careens into its next great slump. There is ample skepticism about free markets and free trade, and a window of opportunity exists for activists to promote anti-capitalist alternatives. The political task activists face today is how to tap into this sentiment, to turn concern into the kind of broad-based action that could challenge the corporate agenda of trade liberalization.

For those grappling with this current situation, history provides an important lesson. 1968 is the year most progressive historians cite as the last great challenge to the power of the world economic élite. Chris Harman has referred to this period as the "fire last time." In May 1968, France ground to a halt with 10 million workers on strike. Student activists initiated a conflict that ultimately led to the ousting of Charles De Gaulle. The tremors of this ground-shaking period in world history were felt all over the world. The anti-war movement raged in the United States and Canada; the "Hot Autumn" in Italy shortly thereafter saw unprecedented mass action; students and workers in Czechoslovakia bravely took on a Stalinist regime. It was a time when a cauldron of dissent nearly bubbled over, when the establishment trembled at the thought of where the activity in the streets might lead.

The significance of the "fire last time," when studied in the context of today's fight against trade liberalization, is the lesson it imparts about the power and potential of collective action. As previously mentioned, the unique feature of the movement against trade liberalization has been the solidarity it has created among grass-roots activists across social movements. This mood of solidarity has created the broad-based united front that has made the fight against free trade effective, but it will only last as long as the commitment to collective action remains.

The only way forward is to mobilize in ever-greater numbers, to establish the confidence this movement needs to not only shut down trade meetings, but to change the capitalist economic system that privileges corporate profit over human needs. Mobilizing people in greater numbers will require activists to maintain an open mind in appealing to others to join the struggle; the fight against trade liberalization must not become the preserve of only the most informed.

For this new movement to become the "fire this time," it must rely on its strength in numbers. The most significant power the corporate élite has in this struggle is not only its economic clout, but its ability to divide citizens against one another, to split natural allies and diffuse dissent. The 'Spirit of Seattle' is latent in every human being who realizes that the corporate direction our world is taking is both unjust and unsustainable.

In a speech given to a December 1964 rally at the Berkeley campus of the University of California, Mario Savio, a 21-year-old student, used words that epitomized the same sentiment we must mobilize today:

"There's a time when the operations of the machine become so odious, make you so sick at heart, that you can't take part, can't even tacitly take part. And then you've got to put your bodies upon the gears and upon the wheels, upon the levers, upon all the apparatus, and you've got to make it stop."

(Joel Harden is currently completing his PhD at York University and is the former Chairperson of the Ontario office of the Canadian Federation of Students.)

UNAM — Students on Strike
By Sarah Dopp

Students at Mexico's largest university, the National Autonomous University of Mexico (UNAM), went on strike in April 1999 to protest the university administration's decision to increase undergraduate fees from less than one peso to 1,020 pesos per semester. (The increased cost of tuition is the approximate equivalent of $200 Canadian.) The strike, which shut down the university for 10 months, became a battle to defend public education.

The dramatic fee increase itself is one of many factors confronting students, families and workers in Mexico. The increase is the equivalent to 30 days' pay at the Mexican minimum wage rate. The World Bank estimates that 38 million Mexicans—40% of the population—live on less than $2 a day. Less conservative estimates of Mexico's growing poverty levels place it at between 65% and 70% of the population. Many students attend university on a part-time basis because they must also work. In some cases, students take between five and 10 years to complete a degree.

The UN's Universal Declaration of Human Rights defines education as a basic right. The Mexican Constitution calls for education that is free for all. The reality, however, is increasing ancillary fees, including fees for services such as registration, photocopying, libraries, and computer labs, as well as the costs of textbooks, housing and food, which leads to further limitations of accessibility.

The strike must also be seen within the context of economic globalization and the attack on public education. The tuition fee increase was seen by many to be one of the first signs of the privatization of public services. In recent years the World Bank has recommended tuition fee increases at Mexico's public universities, as well as the promotion of private colleges and creation of loan programs.

"Structural adjustment programs" demanded by international financial institutions, including the World Bank and the International Monetary Fund (IMF), have led to the privatization of public services and reduced public expenditures on services such as education throughout the South. Mexico is one of many countries responding to pressure from the World Bank and IMF.

On April 20, 1999, thousands of students in general assemblies democratically and overwhelmingly approved the strike which effectively shut UNAM down. Over 90% of school activities were suspended and students occupied most of the departments and faculties. The strike was called in response to the adoption of the proposal to increase fees in mid-March and the administration's constant refusal to meet with students.

From the outset, their opponents organized intimidation and counter campaigns and protests; but the students received tremendous support from families, workers, and students at other universities. Violence and force was consistently used by police and agitators to stifle resistance and break the strike. Throughout the 10 months, striking students faced not only academic reprisals for their participation in the strike, but also violence, beatings, mass arrests, and even kidnappings; yet they perservered, demanding education reforms and the resignation of the university president.

All commitments from the university administration to meet and negotiate with students were met with hostility and confrontation. In June, 2000, the university announced that it would maintain the proposal, but make it 'voluntary.' The voluntary tuition plan still allows individual departments to increase fees for exams, labs, and other services—a condition that students would not accept.

On February 6, 2000, as students were meeting to consider continuing negotiations, over 2,000 federal police officers occupied the main campus and forcibly took control. Over 700 students were arrested, bringing the total number of students arrested in the last week of the strike to almost 1,000.

The Mexican student movement has continued its resistance in spite of the violent end to the strike. In the days following the mass arrests, thousands of supporters took to the streets to demand the release of imprisoned students. The university backed down on the fee increase months prior to the raid on the university. It was only in June that the last imprisoned students were released on bail.

(Sarah Dopp is the Coordinator for Operation 2000, a project of the Polaris Institute.)

Playing with numbers:
How U.S. News and World Report mismeasures higher education and what we can do about it
By Nicholas Thompson

My friend Rob took as few classes as possible at Stanford. He had top-notch SAT scores and high-school grades, and he was smart enough to graduate even if he was less at ease in the library than party-hopping in a caveman suit. We took one class together and were assigned Gulliver's Travels—a book I had read before and loved. Our prestigious professor, however, drained the life out of it by lecturing monotonously about his pet theory that Gulliver's voyage was a metaphor for birth. Good students sat with mouths agape; bad students slept. When we broke into small discussion sections, everyone was so stultified that the understudies running the classes simply rehashed the original monologue. To Rob, it was all "cool"; he was on his way to a degree.

Rob may not have been a stereotypically great student. But he was outstanding from the viewpoint of the **U.S. News and World Report** college rankings, the most important arbiter of status in higher education. He went to a top-rated school, and he didn't hurt its score because the **U.S. News** rankings don't measure how much students learn; they don't measure whether students spend their evenings talking about Jonathan Swift or playing beer pong; and they don't measure whether students, like Rob, are just there to get through.

A single magazine's idiosyncratic ranking system may seem peripheral to the larger issues of higher education, but this particular one matters a lot. The **U.S. News** rankings are read by alumni, administrators, trustees, applicants, and almost everyone interested in higher education. The **New York Times** aptly described them as "a huge annual event," and they dominate what is far and away the best-selling college guide available.

Subsequently, the rankings do have a kind of Heisenberg effect, changing the very things they measure and, in certain ways, changing the entire shape of higher education. The problem isn't that the rankings put schools in the wrong order: A better ranking system might put Stanford 1st; it might put it 35th. I can't presume to know where it, or any other school, would rank. What I do know, however, is that a better ranking system, combined with more substantive reporting, would push Stanford to become an even better school—a place where students like Rob would have to focus more on learning than sliding by, and a place with fewer teachers putting their students to sleep. Unfortunately, the **U.S. News** rankings instead push schools to improve in tangential ways and fuel the increasingly prominent view that colleges are merely places in which to earn credentials.

Rank behavior

The first **U.S. News** rankings appeared in 1983. The magazine grouped colleges into categories like "national universities" and "regional liberal arts colleges" and sent a survey asking for the opinions of university presidents on the five best schools in their category. There was nothing scientific or subtle about the survey, and most people just shrugged it off. Donald Kennedy, president of then-first-ranked Stanford, said, "It's a beauty contest, not a serious analysis of quality."

That issue still sold remarkably well and in 1985 and 1987 **U.S. News**, under new owner Mortimer Zuckerman, again published rankings based solely on university presidents' perceptions. Then in 1988, **U.S. News** decided to take the rankings more seriously and to try to develop a franchise much like People's "50 Most Beautiful People" or the "Forbes 400." So Zuckerman placed Mel Elfin, an influential Washington journalist recently lured away from **Newsweek**, in charge of developing a more respectable system.

Elfin found his sidekick a year later in Robert Morse, an intelligent, soft-spoken man who, if he were an actor cast as an introverted accountant, would be criticized for overplaying his role. The team got to work: Morse crunching the numbers, Elfin packaging the rankings with stories on higher education and creating the institution christened "America's Best Colleges."

Morse, Elfin, and, later, Managing Editor Alvin Sanoff, rapidly created a franchise: Every September since 1988, the magazine has produced an eagerly anticipated list that precisely orders every college in the country. According to last September's rankings, for example, St. Mary's College of California is the eighth best western regional college, just slightly better than Mt. St. Mary's College, California, but well ahead of Our Lady of the Lake University in Texas—a school ranked down in the second of three tiers that the magazine groups institutions into once the top 50 schools in a category have been nailed down. "America's Best Colleges" sells about 40% more than **U.S. News'** standard weekly issues, and the magazine also produces a hot-selling accompanying book. Last year, eight million people visited **U.S. News'** web-site when it posted the rankings.

The rankings are opaque enough that no one outside the magazine can figure out exactly how they work, yet clear enough to imply legitimacy. For the past 12 years the main ranking categories have remained fairly constant: student selectivity, academic reputation in the eyes of other university presidents and admissions deans, student retention and graduation rates, faculty quality rated by pay and Ph.Ds, financial resources, and alumni giving. A category introduced in 1996 measures a university's "value added," assessed by the difference between actual and expected graduation rates (if you let in highly qualified students, your expected graduation rate is high). In short, the perfect school is rich, hard to get into, harder to flunk out of, and has an impressive name.

Beyond the rough guidelines, each category is then broken up further. Under the rules of the 2000 survey, "student selectivity" is based on some unexplained combination of the SAT scores of the 25th and 75th percentile of the entering freshman class, their class ranks, the percentage of applicants accepted, and "yield," the percentage of admitted applicants who enroll.

These numbers are hard to parse, but it's difficult to accuse **U.S. News'** ranking system of being a simple beauty contest; it's now a **complicated** beauty contest and its scientific air contributes greatly to the attention people pay it. As Groucho Marx said: "Integrity is everything. If you can fake integrity, you've got it made."

Morse Code

Of course, there is no one definitive way to judge colleges, and **U.S. News** does consistently encourage students to take the rankings with salt. Cal-Tech, for example, was a surprise 1999 choice as the top-rated national university, but even its name suggests that it caters to technophiles, not poets, marines, or aspiring history professors. It also didn't seem like a great place to the seven African-Americans accepted last year: none of them chose to attend. **U.S. News** understands this and sprinkles lines throughout the issue warning students of the importance of "researching the intangibles." But it also understands that, in a status-conscious era, rankings sell.

So, the magazine trudges forward, annually tweaking its algorithm. Last year, for example, criticism from rural schools persuaded the magazine to include a cost-of-living adjustment in the calculation of faculty salaries so as not to make the faculty seem cut-rate at schools where groceries and apartments cost less. This and other small changes have made the rankings better, and the editors have often been praised for their willingness to listen to criticism from universities, even as they are criticized for closing decisions about the rankings off from the rest of the **U.S. News** staff and creating a private fiefdom isolated from the rest of the magazine.

According to one former senior reporter who worked on the rankings in the early '90s: "We were roped around the neck to get us to write the serious journalistic stories in the issue, but none of us had a clue how the rankings worked."

According to another former staff writer who contributed to the "Best Colleges" issue: "The rankings are completely ridiculous. But they totally pay your salary."

But further from home, the rankings are taken much more seriously. According to research done by James Monk and Ronald Ehrenberg for the National Bureau of Economic Research, a one-place change in a school's ranking one year increases its admittance rate by 0.4%. In other words, if a school that needs to admit 15% of its applicants to fill its class moves from 5th place to 10th place, they will need to admit 17% the next year.

Monk and Ehrenberg also found that the rankings have a statistically significant impact on both yield and SAT scores of incoming freshmen. Furthermore, foundations and bond-rating organizations like Moody's use the rankings when evaluating institutions.

Ranking placement also has a demonstrably larger impact on institutions outside the highest grouping. Schools in the top subset may bounce around by a couple of places at most each year, but they tend to have all the applicants they can handle, anyway. Down lower, one tiny change in a school's data or in **U.S. News'** methodology can bump it from the second "tier," where its score is identical to the 51st best school in the country, to the third tier where its score is identical to the 176th.

The Heisenberg Effect

Not surprisingly, there is evidence that schools alter policies for the sake of rankings. This isn't automatically bad. But because **U.S. News** doesn't measure the most important thing on campus—actual learning—it is pushing colleges to prioritize in ways that are not necessarily the best. In a sense, the rankings are like a professor who ignores the content of her student's papers and instead bases her grades only on spelling and punctuation.

Since **U.S. News** began factoring in yield, the percentage of admitted students who choose to attend a given school, the number of colleges with "early decision" programs has shot up. Normally, students apply to college in the early winter of their senior years and then hold their breath until April when the verdicts come back. Under early decision, applicants apply to one school at the beginning of their senior year, promising to attend if admitted in December or January. Thus, if a college accepts half of its class under early decision, as many now do, it is guaranteed a much higher yield rate because all early decision students are required to attend.

Early decision programs have their advantages, but they also make it much more difficult for students to compare financial aid offerings, and thus give an advantage to students who don't need to worry about financial aid. In addition, early decision has essentially pushed the application cycle forward a year. In 1980, 19% of all the students enrolled in the Princeton Review's SAT training course entered before January 1 of their junior year. By this year, that number had climbed to 52%.

Yield only makes up a small percentage of an overall **U.S. News** score, and there were a number of factors pushing the fad among elite institutions—including the fact that it makes the admissions office's job easier by spreading work out—but the **U.S. News** rankings were nevertheless, as confirmed by multiple university officials, a significant factor.

The introduction of **U.S. News'** category of "percentage of alumni who give" also significantly affected fund-raising. When I was at Stanford, student groups were paid $25 an hour to solicit donations from alumni and, on the one shift I worked, were specifically told to mention that any donation would increase our ranking. Prof. Ronald Ehrenberg of Cornell University described his university's two-tiered approach to improve its score in this category: increase the number of alumni who give and decrease the number of living alumni.

The first goal was achieved by increasing the number of contributing alumni by aggressively pursuing small donations. The second goal was achieved by removing the names from the database of people who attended Cornell at one point but are unlikely to donate (for example, people who left the school before earning degrees). At one West Coast college, I was told, alumni who have not given money in five years have been reclassified as dead.

Administrators will deny until their ears start smoking that rankings influence their actions. And in fact few administrators actually sit down with the book and decide that they are going to change specific policies. What happens is that the rankings grease the skids for changes in specific directions, and decisions are gradually made that move the school those ways. A good example comes from Wesleyan University, where Vice-President for University Relations Barbara-Jan Wilson described to me a successful campaign to increase the number of teachers hired. When she went to the trustees, she argued, in part, that an increase would "be a good thing in the national media," which, she said, meant **U.S. News.**

The rankings are one of the main ways that alumni and trustees keep track of their school's progress, and they are an indicator of the status society attaches to their degrees. Would the trustees have accepted Wilson's proposal if the rankings didn't exist? It's hard to know. What is clear, however, is that the schools seem to take the rankings so seriously that it would be surprising if they weren't having a large effect.

At Whitman College, for example, the president's fax cover sheets proclaim that the university is "the only Northwest college in **U.S. News'** top tier among national liberal arts colleges." The Monthly recently received a letter from Connecticut College beginning, "[We] would very much like to establish a recruiting relationship with your organization. We are ranked among the top 25 national liberal arts colleges by **U.S. News and World Report.**" It is indeed ranked exactly 25th, tied with four other schools.

The Meritocracy

There's a certain irony to the way that universities trip over themselves to improve their rankings. Not only are many of the best minds at colleges across the country preoccupied with what is essentially a silly enterprise, but the books were cooked to begin with. Since the beginning, **U.S. News** has operated a system with the top schools pre-selected and the rest jumbled behind.

When Elfin was first charged with creating a ranking system, he seems to have known that the only believable methodology would be one that confirmed the prejudices of the meritocracy: The schools that the most prestigious journalists and their friends had gone to would have to come out on top. The first time that the staff had drafted up a numerical ranking system to test internally—a formula that, most controversially, awarded points for diversity—a college that Elfin cannot even remember the name of came out on top. He told me: "When you're picking the most valuable player in baseball and a utility player hitting .220 comes up as the MVP, it's not right."

Elfin subsequently removed the first statistician who had created the algorithm and brought in Morse, a statistician with very limited educational reporting experience. Morse rewrote the algorithm and ran it through the computers. Yale came out on top, and Elfin accepted this more persuasive formula. At the time, there was internal debate about whether the methodology was as good as it could be. According to Lucia Solorzano, who helped create the original **U.S. News** rankings in 1983, worked on the guide until 1988, and now edits **Barron's Best Buys in College Education,** "It's a college guide and the minute you start to have people in charge of it who have little understanding of education, you're asking for trouble."

To Elfin, however, who has a Harvard master's diploma on his wall, there's a kind of circular logic to it all: The schools that the conventional wisdom of the meritocracy regards as the best are in fact the best—as confirmed by the methodology, itself conclusively ratified by the presence of the most prestigious schools at the top of the list. In 1997, he told the **New York Times**: "We've produced a list that puts Harvard, Yale and Princeton, in whatever order, at the top. This is a nutty list? Something we pulled out of the sky?"

We're Number One

The walls around the system that confirmed the top Ivies began to crack in 1996 when Zuckerman hired James Fallows (a contributing editor of **The Washington Monthly)** to edit the magazine. Fallows hired former **New Yorker** writer Lincoln Caplan and, when Elfin left in January of '97, Fallows put Caplan in charge of special projects at the magazine, which included the annual development of the rankings. The two began to make a series of changes that improved the rankings, most noticeably by eliminating one decimal place in the scoring (schools now get grades like 77 instead of 76.8) to create more ties and reduce a spurious air of precision.

Caplan also hired a statistical expert named Amy Graham to direct the magazine's data gathering and analysis. Although both Caplan and Graham have left the magazine, and both declined to be interviewed, sources within **U.S. News** claim that, after looking deeply into the methodology of the rankings, Graham found that **U.S. News** had essentially put its thumb on the scale to make sure that Harvard, Yale, and Princeton continued to come out on top, as they did every year until 1999 after Elfin selected a formula.

This was done in large part by rejecting a common statistical technique known as standardization and employing an obscure weighting technique in the national universities category. Consider the data from the 1997 book, the last year the numbers for overall expenditures were posted publicly. Cal-Tech spent the most of any college at $74,000 per student per year, Yale spent the fourth-most at $45,000, and Harvard spent the seventh-most at $43,000. According to the **U.S. News** formula applied in every single category except for national universities, the absolute rates of spending would be compared and Cal-Tech would be cred-

Missing Pieces II   255

ited with a huge 40% category advantage over Yale. Under the formula used solely in this category, the difference between Cal-Tech and Yale (first place and fourth place) was counted as essentially the same as the difference between Yale and Harvard (fourth place and seventh place) even with the vast difference in absolute spending.

According to sources close to the magazine, a bitter internal struggle broke out when it became clear that Cal-Tech was going to come out on top in the late spring of 1999 after the rankings had been changed to count every category the same way. Fallows' replacement, Stephen Smith, and new Special Projects Editor Peter Cary were both reportedly shocked to see that, under the new formula Graham had recommended, the conventional wisdom of the meritocracy would be turned upside down, and there were discussions about whether the rankings should be revised to change the startling results. (Morse and Cary both deny this.)

Eventually, a decision was made to keep the new formula and **U.S. News** received a hefty dose of criticism from baffled readers. Morse declined to say how the formula has been changed for the rankings that will be printed this year. But if Cal-Tech's ranking drops and one of the three Ivies recovers its crown, read the small print carefully. Cal-Tech's advantage over the second-ranked school last year was an astronomical seven points (more than the difference between #2 and #8). The methodology would have to be monkeyed with substantially to drop Cal-Tech out of the top spot.

Learning

There are good things about the **U.S. News** rankings: They help high school students without college counsellors figure out ballpark quality estimates of the schools they're considering; and they have standardized the information that universities do make public. As Harrison Rainie, a longtime **U.S. News** editor who worked briefly as special projects editor after Caplan and before Cary says, "they helped create a common vocabulary. They made colleges count the number of part-time and full-time students the same way. They got colleges to define graduation rates the same way. ...Colleges were using whatever numbers that they could justify under whatever definitions they felt like choosing."

The rankings should also be given credit for intending to serve a worthy purpose. Over the past decades, colleges have become vastly more expensive and vastly more important to the American workforce. But they have not become commensurately more transparent. Colleges are reluctant to release information—like financial data or independent reports on teacher quality and student satisfaction—that could be useful to potential students and the public. Part of this reticence comes from a genuine belief that higher education functions best when left alone; part of it comes from an effort to use the ivory tower as an excuse to obscure information that might be viewed critically. **U.S. News** wanted to open some of the windows that colleges close and let students see in.

But to make the **U.S. News** rankings into something with a salutary effect overall—

the kind of rankings that encourage good behavior by universities and truly help applicants—there need to be systemic changes. Specifically, the magazine needs to make a concerted effort to measure **actual** education. But **U.S. News** has never been able to change its system, for two main reasons. First, with every change it makes, the magazine gets hammered by people who charge it with simply trying to generate interest each year by making schools bounce around. Secondly, when **U.S. News** changes its methodology it implicitly admits that its previous systems were inferior; if the ranking methodology is better this year, it must have been worse last year. A major change would throw 15 years' work into question.

The second reason was particularly acute when Mel Elfin, who had an almost paternal devotion to the rankings, held the reins. Elfin was Washington bureau chief of **Newsweek** for almost 20 years; he's been to China with Nixon; he has pictures of himself sitting with every president from Johnson to Reagan on his wall. But when I asked him whether, looking back, the rankings were his greatest accomplishment, he repeated twice: "This is what's going to last." He wasn't the kind of guy who was going to let the project into which he invested so much be turned upside down.

In some ways, Morse and Elfin treated critics of the rankings as enemies of the faith. When Reed College refused on principle to submit data in 1995, **U.S. News** summarily dropped it to the lowest tier; despite having the 18th best academic reputation of all national liberal arts colleges in **U.S. News'** reputational survey, Reed was listed right next to Richard Stockton College of New Jersey, which had the 153rd place.

One of the most eloquent critics of the rankings, Stanford President Gerhard Casper, sent a personal letter in 1996 to Fallows, that was eventually made public, saying: "I am extremely skeptical that the quality of a university—any more than the quality of a magazine—can be measured statistically. However, even if it can, the producers of the **U.S. News** rankings remain far from discovering the method." Elfin wasn't CC'd and the criticism and its form did not please him. Casper announced his retirement this year and, when I met Elfin for our interview, he almost immediately told me that: "Casper's gone and that's changed things." At the most recent meeting of the National Association of College Admissions Counsellors, Stanford Associate Admissions Director Jonathan Reider asked Morse a critical question about the rankings. Morse interrupted him with a caustic: "Your president's just quit."

Measuring Mr. Chips

When I asked Morse and Cary why they didn't include more measures of actual education, they gave me four reasons: colleges don't make the data available, it would be too expensive to gather, much of it simply cannot be quantified, and, as Cary told me, "if we were to tread into it...we'd get into a dozen, scores of questions."

The last two concerns are valid, but also, in a sense, refute the whole enterprise. If the rankings are subjective and leave things out, **U.S. News** should say so. If, as Cary said to me, the rankings can't "be everything to everybody," the magazine should give schools much less precise rankings, or not even rank at all: Just publish the data without running it through the algorithm that produces the ordinal rankings. At the least, it should point out right in the middle of the table that it has left out extremely important data.

U.S. News also doesn't have a terribly strong excuse in the contention that colleges give out little data: every college studies student satisfaction and teacher quality, so the data's out there. And, as Harrison Rainie pointed out, one of the virtues of **U.S. News** is that it has been able to convince colleges to standardize data and make it public in other categories.

Expense is the best of the four arguments, and the previously noted NORC report did caution that the authors could not think of a financially reasonable way to gather the necessary data. But Robert Zemsky at the University of Pennsylvania's Institute for Research on Higher Education has recently completed a survey of students six years after their graduations from 80 schools, compiling data on everything from general employment information, to whether respondents voted in the last election cycle, to complicated scenario-based questions that gauge confidence in certain job tasks and skills. How did Zemsky get his data? In large part because colleges were so eager to find reliable data on graduates that they helped fund the surveys.

Another complementary research project comes from the National Survey of Student Engagement, an organization working to survey undergraduates to find out which colleges use "good practices." Students are asked, for example, how often they talk to professors outside of class, how much time they spend doing homework, and whether or not they would attend the same institution again. **U.S. News** could tap into either data set or it could develop its own.

Virtual Reality

Of course, even with all of Zemsky's research and NSEE's survey data included, rankings inevitably fall short: Numerical lists are a fundamentally flawed way to measure the quality of a college, an argument that university presidents, usually when their schools drop in the ratings, have been making for years. It's hard enough to quantify the quality of one person's education, much less the quality of an entire college. There's too much complexity, subtlety, and individuality to justify more than a rough score.

This isn't to say that **U.S. News** should abandon its system. The good should be the enemy of the pretty bad (which is why **U.S. News** should improve), but the perfect shouldn't be the enemy of the good. But it is to say that journalists should therefore work toward two goals: turning over the rocks that **U.S. News** leaves untouched, and disabusing people of the notion that these rankings should play such a prominent role in higher education.

The data that **U.S. News** glides by isn't the sort that comes easily; it's buried deep. Do the big shot professors actually teach? How many hours? Are they good teachers? Are there unknown professors who are better teachers? Or is it the graduate students who teach? What is the intellectual atmosphere like on campus? How frequently do students stay up arguing about Faulkner, aid to Ghana, or whether a wheel chair can be built that goes up and down stairs? What about the campus support and counselling system for students who begin to fail? Some journalists do a good job searching for answers to these questions, and there are guides, like the **Princeton Review**'s, that take a stab at sorting through them for hundreds of colleges. But the overall trend that **U.S. News** feeds into has been to treat universities as though they are in the business of conferring degrees—personnel offices for the rest of America—and less as intellectual environments where students really learn.

In fairness to journalists, of course, these are not questions that are easily answered, and there's good reason for that. Universities often don't want students to know. They don't want to make it easy for reporters to look into issues of teacher quality or the intellectual atmosphere on campus, because what they'd find wouldn't be pretty and they know that reporters would find a few too many students like Rob, and a few too many professors like mine on Gulliver's Travels. As the Carnegie Foundation for the Advancement of Teaching wrote in a blistering report on research universities in 1998: some professors "are likely to be badly trained or even untrained teaching assistants who are groping their way toward a teaching technique; some others may be tenured drones who deliver set lectures from yellowed notes, making no effort to engage the bored minds of the students in front of them."

As for disabusing readers of the notion that rankings should have a central function in educational evaluation, there's a very good example of the kind of journalism needed that comes straight from the magazine itself: **U.S. News'** very own 1999 guide to "Outstanding High Schools." This 40- page report investigated high schools in six major metropolitan areas and evaluated them through a series of quantitative measures based on test scores and dropout rates controlled for family circumstances. Most important, after making their best rough analysis, **U.S. News** simply listed the schools they considered the most outstanding; they didn't rank them. Thus, instead of focusing on the horse-race element, readers focused on the list of traits common among outstanding schools—for example, mentoring programs for new teachers and partnerships with parents. The report focused on extensive profiles of schools that succeeded in each category.

In a sense, the **U.S. News** rankings serve as a test; administrators are teaching to it, and society, including students, puts too much stock in the results. And, as in all levels of education, there's no problem with that—if the test measures the right things as well as possible, if people recognize that no test can measure everything, and if there are well-developed methods for describing what the test leaves out.

Unfortunately, **U.S. News** falls far short of the first goal, and we all fall short of the others.

(Nicholas Thompson is an editor of The Washington Monthly, where this report was first published. When he was a student, Thompson worked on a campaign opposing the rankings. For more information, see www.washingtonmonthly.com)

Appendix

Appendix

Overall Rankings

Province	Equity Rank	Quality Rank	Affordability, Access and Opportunity Rank	Accountability Rank	Overall Rank	Last Year's Overall Rank
NF	10	6	7	3	7	9
PEI	9	5	5	5	6	8
NS	3	8	3	9	4	3
NB	7	1	8	8	6	3
PQ	5	3	1	2	2	2
ON	6	10	7	10	10	10
MB	2	5	3	5	3	6
SK	8	9	9	6	9	7
AB	4	8	10	8	8	5
BC	1	2	4	1	1	1

Equity

Province	% of International Students (College 1995-1996)	% of International Students (University 1996-1997)	% of Women Faculty 1998	% Poor Households with PSE (1997)	Unemployment rate (1999)	Equity Rank	Last Year's Equity Rank
NF	10	9	10	9	10	10	10
PEI	9	10	3	7	9	9	9
NS	7	3	1	4	7	3	2
NB	6	8	2	6	8	7	6
PQ	8	1	9	1	6	5	4
ON	2	7	8	8	1	6	4
MB	4	4	6	2	2	2	8
SK	5	7	5	10	4	8	7
AB	3	5	7	5	3	4	3
BC	1	2	4	3	5	1	1

Quality

Province	% University Faculty Change 92/93 - 98/99	% College Faculty Change 92/93 - 96/97	Change in Prov. Expenditure on PSE (99/00)	Avg. Student / Faculty Ratio (1996-1999)	Per Capita University Operating Grants (1999-2000)	Quality Rank	Last Year Quality Rank
NF	10	8	7	2	1	6	8
PEI	1	6	10	1	7	5	8
NS	5	9	9	4	4	8	5
NB	3	1	4	5	2	1	3
PQ	7	3	1	8	5	3	1
ON	8	5	8	10	10	10	10
MB	9	4	6	3	3	5	7
SK	6	10	5	7	6	9	4
AB	4	7	2	10	8	8	6
BC	2	2	3	6	9	2	1

Affordability, Access, Opportunity

Province	Avg. Undergrad University Tuition (2000-2001)	Avg. College Tuition (1999-2000)	% Change in University Tuition (90/91-99/00)	% Change in College Tuition (90/91-99/00)	Avg. % 18-24 Year Olds' Participation Rate	Afford., Access & Opp. Rank	Last Year's Afford., Access & Opportunity Rank
NF	4	4	9	9	4	7	5
PEI	6	8	3	4	8	5	8
NS	10	2	7	2	1	3	3
NB	7	10	2	10	2	8	7
PQ	1	1	5	1	7	1	1
ON	9	5	8	5	3	7	6
MB	3	3	4	6	6	3	4
SK	5	9	6	7	5	9	8
AB	8	6	10	8	9	10	10
BC	2	7	1	3	10	4	2

Accountability

Province	% of PSE funding from Gov't (1998-1999)	% of PSE funding from Student Fees (1998-1999)	% of PSE funding from Private Sources (1998-1999)	Needs Based Point System	Accountability Rank	Last Year's Accountability Rank
NF	2	6	1	8	3	7
PEI	3	7	2	6	5	4
NS	10	10	3	10	9	9
NB	8	8	5	6	8	3
PQ	1	1	8	6	2	1
ON	9	9	10	10	10	10
MB	4	4	9	1	5	6
SK	5	2	6	6	6	8
AB	7	5	7	8	8	5
BC	6	3	4	1	1	2

Equity

% of International College Students

Province	% of Students who are non-Canadian	Rank	Last Year's Rank
NF	0.2	10	9
PEI	0.5	9	10
NS	0.7	7	4
NB	0.8	6	8
PQ	0.6	8	3
ON	4.9	2	5
MB	2.7	4	2
SK	1.6	5	7
AB	3.7	3	5
BC	14.7	1	1

% of International University Students

Province	% of Students who are non-Canadian	Rank	Last Year's Rank
NF	2.7	9	9
PEI	0.04	10	10
NS	5.3	3	4
NB	3.4	8	8
PQ	8.8	1	3
ON	4.0	7	5
MB	5.1	4	2
SK	4.0	7	7
AB	4.4	5	5
BC	7.8	2	1

% of Women Faculty

Province	Percentage of Women Faculty	Rank	Last Year's Rank
NF	25.1	10	5
PEI	30.7	3	2
NS	34.4	1	1
NB	32.9	2	3
PQ	25.3	9	8
ON	26.0	8	4
MB	27.3	6	8
SK	29.7	5	10
AB	27.0	7	7
BC	29.8	4	6

% of Poor Households with Completed PSE

Province	% Poor Households with Completed PSE	Rank	Last Year's Rank
NF	12.8	9	n/a
PEI	13.6	7	n/a
NS	16.1	4	n/a
NB	14.1	6	n/a
PQ	18.1	1	n/a
ON	13.3	8	n/a
MB	18.0	2	n/a
SK	12.7	10	n/a
AB	15.1	5	n/a
BC	16.7	3	n/a

Unemployment Rate (% 1999)

Province	Unemployment Rate	Rank	Last Year's Rank
NF	16.9	10	n/a
PEI	14.4	9	n/a
NS	9.6	7	n/a
NB	10.2	8	n/a
PQ	9.3	6	n/a
ON	5.3	1	n/a
MB	5.6	2	n/a
SK	6.1	4	n/a
AB	5.7	3	n/a
BC	8.3	5	n/a

Quality

% University Faculty Change

Province	Percentage Faculty Change - Univ 1992/93-1998/99	Rank	Last Year's Rank
NF	-18.6	10	10
PEI	0.6	1	1
NS	-7.2	5	5
NB	-5.2	3	4
PQ	-9.8	7	3
ON	-11.7	8	7
MB	-15.9	9	8
SK	-7.9	6	6
AB	-7.0	4	9
BC	-1.6	2	2

% College Faculty Change

Province	Percentage Faculty Change - College 1992/93 - 1996/97	Rank	Last Year's Rank
NF	-39.9	8	10
PEI	-31.7	6	1
NS	-42.3	9	5
NB	37.2	1	4
PQ	7.1	3	3
ON	-24.1	5	7
MB	-3.9	4	8
SK	-57.3	10	6
AB	-33.9	7	9
BC	25.4	2	2

Change in Provincial Expenditure on PSE

Province	Provincial Expenditure on PSE (1999-2000)	Rank	Last Year's Rank
NF	314	7	8
PEI	269	10	10
NS	277	9	4
NB	329	4	6
PQ	418	1	1
ON	286	8	7
MB	316	6	8
SK	320	5	5
AB	349	2	2
BC	347	3	3

Per Capita University Operating Grants

Province	University Operating Grants - $ per Capita	Rank	Last Year's Rank
NF	220.63	1	n/a
PEI	169.77	7	n/a
NS	200.84	4	n/a
NB	203.52	2	n/a
PQ	198.69	5	n/a
ON	138.72	10	n/a
MB	201.57	3	n/a
SK	179.78	6	n/a
AB	166.25	8	n/a
BC	165.91	9	n/a

Student/Faculty Ratio

Province	Avg. Number of Students per Faculty Member 1996-1999	Trend	Rank	Last Year's Rank
NF	16.1	Increasing	2	1
PEI	13.9	Increasing	1	5
NS	16.5	Increasing	4	7
NB	17.1	Decreasing	5	1
PQ	19.3	Increasing	8	7
ON	20.0	No Change	10	10
MB	16.2	Increasing	3	1
SK	18.6	Increasing	7	1
AB	20.0	Increasing	10	9
BC	18.4	Increasing	6	5

Affordability, Access, Opportunity

Average Undergrad. University Tuition

Province	Avg. Undergrad Tuition Cost	Rank	Last Year's Rank
NF	3300.00	4	5
PEI	3480.00	6	7
NS	4408.00	10	10
NB	3519.00	7	6
PQ	1898.00	1	1
ON	3971.00	9	9
MB	2873.00	3	3
SK	3304.00	5	4
AB	3841.00	8	8
BC	2520.00	2	2

Average College Tuition

Province	Avg. College Tuition Cost	Rank	Last Year's Rank
NF	1,452.00	4	2
PEI	2,000.00	8	10
NS	1,200.00	2	3
NB	2,400.00	10	8
PQ	FREE	1	1
ON	1,684.00	5	5
MB	1,432.00	3	4
SK	2,005.00	9	9
AB	1,689.00	6	7
BC	1,750.00	7	6

% Change in University Tuition

Province	% Change in Undergrad University Tuition	Rank	Last Year's Rank
NF	145.5	9	8
PEI	89.1	3	3
NS	126.9	7	6
NB	85.4	2	2
PQ	110.4	5	9
ON	140.2	8	7
MB	103.0	4	4
SK	116.6	6	4
AB	208.8	10	10
BC	45.9	1	1

% Change in College Tuition

Province	% Change in College Tuition	Rank	Last Year's Rank
NF	200.0	9	7
PEI	79.0	4	4
NS	57.0	2	2
NB	380.0	10	10
PQ	n/a	1	1
ON	128.0	5	5
MB	137.0	6	6
SK	178.0	7	8
AB	195.0	8	9
BC	65.0	3	3

18-24 Year Old Participation Rate

Province	18-24 Year Olds, Participation Rate %	Rank	Last Year's Rank
NF	19.4	4	6
PEI	15.4	8	8
NS	29.3	1	2
NB	22.3	2	4
PQ	16.4	7	1
ON	19.5	3	3
MB	18.7	6	10
SK	19.1	5	7
AB	15.3	9	5
BC	13.2	10	9

Accountability

% of Total PSE Budget Received from Gov't Funding

Province	% of Total PSE Budget Received from Gov't Funding	Rank	Last Year's Rank
NF	63.0	2	2
PEI	62.7	3	3
NS	46.6	10	10
NB	52.6	8	7
PQ	67.7	1	1
ON	47.2	9	9
MB	61.4	4	4
SK	56.9	5	6
AB	55.5	7	8
BC	56.1	6	5

% of Total PSE Budget Received from Student Fees

Province	% of Total PSE Budget Received from Student Fees	Rank	Last Year's Rank
NF	21.6	6	n/a
PEI	21.9	7	n/a
NS	28.5	10	n/a
NB	22.6	8	n/a
PQ	13.1	1	n/a
ON	25.3	9	n/a
MB	18.2	4	n/a
SK	16.8	2	n/a
AB	19.7	5	n/a
BC	17.1	3	n/a

% of Total PSE Budget Received from Private Sources

Province	% of Total PSE Budget Received from Private Sources	Rank	Last Year's Rank
NF	3.7	1	2
PEI	3.8	2	1
NS	5.6	3	3
NB	6.4	5	4
PQ	9.8	8	7
ON	12.2	10	10
MB	9.9	9	8
SK	7.5	6	6
AB	9.2	7	9
BC	6.2	4	5

Needs-Based Point System

Province	Tuition Fee Freeze (Max. 1)	Tuition Roll-Back (Max. 2)	Grants Increase (Max. 2)	Existing Grants (Max. 1)	Points Total	Rank	Last Year's Rank
NF	1	0	1	0	2	8	n/a
PEI	1	0	2	0	3	6	n/a
NS	0	0	0	0	0	10	n/a
NB	0	0	2	1	3	6	n/a
PQ	1	0	0	1	3	6	n/a
ON	0	0	0	0	0	10	n/a
MB	0	2	2	0	4	1	n/a
SK	0	0	2	1	3	6	n/a
AB	0	0	1	1	2	8	n/a
BC	1	0	2	1	4	1	n/a